Rising to the youth employment challenge

New evidence on key policy issues

Niall O'Higgins

International Labour Office, Geneva

O'Higgins, Niall.

Rising to the youth employment challenge: New evidence on key policy issues / Niall O'Higgins; International Labour Office – Geneva: ILO, 2017

ISBN 978-92-2-130865-2 (print)

ISBN 978-92-2-130866-9 (web pdf)

International Labour Office.

youth employment / employment policy / labour market analysis / minimum wage / self-employment / labour contract / informal employment

13.01.3   *ILO Cataloguing in Publication Data*

This publication was produced by the Document and Publications Production, Printing and Distribution Branch (PRODOC) of the ILO.

Graphic and typographic design, layout and composition, copy editing, proofreading, printing, electronic publishing and distribution.

PRODOC endeavours to use paper sourced from forests managed in an environmentally sustainable and socially responsible manner.

Code: DTP-CORR-SCR-ATA

Rising to the youth employment challenge

New evidence on key policy issues

Foreword

Across the globe, young women and men are making important contributions as productive workers, entrepreneurs, consumers, citizens, members of society and agents of change. All too often, the full potential of young people is not realized because they do not have access to productive and decent jobs that match their qualifications and meet their aspirations. Many young people face high levels of economic and social uncertainty. A difficult transition into the world of work has long-lasting consequences not only on young people themselves but also on their families and communities. It also impacts more structurally on the evolution of labour markets and the future of work and society.

The ILO's Employment Policy Department (EMPLOYMENT) is engaged in global advocacy and in supporting member States in placing more and better jobs at the centre of economic and social policies and growth and development strategies. Policy research and the generation and dissemination of knowledge on a broad range of topics are essential components of the Employment Policy Department's activities. This book is one in a series of publications which analyse evidence and collect and disseminate key findings on *what works for youth employment* so as to inform more effective youth employment policy-making in a timely and accessible manner.

In 2012, in response to the unprecedented youth employment crisis, the International Labour Conference issued a resolution making a call for urgent and targeted action on youth employment through a set of policy measures (ILO, 2012a). The resolution provides guiding principles and a tested package of interrelated policies from macroeconomic frameworks to labour market interventions for countries wanting to take immediate and targeted action to address the crisis of youth labour markets.

The analyses incorporated in this book focus on specific policy instruments recently used to improve the employment prospects of young people. There is no attempt to be exhaustive. The field is vast and there are already many overviews of the general issues. Rather, the chapter themes were selected on the basis of (a) their substantive importance for the effective design and implementation of strategies; (b) a perceived need to shed additional light on specific areas where evidence is patchy or where actions and pronouncements may hitherto have tended to be guided by assumptions rather than analysis; and (c) a judgement that in some cases, as in the discussion of contractual arrangements in Chapter 6, an innovative approach to a well-studied subject may aid understanding of relevant issues.

The book contains a range of analyses and reviews of the evidence, adopting a variety of appropriate methodologies to examine a series of specific questions related to youth employment policy with a view to producing specific policy recommendations to support the more effective integration of young people into decent work.

The policy issues covered here have also been selected with reference to the five pillars of the ILO's multi-pronged approach to youth employment policy as advocated in the aforementioned 2012 ILO call for action (ILO, 2012a). These pillars are:

1. employment and economic policies for youth employment;
2. employability – education, training and skills, and the school-to-work transition;
3. labour market policies;
4. youth entrepreneurship and self-employment; and
5. rights for young people.

After a brief discussion of some of the major global issues in youth labour markets in Chapter 1, six thematic chapters focus on new evidence on key policy issues. Chapter 2 on macroeconomic and sectoral policies uses panel econometric models to analyse issues related to pillar 1, employment and economic policies. Chapter 3 on minimum wages and youth employment deals primarily with the effects of interactions between labour market institutions and policies, and is thus concerned with issues grouped under pillars 1 and 3 of youth employment policy as identified by the 2012 resolution. Such institutions also have implications for pillar 5, young people's rights at work. Chapter 4, which focuses on active labour market policies in general and wage subsidies in particular, speaks directly to pillar 3 on labour market policies, but also raises issues of relevance to pillar 2 on employability. Chapter 5 speaks directly to the resolution's pillar 4 on youth employment policy, namely self-employment among young people, and examines the effectiveness of programmes to promote youth entrepreneurship. The issues it raises also have some bearing on pillar 5 concerning rights at work. This key pillar is also the unifying theme underlying the last two analytical chapters, Chapters 6 and 7. Chapter 6 looks at contractual arrangements aimed at facilitating the entry of young people into employment, while Chapter 7 turns to look at what may reasonably be seen as the low- and middle-income country counterpart to non-standard employment in high-income countries: informal employment.

The eighth and final chapter draws together some of the major findings of the six thematic chapters and suggests ways in which these can be brought together – in a complementary fashion – in order to better promote the integration of young people into decent work. This is by no means the end of the story; we still know far too little about some key issues, and the book ends by offering a perspective on what more needs to be done in continuously building evidence and evaluating the impact of policies.

The new evidence and key findings presented here are intended for use by policy-makers, social partners, development practitioners, academics and labour market analysts interested in rising to the challenge of youth employment.

Azita Berar Awad
Director
Employment Policy Department

Acknowledgements

This book is based on a range of contributions to the ILO's research programme on youth employment. The lead author is Niall O'Higgins (ILO-YEP), who drafted the manuscript on the basis of contributions and analyses co-authored with a variety of contributors. The development of the book was the result of detailed discussions with Azita Berar Awad, Sukti Dasgupta and Valter Nebuloni. Contributing authors to the chapters are as follows:

Chapter 1 – Overview: **Niall O'Higgins**, ILO.

Chapter 2 – Macroeconomic and sectoral issues in youth employment policy: **Niall O'Higgins**, ILO, **Monique Ebell**, National Institute of Economic and Social Research, and **P.N. (Raja) Junankar**, University of New South Wales, Sydney.

Chapter 3 – Labour market institutions and youth labour markets: **Niall O'Higgins**, ILO, and **Valentino Moscariello**, OECD.

Chapter 4 – Active labour market programmes: **Katalin Bördős** and **Márton Csillag**, Budapest Institute for Policy Analysis, **Niall O'Higgins**, ILO, and **Ágota Scharle**, Budapest Institute for Policy Analysis.

Chapter 5 – Self-employment and entrepreneurship: **Brendan Burchell**, **Adam Coutts** and **Edward Hall**, University of Cambridge, **Niall O'Higgins**, ILO, and **Nick Pye**, University of Cambridge.

Chapter 6 – Contractual arrangements for young workers: **Ana Jeannet-Milanovic** and **Niall O'Higgins**, ILO, and **Annika Rosin**, University of Turku.

Chapter 7 – The quality of work: **Niall O'Higgins** and **Jonas Bausch**, ILO, and **Francesca Bonomelli**, Ministry of Education, Chile.

Chapter 8 – Towards more effective youth employment policies and programmes: **Niall O'Higgins**, ILO.

Francesca Bonomelli also provided excellent research assistance in the production of tables and figures throughout the book. Gillian Somerscales edited the entire text excellently.

Useful comments were provided on specific chapters and/or issues by ILO colleagues Mariya Aleksynska, Patrick Belser, Janine Berg, Laura Brewer, Kazutoshi Chatani, Paul Comyn, Sukti Dasgupta, Veronica Escudero, Colin Fenwick, Frédéric Lapeyre, Nomaan Majid, Marta Makhoul, Massimiliano La Marca, Valter Nebuloni,

Yoshie Noguchi, Aurelio Parisotto, Clemente Pignatti, Markus Pilgrim, Maria Prieto, Marco Principi, Gianni Rosas and Valerio De Stefano; these contributed much to improving the quality of the manuscript. The entire manuscript was reviewed by Matthieu Cognac, Sara Elder, Susana Puerto Gonzalez and two anonymous external peer reviewers.

Stephen Bazen, Aix-Marseille University, Werner Eichhorst, Bonn Institute of Labour Economics, and Seamus MacGuiness, Economic and Social Research Institute, Dublin, also provided extremely helpful comments on background papers presented at workshops at the ILO in November 2015 and February 2016.

Contents

List of figures

List of tables

List of boxes

Abbreviations

ALMP	active labour market programme/policy (according to context)
AP	Asia and the Pacific
CAE	*contrat d'accompagnement dans l'emploi*
CAPB	cyclically adjusted primary balance
CEDEFOP	European Centre for the Development of Vocational Training
CIE	*contrat initiative emploi*
CUI	*contrat unique d'insertion*
EC	European Commission
ECA	Europe and Central Asia
EECA	Eastern Europe and Central Asia
EPL	employment protection legislation
EPLex	Employment Protection Legislation database (ILO)
ESJSA	employment services and job search assistance
ETUC	European Trade Union Confederation
EU	European Union
GDP	gross domestic product
GNI	gross national income
HICs	high-income countries
HP-filter	Hodrick–Prescott filter
ILC	International Labour Conference
ILO	International Labour Office/Organization
IMF	International Monetary Fund
ISCED	International Standard Classification of Education
IVET	initial vocational education and training
LAC	Latin America and the Caribbean
LICs	low-income countries
LMICs	low- and middle-income countries
MENA	Middle East and North Africa
MICs	middle-income countries
NEET	not in employment, education or training
OECD	Organisation for Economic Co-operation and Development
OLS	ordinary least squares
PEPs	public employment programmes
PES	public employment service(s)
PPP	purchasing power parity
RCT	randomized controlled trial
SEJ	Subsidio al Empleo Joven (Chile)

SSA	sub-Saharan Africa
SVIP	Stage d'Initiation à la Vie Professionnelle (Tunisia)
SWTS	School-to-Work Transition Survey(s) (ILO)
SYETP	Special Youth Employment Training Programme (Australia)
TEI	technical education institutes
TUC	Trades Union Congress (United Kingdom)
UN	United Nations
W4Y	Work for Youth
YEP	Youth Employment Programme (ILO)

1. Overview

1.1. Introduction

Young people today face a difficult process in seeking to enter the world of work. The global recession has left its mark and, after falling for some years, youth unemployment rates are once again on the increase (ILO, 2016a); ILO estimates suggest that the global youth (age 15–24) unemployment rate was 12.8 per cent in 2016 (slightly up from 12.7 per cent in 2015). Similarly, the number of unemployed young people increased slightly between 2015 and 2016 from 69.4 to 69.6 million. Owing largely to the falling size of the youth cohort, this is down from the peak of 76.5 million in 2009, but nevertheless the current youth unemployment rate remains significantly above its pre-recession level of 12.0 per cent in 2007.[1]

Unemployment, moreover, is only the tip of the iceberg; the quality of employment available to young people is increasingly an issue for concern. In low- and middle-income countries (LMICs) vulnerable and/or informal types of employment have come to dominate young people's labour market experiences, while in higher-income countries (HICs) temporary and other non-standard forms of employment are increasingly becoming the norm.

In this context, the problem of how best to promote young people's entry into decent work is becoming ever more pressing and also more complex. Moreover, the specific challenges posed in promoting decent work for young people vary widely across national and regional contexts as well as across the different characteristics of young people themselves. This volume looks at some specific issues concerning the promotion of decent work among young people as they enter, and once they have entered, the labour market.

The book is aimed at all those interested in the design and implementation of effective policies to promote decent work for young people. In addition to reviewing the existing evidence, the book also contains original analysis, and in the course of presenting this it has been necessary to include some technical detail. However, the book's contents overall are designed to be accessible to all those familiar with the issues related to youth employment policy, and are expected to be of interest inter alia to policy-makers, officials in ministries of labour and employment services, and also to ILO officials charged with providing support to constituents on youth

---

[1] ILO modelled estimates, Nov. 2016, http://www.ilo.org/ilostat/faces/wcnav_default Selection?_adf.ctrl-state=19seyhsqpo_4&_afrLoop=246216283995722&_afrWindowMode=0&_afrWindowId=19seyhsqpo_30#! [6 Feb. 2017].

employment policy; given that it also proposes original analysis, it is hoped that the book will appeal in addition to both specialist and non-specialist academics.

The next section of this opening chapter provides a very brief overview of some of the features of youth labour markets from a global perspective. It seeks to draw out some of the key elements in the school-to-work transition process in the world today. In doing so, it does not enter into the widely varying detail of specific national and regional realities; these are returned to in the thematic chapters below.

1.2. Some key features of youth labour markets

Just as entry into stable employment has become a lengthier and more complex process, so the notion of what constitutes a young person has also undergone some modification. The standard United Nations (UN) definition of a young person as one aged between 15 and 24 years no longer fully covers the typical period of transition from education to employment which the concept of youth was originally intended to capture (Ryan, 2001). These days, more young people stay in education to higher levels, and the transition process itself is becoming more drawn out, so that a significant number of young people do not complete that transition until their late twenties.[2] Information from the ILO's School-to-Work Transition Survey (SWTS)[3] illustrates that, in LMICs, nearly one in three young men and around one in two young women aged between 25 and 29 were not working, either because they were still in education or training, and so had not yet begun the transition process, or because they were neither in employment nor in education or training (NEET), and so had not completed it.[4] In this context, it makes sense on occasion to broaden the coverage, and accordingly those aged 25–29 are sometimes included in the analysis; however, where

---

[2]   It is also true, of course, that many countries use (and many have long used – see also O'Higgins, 2001) a broader definition; it is not unusual, particularly in some African and Asian countries, for a person to be classified as "young" well into their thirties, although more often than not this has to do with institutional classifications such as, for example, the cut-off age for belonging to the youth wing of a political party.

[3]   The two rounds of the SWTS are used throughout this book as a source of information on the school-to-work transition in LMICs. The survey was implemented in 34 LMICs between 2012 and 2015. In 19 of these it was undertaken twice. The full data set containing 53 surveys was employed as the basis for figures, tables and analysis, except where indicated otherwise. A description of the SWTS data is provided in the appendix at the end of the book. More details and a variety of reports using the data as well as the data themselves are all available at http://www.ilo.org/w4y.

[4]   Author's calculations, based on the SWTS. Of course, a significant proportion of these young people, and above all young women, will never complete the school-to-work transition. Moreover, to further complicate matters it is becoming increasingly common for young people to move back to "previous" states (education, training or NEET) after they have been employed, and/or to be simultaneously in more than one of these states – for example, combining some form of education or training with work. Certainly the traditional view of the transition being the period between school (the starting point) and work (the end point), is becoming increasingly inaccurate.

standard statistics are referred to, these are typically made available for the more traditional 15–24 age group. It will be clear from the text which specific definition is being used in each context.

In part to illustrate the increasing length and variability of the school-to-work transition, but also to give a first summary impression of the process in different regions, figure 1.1 reports the distribution of young men and young women between the three broad categories – in education, NEET and in employment – for the 34 countries included in the SWTS.[5] Some initial observations may be made on the basis of this overview. First, by age 25, over 30 per cent of young men and more than half of young women are either still in education or NEET. Moreover, even at age 29 a significant minority – over 5 per cent – of young people are still in education. Both of these factors tend to favour the extension of the "youth" category to all those still in their twenties.

For both young men and young women, the proportion of NEETs tends to grow with age up to a point; among young men the percentage of NEETs in the population peaks at age 23, while for young women the rising trend continues into their late twenties – for fairly obvious reasons.

It is also worthy of note that at so young an age as 15 a significant minority – around 12 per cent – of young people have already left school and are either employed or NEET. There does not seem to be a significant gender imbalance in this proportion at the global level, although of course there are substantial differences at regional and country levels (ILO, 2015a). Perhaps the main point emerging from the figures is that the substantial proportion of NEETs throughout the age distribution – particularly of young women – suggests that the transition from school to work is by no means straightforward.

Countries vary widely in the characteristics of their youth labour markets, the nature and duration of the education-to-employment transition, and the forms of employment and/or economic activity in which young people are involved. That said, and while the importance of this heterogeneity should not be underestimated, it is also true that there are some significant common features which characterize youth labour markets at both global and regional levels and which are worth mentioning here.

One such common feature in high-income countries (HICs), and above all in some parts of Europe, is the trend towards non-standard forms of employment. In 2015, 25.0 per cent of young workers were in temporary employment – as opposed to 9.5 per cent of workers aged 25–54 years – in member States of the

---

[5] For the most part, this section limits itself to reporting some broad aggregates, with few regional or country-specific details. Of course, there is much heterogeneity among regions and even more among countries. The ILO (2015a, 2016a) provides more discussion of regional differences regarding the principal labour market indicators, and more detailed country information on some relevant indicators for LMICs in the SWTS is provided in the appendix to this book. Cross-country differences underlie much of the book's analysis, of course, and are discussed further where relevant in the appropriate chapters.

**Figure 1.1. Education/employment status of young people (age 15–29)
by single-year age group in LMICs**

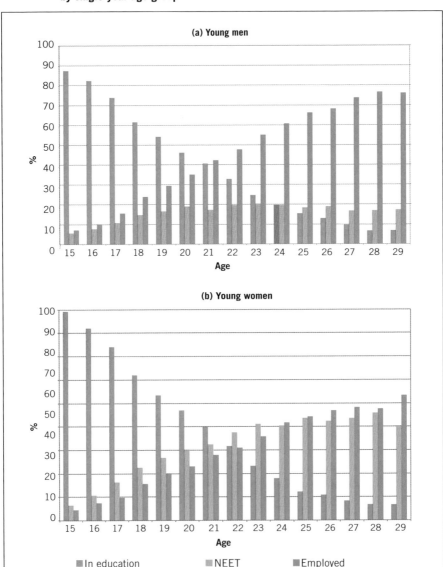

Note: The figure reports the average value for each country over the survey period 2012–15. The precise dates of the average vary across countries. For details on the aggregation procedure and other details on the surveys, see the appendix. The specific countries included are, grouped by region: Benin, Congo, Liberia, Madagascar, Malawi, Sierra Leone, United Republic of Tanzania, Togo, Uganda, Zambia; Egypt, Jordan, Lebanon, Occupied Palestinian Territory, Tunisia; Brazil, Colombia, Dominican Republic, El Salvador, Jamaica, Peru; Armenia, Kyrgyzstan, the former Yugoslav Republic of Macedonia, Republic of Moldova, Montenegro, Russian Federation, Serbia, Ukraine; Bangladesh, Cambodia, Nepal, Samoa and Viet Nam.

Source: Author's calculations based on SWTS data.

Figure 1.2. Temporary employment among young people (age 15–24) in HICs, 2015

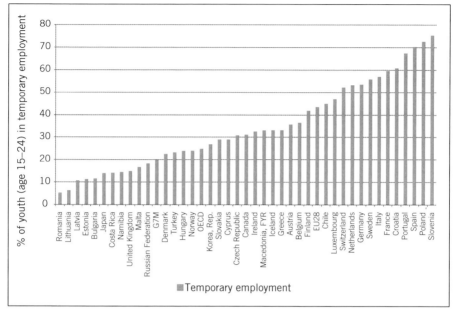

Source: OECD Temporary employment (indicator), doi: 10.1787/75589b8a-en (accessed 3 Jan. 2017).

Organisation for Economic Co-operation and Development (OECD).[6] In the European Union (EU), the numbers were 43.8 per cent and 12.3 per cent respectively.[7] Thus, by 2015, almost one in every two young European workers was in temporary employment, and young workers were nearly four times as likely as those of prime working age (25–54) to find themselves in this situation. (For a breakdown by country, see figure 1.2.) Among the young in HICs, part-time work in general and involuntary part-time work in particular have followed a similar upward trend (ILO, 2016b).

If in many developed economies youth people are over-represented in temporary work, in LMICs it is informal and/or vulnerable employment that dominates young people's labour market experiences. The SWTS data suggest that in sub-Saharan Africa (SSA) the percentage of young workers in informal jobs is 90.7 per cent, in the Middle East and North Africa (MENA) 75.4 per cent, in Latin America and the Caribbean (LAC) 72.9 per cent, in Eastern Europe and Central Asia (EECA) 54.3 per cent and in Asia and the Pacific (AP) 90.5 per cent.[8]

---

[6] https://data.oecd.org/emp/temporary-employment.htm.

[7] https://data.oecd.org/emp/temporary-employment.htm.

[8] School-to-Work Transition Surveys, W4Y project, Youth Employment Programme, ILO, http://www.ilo.org/employment/areas/youth-employment/work-for-youth/WCMS_191853/lang--en/index.htm.

Figure 1.3. Informal employment among young people in LMICs

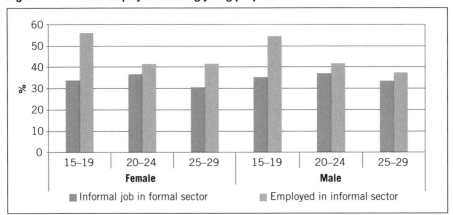

Note: The figure reports average values over the survey period 2012–15. The precise dates of the average vary across countries. For countries covered, see note to figure 1.1 above.
Source: Author's calculations based on SWTS data.

Figure 1.4. Vulnerable employment among young people in LMICs

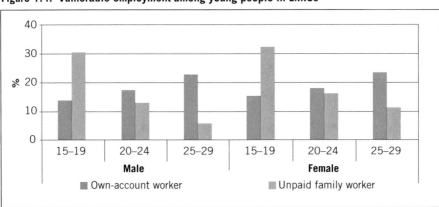

Note: The figure reports average values over the survey period 2012–15. The precise dates of the average vary across countries. For countries covered, see note to figure 1.1 above.
Source: Author's calculations based on SWTS data.

Both informal employment (figure 1.3) and vulnerable employment (figure 1.4) decline with age in percentage terms.[9] However, whereas for vulnerability this is largely

---

[9] Those in vulnerable employment comprise all own-account workers and all unpaid family workers. Those in informal employment comprise all unpaid family workers and the vast majority of own-account workers, in addition to some employers (and their employees) and also a significant number of employees. More specifically, informally employed young workers include two broad categories: those working in their own or someone else's informal business, and those who are employed informally in formal firms. For the full definition of informality, see Chapter 7 of this book.

due to young people gradually moving out of unpaid family work as they get older, it is much less likely that young people in informal employment will move on to formal work.

The issue of the quality of employment is a theme running through this book, and is also treated explicitly in Chapters 5 on self-employment, 6 on contractual arrangements and 7 on informal employment.

1.3. A look at what follows

The analyses incorporated in this book are concerned with a variety of specific issues concerning the effective design and implementation of strategies to improve the employment prospects of young people. There is no attempt to be exhaustive. The field is vast and there are already many overviews of the general issues. Rather, the chapter themes were selected on the basis of (a) their substantive importance; (b) a perceived need to shed additional light on specific areas where understanding is patchy or where actions and pronouncements may hitherto have tended to be guided by assumptions rather than analysis; and (c) a judgement that in some cases, as in the discussion of contractual arrangements in Chapter 6, an innovative approach to a well-studied subject may aid understanding of relevant issues. A balance has been sought between analyses of issues in developed and in developing countries. Different policy options are appropriate in different countries according to their income and level of development, and the individual chapters have varying importance and relevance for countries at different stages in development. As far as possible, the chapters explicitly consider the relevance of the respective themes for countries differentiated, in particular, by per capita income level. In some cases, for example in respect of the discussion of fiscal policy in the first part of Chapter 2, the availability of evidence or base data limited the approach to a particular selection of countries. However, the analysis thereby generated is of much broader interest and relevance.

The most consistent finding concerning the determinants of youth employment and unemployment is that aggregate demand – the state of the macroeconomy – plays a key role. From their beginnings in the 1980s to date, every single econometric study of the determinants of youth (un)employment, has found an important and statistically significant role for aggregate demand, however measured.[10] Perhaps because it is the constant background to all activity and analysis, the importance of the state of the economy is often neglected in policy discussions where the focus all too often is on the microeconomic determinants of the demand for, and above all the supply-side characteristics of, young jobseekers. With this in mind, Chapter 2 looks at the role of the macroeconomy in determining youth labour market outcomes. More specifically, in the light of the recent renewal of interest in "Keynesian" expansionary fiscal policy

---

[10]   See, for example, Ryan (2001) for a brief review of these studies before the turn of the century. More recent studies tend to focus on other factors – such as institutional arrangements – and look at a broader range of countries, including LMICs; however, the overarching importance of aggregate demand has never been put into doubt.

as a means to redress the fall in aggregate demand following the global financial crisis of 2008, the chapter first examines the potential impact of discretionary fiscal expansion as a means to promote youth employment and reduce youth unemployment in the presence of insufficient aggregate demand. Despite the potential importance of fiscal policy in mitigating the negative consequences of insufficient aggregate demand for youth labour markets, as opposed to those for the labour market as a whole, the specific effects of discretionary fiscal policy on youth labour market outcomes have not – with the partial exception of one study by the International Monetary Fund (IMF, 2014), discussed further below – been the subject of study. The first part of Chapter 2 seeks to fill this gap.

The results of the analysis reported in the first part of the chapter clearly establish the usefulness of discretionary fiscal policy in promoting youth employment, particularly during recessions. This is not an entirely unexpected result; but, as suggested above, it is all too often forgotten in discussions of the youth employment "problem". The analysis also shows, however, that such a strategy will only be effective if government finances are in relatively good shape in the period leading up to the recession, and if the discretionary fiscal policy is implemented without delay once recession hits.

In the second part of the chapter, the potential for sectoral development policies to promote youth employment is discussed. Again, there has been relatively little evidence-based analysis of the potential for sectoral strategies to promote the integration of young people into decent work; the discussion here reaffirms that potential. However, although the econometric analysis provides support for the notion that promoting employment and productivity in traditionally low-productivity occupations is the way to go, a more detailed examination of country-specific experiences and the relevant literature leads to the conclusion that there is no sectoral "silver bullet" for youth employment. Thus, while sectoral strategies of various forms have proved successful in different contexts, there is no unique path to successful youth-oriented development.

An important theme running through the book – along with the growing precariousness of youth employment – concerns the importance of interactions and complementarities between institutions, policies and the broader economic context. Indeed, the analysis of discretionary fiscal policy in Chapter 2 notes the important role of sound budgetary policy in times of growth as a necessary condition for effective countercyclical expansionary fiscal policy during times of recession.

In Chapter 3, which reports the results of a meta-analysis of the youth employment effects of minimum wage legislation, the role of interactions between labour market institutions takes centre stage. The chapter first confirms that, for the most part, the disemployment effects of minimum wages are either small or nil. This finding is in line with the review of minimum wages undertaken under similar circumstances nearly two decades ago (O'Higgins, 2001, ch. 5).

The main contribution of Chapter 3, however, concerns the role of other labour market institutions in determining the size of the disemployment effects of minimum wages in youth labour markets. In addition to the small average size of the disemployment effect, one of the main characteristics of estimates of the effects of minimum wages on youth employment is their substantial heterogeneity across location and time. In seeking to explain some of this variation, a meta-analysis[11] is used to explicitly consider the role of interactions between labour market institutions in determining the youth employment effects of minimum wages. It finds that any disemployment effects that do exist are moderated in countries that have more protective employment legislation, and also – in HICs – where collective bargaining is both more coordinated and less centralized.

Chapter 4 looks at wage subsidy programmes and derives a number of specific findings on their features which may be incorporated into the design of such programmes to improve their effectiveness. There has been a resurgence of interest in wage subsidy programmes of different forms in recent years with the increasing recognition of the need to increase the demand for young workers, particularly in the light of the recent global economic and financial crisis. The chapter seeks to redress the balance in contemporary discussions of ALMPs, which have often tended to focus primarily on the role of training programmes. In doing so, it clearly establishes the importance, for the long-run effectiveness of wage subsidy programmes, of incorporating elements which promote the formal or informal acquisition of employment-related skills and competences by the young participants.

Chapter 5 discusses self-employment among young people, and examines the effectiveness of programmes to promote youth entrepreneurship. While it reaffirms the role frequently played by self-employment, across high-, middle- and lower-income countries, as the "employer" of last resort, the analysis of the ILO's SWTS data in LMICs also suggests a more nuanced picture. It is important to distinguish between "freely chosen" and profitable self-employment, which is often associated with involvement in family business and with more educated young people, from the survival strategies of more disadvantaged young people. The promotion of entrepreneurship programmes is an area in which international organizations have been particularly active. Where opportunities for wage employment are severely limited, as in many LICs, such programmes may be seen as one of relatively few options. However, while programmes promoting entrepreneurship can have a positive effect on young people's longer-term employment and income prospects, the chapter notes that this requires fulfilment of quite a restrictive set of conditions. Ideally, such programmes should be part of a more general toolkit of programmes and policies designed to integrate young people into good-quality employment. On their own, they are unlikely to provide a successful general solution to the challenge of promoting decent work among young people.

The last two analytical chapters, Chapters 6 and 7, consider issues of relevance primarily to pillar 5, rights at work. Chapter 6 looks at contractual arrangements aimed at facilitating the entry of young people into employment. Unusually, it also

---

[11] For those not familiar with the term, meta-analysis and its rather grander sister, systematic review, are forms of quantitative literature review where the findings of single studies are used as observations in a statistical analysis of an aggregation of studies on a particular issue which meet specific criteria. It is a very useful tool, inasmuch as it allows one to use statistical analysis to make sense of the variety of findings related to a specific case, such as here.

considers work-based training arrangements, including apprenticeships, which may in practice be seen as forms of contractual arrangement with the potential to facilitate the entry of young people into long-term stable employment. This is important inasmuch as recent years have seen the emergence of less formal work-based learning arrangements such as traineeships and/or internships. While these arrangements may provide a basic and flexible form of on-the-job competence-building, they can run the risk of becoming cheap "make work" programmes with few positive outcomes for young people. The chapter is thus concerned not only with issues arising under pillar 5, but also with those covered by pillar 2 on employability. Underlying the analysis is the concern that the spread of "non-standard" contractual forms has had the effect of removing or at least reducing the protections available to young workers in HICs. These arrangements take many forms, and the chapter identifies those that appear to be more effective in promoting the longer-term integration of young people into stable employment. Some of the findings are perhaps surprising; for example, in addition to the standard finding that dual apprenticeships work "best",[12] the chapter also finds a positive role – in some circumstances – for traditional informal apprenticeships.

Chapter 7 looks at informal employment, which is clearly the dominant form of youth employment in LMICs, and as such is an obvious choice for inclusion here. Moreover, although there are a number of single-country analyses of various aspects of youth informality, there have been relatively few evidence-based considerations of the characteristics, determinants and consequences of, and possible remedies to, informal employment among young people.[13] As in Chapter 6 on contractual arrangements, the concern is primarily with issues related to pillar 5 on rights at work. Just as non-standard contractual forms of employment have come to dominate the early labour market experiences of young people in HICs, as noted above, informal employment is the predominant form of employment for young people living in LMICs. Of course, informal employment exists also in HICs, as do non-standard contractual forms of formal employment in LMICs; however, in both cases these are minority forms of employment.

One of the key features of informality is its variety. By definition, the key characteristic of informality is absence of formality, that is, of regulation; thus it is not surprising that informal employment comprises a huge variety of types of job and situation, of which the only common feature is the absence of formal regulation. The chapter reviews evidence on informality and young people and uses the SWTS data to dig a little more deeply into how informality affects young people and how this varies across regions and countries, and according to individuals' characteristics. In particular, the analysis considers the extent to which – as some have suggested – informality may act as a stepping stone to stable formal employment. For less educated

---

[12]   See any standard general treatment of the youth employment problem. See, for example, O'Higgins, 2001.

[13]   A partial exception is the paper by Shehu and Nilsson (2014) which provides a starting point for the chapter's analysis.

youth, this suggestion is conclusively refuted by the analysis of the chapter, as is the idea that informality is in any sense freely chosen. For the more highly educated, however, the situation is somewhat more ambivalent. While clearly inferior to formal employment, informality is more easily escaped by more highly educated young people, for whom the wage penalty associated with informality is also smaller. The chapter considers possible policy remedies and discusses a number of initiatives being proposed and implemented by the ILO in this area.

The eighth and final chapter draws together some of the major findings of the six themed chapters and suggests ways in which these can be brought together – in a complementary fashion – in order to better promote the integration of young people into decent work. The book ends by offering a perspective on what needs to be done in the future.

2. Macroeconomic and sectoral issues in youth employment policy

2.1. Introduction

One of the most consistent, indeed universal, findings in the literature on the causes of youth labour market outcomes is that aggregate demand is a fundamental determinant of the state of the youth labour market. It is firmly established that what happens to young people as they enter the labour market is very much dependent on what is going on in the economy as a whole.[1] In particular, youth unemployment and NEET rates are very closely related to aggregate demand. Matsumoto et al. (2012) have looked explicitly at the role of the macroeconomy in determining youth employment and unemployment and have found that, as one might expect, growth in gross domestic product (GDP) is strongly related to youth employment and inversely related to youth unemployment; however, they also find that a greater volatility of GDP is in itself damaging to youth labour market outcomes. That is, not only do growth rates themselves matter, so too does the extent to which they vary over time. O'Higgins (2012) also finds that the elasticity of the youth employment rate in relation to variations in real GDP increased during the recent financial crisis, while Choudhry et al. (2012) have found that the impact of an economic shock may vary according to the type of shock (e.g. whether financial or non-financial) and also across different types of person, and in particular may impact the youth and aggregate labour markets to varying extents.

Research by the ILO (ILO, 2013a) also reaffirmed the importance of expansionary fiscal policy in counteracting, or at least mitigating, the negative effects of the global economic crisis, raising employment rates and reducing unemployment at the aggregate level. In the period immediately following the onset of the recent global recession, many countries implemented some form of discretionary countercyclical fiscal policy in addition to the countercyclical response of automatic stabilizers. Among North American and European countries, this almost universally took the form of de facto expansionary fiscal policy. Indeed, "the fiscal response of the advanced economies to the global financial crisis showed the importance of discretionary actions in mitigating the effects on activity of a severe and protracted slump"

---

[1]   There are many studies confirming this. See e.g. World Bank, 2006; O'Higgins, 2001, 2010. That is not to say, of course, that macroeconomic conditions are the only significant factor (O'Higgins, 2012).

13

(IMF, 2015, p. 21).[2] From 2010 on, the policy priority in many of these countries moved towards a concern with debt and deficit levels. By the third quarter of 2011, the majority of HICs had adopted fiscal consolidation measures – that is, "austerity", as it has come to be known (ILO, 2013a). The ILO's *World of Work Report 2013* argues plausibly that the consequences of cuts in public expenditure and increases in (primarily indirect) taxation during this period, along with the relaxation of employment protection legislation (EPL), impeded recovery in many cases (ILO, 2013b). Similarly, in the United States, Ball et al. (2014) have argued persuasively that, in the context of a liquidity trap with interest rates effectively at zero, in addition to – and partly because of – the positive effects of expansionary fiscal policy on economic and employment growth, properly designed fiscal stimulus is likely to reduce rather than increase the long-run debt burden. In the United Kingdom, a number of commentators have argued that the introduction of austerity measures in 2010 was both unnecessary and counterproductive in that they prematurely interrupted the recovery from the recession (e.g. Sawyer, 2012).

Relatively little attention has been paid, however, to the potential of macroeconomic policy specifically to improve labour market outcomes for young people. The next section analyses the potential for discretionary fiscal policy to influence youth labour market outcomes, while the subsequent section looks at the potential for sectoral policies to improve the labour market situation of young people.

2.2. Fiscal policy and youth labour markets

The idea that countercyclical expansionary fiscal policy could be used to stimulate GDP growth and consequently employment during a recession is of course closely associated with Keynes (and Kalecki), but its origins are rather older.[3] In the past two decades or so, there has been a steady growth in the literature looking at the size (and sometimes also the sign) of the fiscal multiplier, that is, the effect of expansionary fiscal policy on GDP. Such efforts have proliferated since the onset of the recession and the adoption of de facto discretionary countercyclical fiscal policy in most OECD countries. The findings have been neatly summarized in a recent meta-analysis (Gechert, 2015) which suggests that the fiscal multiplier is of the order of 1, with larger multipliers associated with increased government expenditure as opposed to reductions in taxation; and that fiscal expansion based on increased government investment expenditure appears to be the most effective of all. A fur-

---

[2]   Although the text continues – quoting Blanchard et al. (2010): "it also illustrated one of the limitations of discretionary fiscal measures, namely that 'they come too late to fight a standard recession'" (IMF, 2015, p. 21).

[3]   See e.g. Barber, 1985, for a review of pre-Keynesian work which advocated fiscal stimulus to counteract a recession. Closely related under-consumption theories go back further to the Birmingham School of economists in the first half of the nineteenth century. The Birmingham School argued that the economic downturn of the time was caused by the end of the stimulus associated with spending during, and related to, the Napoleonic Wars.

ther finding common to much of the literature is that fiscal expansion is particularly effective during times of recession, as was indeed suggested by Keynes (1936).

The aforementioned paper by Gechert, along with a number of other analyses, may be contrasted with a view put forward by Feldstein (1982), with subsequent empirical support from work by Giavazzi and Pagano (1990, 1996) and later still by Alesina and others in a series of papers during the 1990s and early 2000s (Alesina and Perotti, 1995; Alesina and Ardagna, 1998; Alesina et al., 2002). The basic idea of this line of analysis is that traditional Keynesian stimuli can be contractionary and, conversely, that austerity can be expansionary. The intuition underlying these papers concerns the effects of specific government policy changes on individuals' expectations; thus, for example, business and consumer confidence may be boosted by reduced government expenditure because the reduction is seen as an indicator of future long-term reductions in the tax burden. Increased private consumption and investment will consequently more than offset the contractionary reduction in government expenditure (or taxation).

This view has been refuted by numerous studies; for example, the IMF (2014) has demonstrated convincingly, in its examination of fiscal consolidations in HICs between 1980 and 2009, that fiscal consolidations were in fact contractionary, with a deficit reduction equal to 1 per cent of GDP leading to a contraction of 0.5 per cent in output and an increase in unemployment of 0.3 percentage points.

It has also been observed by several commentators that whereas in the past fiscal consolidation was typically mitigated by expansionary monetary policy, such an option – with real interest rates at or close to zero – is not available today. Moreover, a number of authors have pointed to the endogeneity bias inherent in the approach of Alesina and colleagues based on analysis of the cyclically adjusted primary balance (CAPB); during a period of strong economic growth, governments faced with labour and capacity constraints may well opt to reduce the budget deficit, which would lead to an association between CAPB and contractionary policy, but with the direction of causation pointing in the opposite direction (Baker and Rosnick, 2014). It has also been observed that the cyclical adjustments of the CAPB will not take into account changes in asset values with consequent effects on capital gains taxation, here too leading to a direct association between consolidation and expansion, but once again with causation running in the opposite direction (Guajardo et al., 2011).

To summarize, the balance of the currently available evidence suggests a constructive role for expansionary fiscal policy in mitigating and even reversing crisis-induced falls in real GDP. The second question that arises is whether this translates into increased employment and, of specific concern here, increased youth employment and reduced youth unemployment. Over the past decade or so, particularly following the onset of the global crisis, a number of papers produced by the ILO have looked at the relationship between economic and employment growth (e.g. Kapsos, 2005; ILO, 2012a, 2013a), and the potential for and advisability of using expansionary fiscal policy to boost employment was reaffirmed in the ILO's *World of Work Report 2013* (ILO, 2013b). The IMF's analysis (IMF, 2014) provides further evidence of the negative effects of fiscal consolidation on employment – although these are weaker when the reduction in the deficit is the result of reduced government expenditure (as opposed to increased taxation), and the adjustment does not take place following a protracted recession – with positive (non-Keynesian) employment effects discernible after three years. A similar pattern of effects is also reported for youth unemployment. As yet, with the partial exception of the IMF paper, little work has been done on the specific relation between fiscal policy and youth labour market outcomes.

2.2.1. Discretionary fiscal policy and youth labour market outcomes

In this section we report the results of an ILO analysis of the short-run impact of discretionary fiscal policy on youth labour market outcomes.[4] The analysis covers 19 European countries over the period 2001–13.[5] Discretionary fiscal policy was identified following the method used by, among others, Fatás and Mihov (2003, 2006), Afonso et al. (2010) and, in particular, Agnello et al. (2013). At the first stage, the relevant fiscal variables are regressed on their own lagged value, real GDP, the inflation rate and its square, public debt and a linear time trend, for each country separately. The purpose is to distinguish between persistence, automatic responsiveness and discretion in fiscal policy. Specifically, using this approach, the residual from the first-stage country-specific regressions can be employed as a measure of discretionary fiscal policy.[6] The second stage involved regressing the relevant labour market indicator on the resultant measures of discretionary fiscal policy, HP-filtered real GDP and government debt,[7] and the three main components of the OECD employment protection index, in order to take some account of cross-country institutional differences likely to influence youth labour market outcomes.

The impacts of discretionary fiscal policy on several indicators of youth labour market outcomes were analysed, distinguishing between the effects of expansionary policy during recessions and expansions, as well as between policies financed by reducing the (trend) budget surplus and those financed by increasing the deficit (table 2.1).

---

[4]   A more detailed analysis is available in Ebell and O'Higgins, 2015.

[5]   The data employed are quarterly (2001.I–2013.IV) and the 19 countries covered are: Austria, Belgium, Czech Republic, Denmark, Finland, France, Germany, Greece, Hungary, Ireland, Italy, the Netherlands, Norway, Poland, Portugal, Slovakia, Spain, Sweden and the United Kingdom. With the exception of Norway, all the countries are members of the EU. The specific choice of countries was determined by the availability of data; only European countries with a complete or almost complete set of observations were included.

[6]   At an earlier stage of this work a Hodrick–Prescott filter (HP-filter) was used on the fiscal policy variables; that is, they were de-trended using the methodology named after Hodrick and Prescott (1980, 1997). This arguably accounts for persistence in fiscal policy, but not for the effects of automatic stabilizers, which are non-discretionary, at least in the short run. Using this approach, the results were qualitatively similar although coefficients were less well defined.

[7]   That is, real GDP and public debt (as a percentage of GDP) were included in HP-filtered form. Apart from removing the trend component and hence avoiding problems of spurious correlation arising from common trends, the resultant HP-filtered index of government debt may be interpreted as a measure of the output gap.

Table 2.1. The effects of expansionary fiscal policy on youth labour market indicators: The role of the state of the economy and the state of public finances

| | Effects of expansionary fiscal policy | | | |
| | Budget in surplus | | Budget in deficit | |
	During expansion	During recession	During expansion	During recession
Youth unemployment rate	_*	___***	++	++**
Youth employment rate	0	+++***	__***	_*
Ratio of youth/adult unemployment rates	_***	_***	0	0
Long-term unemployment	__**	__**	+	__*
Temporary employment	__***	0	0	+

Note: The direction of the effects of expansionary fiscal policy on the various indicators is shown by plus/minus signs (and zero); the size of the effects is indicated by the number of plus or minus signs. Statistical significance is indicated by asterisks (with * denoting $p < .10$, ** denoting $p < .05$ and *** denoting $p < .01$).

Source: Author's calculations based on results reported in Ebell and O'Higgins (2015).

The effects of expansionary fiscal policy vary with the state of the economic cycle and the state of public finances; the best time to adopt an expansionary stance is when the budget balance is above trend and the economy is in recession. Under these circumstances, an expansionary fiscal stance is associated with a substantial fall in youth unemployment and a corresponding increase in youth employment; it is also associated with a fall in the prevalence of long-term unemployment among young people, an important gain. On the other hand, expansionary policy during recession seems to have little or no effect on the prevalence of temporary employment.

Adopting an expansionary stance during a period of economic growth is less effective. So long as the budget balance is above trend, implying a relatively conservative fiscal stance in the past, expansionary fiscal policy still produces positive effects; such a policy is associated with a moderate reduction in youth unemployment and a similarly moderate increase in employment. However, the reduction in long-term unemployment is as pronounced as during a recession, and expansionary fiscal policy in these circumstances also leads to a reduction in temporary employment.

On the other hand, if the public finances are in a relatively poor initial state with the budget balance below trend, any positive benefits from an expansionary fiscal policy are cancelled out or even reversed. In this situation, expansionary policy is largely counterproductive. One possible explanation for this lies in the expectations argument of the "contractionary expansionists" such as Alesina and colleagues mentioned above. It is plausible that, if public finances have been in deficit for some time and hence the budget balance is below trend, a further increase in the deficit is likely to provoke expectations of future remedial (contractionary) action to repair the public finances. In such a scenario, it is likely that people will factor into their current behaviour likely future contractionary action on the part of governments, and thus not respond with enthusiasm to expansionary fiscal policy. In this respect the results give some qualified support to the thesis of Alesina and others who maintain that expansionary fiscal policy can have contractionary effects on the economy. One might observe, however, that even with the budget already in deficit, expansionary fiscal policy does lead to a fall in the prevalence of long-term unemployment.

Finally, we may observe that with the budget in surplus, expansionary fiscal policy leads to a slight improvement of the relative position of young people compared to adults: expansion reduces the ratio of youth unemployment rates to prime-age adult rates. This is encouraging inasmuch as it suggests that expansionary fiscal policy during a recession can slow down the rise in youth unemployment rates in these circumstances, further reducing the increases in youth unemployment which tend in any case to be proportionately slightly less than the corresponding variations in prime-age adult rates (O'Higgins, 2010, 2017).

Overall, the results strongly support the adoption of a truly countercyclical discretionary fiscal policy with an expansionary stance during a recession, and a more conservative position during a boom so as to bolster public finances in preparation for the inevitable slowdown. Moreover, the negative influence of below-trend budget balances suggests that, in the event of a recession, prompt action is required before the effects of the recession in depressing the public finances make themselves fully felt. In this case, expansionary fiscal policy can pre-empt the recession-induced worsening of public finances. Once the budget balance falls below trend, then the fiscal space for and effectiveness of a fiscal expansion may be lost.

2.2.2. Discretionary fiscal policy: Policy recommendations

The evidence presented here shows that countercyclical fiscal policy is an instrument well suited to ameliorating youth unemployment during recessions. Under certain conditions, expanding the budget deficit (or reducing the budget surplus) can mitigate the negative effects of insufficient aggregate demand on both youth and adult labour markets, moderating any reductions in employment and increases in unemployment. Moreover, the evidence also suggests that this counteracting influence is more effective for young people than for prime-age adults. Among other things, this is consistent with the findings cited above regarding the existence of a positive "Keynesian" multiplier (Gechert, 2015), and with previous work by the ILO (in particular, ILO, 2013a) on the positive aggregate employment effects of expansionary fiscal policy and by the IMF (IMF, 2014) on the negative employment effects of contractionary fiscal consolidation.

Specifically, the instrument is most effective if preceded by a relatively conservative fiscal policy in non-recessionary circumstances – that is to say, a fully countercyclical fiscal policy is needed, with fiscal expansion during recessions and contraction during periods of growth. Decreasing the budget surplus, particularly during a recession, leads to substantial reductions in youth unemployment rates. Reducing the discretionary surplus by 1 percentage point relative to trend is associated with an immediate decrease in youth unemployment of between 0.33 and 0.51 percentage points – and, equally importantly, with an increase in the rate of youth employment of between 0.19 and 0.34 percentage points.

Thus the traditional Keynesian prescription of countercyclical fiscal policy is upheld. In order to reduce youth unemployment and increase youth employment, governments should increase expenditure and reduce taxation during recessions, while doing the opposite when the economy is expanding. The fact that the effectiveness of countercyclical fiscal policy in combating youth unemployment is conditional on the prior state of a country's public finances, however, is a strong reminder that expansionary fiscal policy is not a universal remedy for youth unemployment. It is primarily appropriate as a countercyclical measure to adopt during recessions. Moreover, increasing an existing deficit is much less effective than reducing an existing surplus[8] in combating youth unemployment or promoting youth employment rates, and may even be counterproductive; countercyclical fiscal policy is clearly more effective for countries that are already running surpluses at the onset of recession. That is, countries which stabilize their public finances by running surpluses in good times are most able to benefit from reducing those surpluses when a recession hits. Moreover, the results presented here imply that when a recession does appear, the reaction must be swift in order to gain full benefit from the positive effects of expansionary fiscal policy.

The impact of fiscal policy on the ratio of youth to prime-age unemployment rates is rather less marked; this suggests that the impact of fiscal policy does not differ very much between the youth labour market and the labour market for prime-age adults. There is a positive and statistically significant effect, implying that expansionary fiscal policy is more effective for young people than for those of prime age; however, although statistically significant, the size of the coefficient is small. Nevertheless, since youth unemployment is higher in absolute terms (especially in recession), any positive impacts on unemployment will be significantly larger (in absolute terms) for young people.

Further analysis, going into more detail in terms of the destination of expenditure and the source of revenue, would be desirable, though it is not clear how reliable the estimates generated would be. In any event, the evidence already to hand suggests that youth unemployment rates are responsive to fiscal policy (slightly more than) proportionately to adult rates; this suggests in turn that expansionary fiscal policy is likely to reinforce the tendency of youth unemployment rates to react less than adult rates in percentage terms to variations over the cycle.

---

[8] Strictly speaking, the dichotomy is between running budget deficits above and below trend. In the latter case, with a deficit which is below trend – or even negative, i.e. a budget surplus – expansionary fiscal policy will be more effective.

Expansionary fiscal policy can reduce the prevalence of long-term unemployment, again so long as the budget is in surplus, although in this case the effect does not vary with the cycle. Expansionary fiscal policy also tends to reduce the prevalence of temporary employment, but only during periods of growth.

All in all, fiscal policy can play a useful role in ameliorating problems in youth labour markets arising as a result of insufficient aggregate demand. Indeed, the results suggest that expansionary policy during a recession is more effective for young people than it is for adults, and may also go some way towards mitigating some of the specific problems facing European youth labour markets today, such as the increasing duration of unemployment and the decreasing duration of employment contracts. However, it is clear that such demand management policies can – indeed, should – complement, but cannot replace, additional action at the microeconomic and institutional levels. The moderate size of the effects of fiscal policy on youth labour market outcomes and, in particular, on long-term youth unemployment, clearly supports the idea that direct intervention in youth labour markets, through, for example, ALMPs in general and the Youth Guarantee in particular,[9] is also necessary.

2.3. Sectoral development and youth employment

What about the potential for sectoral development policies – in addition to overall macroeconomic demand management – to play a role in promoting decent work for young people?

For many years, there has been a gradual movement of young workers out of agriculture and into industry and, especially, services, so that the agricultural sector now accounts for more than half of youth employment in only a small minority of low-income countries (LICs) (ILO, 2015a), and in several middle-income countries (MICs) it has all but disappeared as a source of employment.[10] Services now dominate youth employment, accounting for more than half of youth employment in four of the five SWTS regions (SSA, MENA, LAC and EECA), and are the largest employer in all five regions.

Data on sectoral employment by age from the ILO's SWTS show a slightly more nuanced picture (figure 2.1). Although services again dominate employment across the three age groups, the agricultural sector is still a significant employer for the youngest workers, accounting for around one-third of teenage employment.

---

[9]   The Youth Guarantee, established by a European Council recommendation in April 2013 (Council of the European Union, 2013), involves the commitment by all Member States to ensure that all young people under the age of 25 receive a good quality offer of employment, continued education, apprenticeship or traineeship within a period of four months of becoming unemployed or leaving formal education. Member States started implementing the Youth Guarantee in 2014, and it has become the main form of ALMP for young people throughout the EU (see http://ec.europa.eu/social/main.jsp?catId=1079).

[10]   In only four of the 34 countries in the complete SWTS data set are the majority of young workers still employed in agriculture; three of these are in SSA (Madagascar, Malawi and Uganda) and one is in AP (Cambodia).

Figure 2.1. Employment of young people in LMICs by industrial sector, age and gender

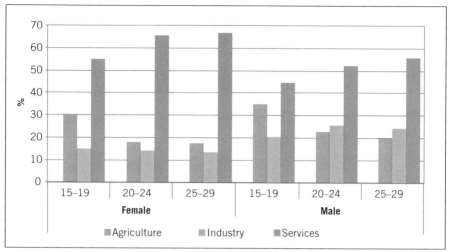

Note: The figure reports average values over the survey period 2012–15. The precise dates of the average vary across countries. For countries covered, see note to figure 1.1 above.

Source: Author's calculations based on SWTS data.

Further examination of the data suggests that this reflects the substantial participation of teenagers in unpaid family work. On the other hand, the majority of all young females and of young men aged 20 and above work in services.

Although the importance of specific sectors for development and, in particular, the role of sectoral development strategies for employment creation, have long been the subjects of much debate (among relatively recent contributions see, for example, McMillan and Rodrik, 2011; Kucera and Roncolato, 2015; Islam and Islam, 2015, ch. 4), the potential for sectoral development policies to promote youth employment has hitherto been rather less studied. At the aggregate level, Arias-Vazquez et al. (2012) argue that the growth of labour-intensive sectors such as agriculture and manufacturing is more likely to lead to growth in employment as a whole than in youth employment specifically. They estimate panel regressions (using 184 surveys from 81 countries) for annualized changes in employment on the weighted growth rates of output of different sectors. They compare the effects of high labour productivity sectors (manufacturing, transport and communications, finance, electricity and utilities, and mining) with low labour productivity sectors (other services, agriculture, retail and wholesale trade, government and public administration,[11] and construction) on employment growth. They also estimate panel regressions on individual data for Brazil, Indonesia and Mexico. They test for differential impact of high and low labour productivity sectors on annual growth of employment, and for the impact

---

[11]   It is not clear on what basis government and public administration is estimated to be a low-productivity sector since it is difficult to measure its output. It is, however, certainly labour-intensive.

Figure 2.2. Youth unemployment rates and manufacturing share in HICs, 1990–2013

Source: World Bank World Development Indicators, ILO modelled estimates.

Figure 2.3. Youth unemployment rates and manufacturing share in MICs, 1990–2013

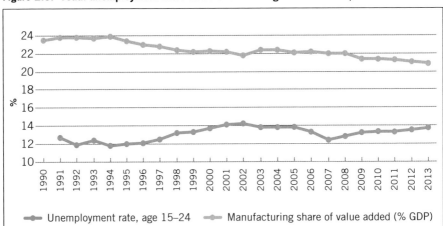

Source: World Bank World Development Indicators, ILO modelled estimates.

of export-led growth on annualized changes in employment. They find that "low productivity growth leads to faster employment growth than does high productivity growth" (p. 13),[12] and that this effect is most marked in MICs. They also find some evidence of a trade-off between employment growth and wage growth.

---

[12] The difference is statistically significant at 10 per cent. However, strictly speaking the coefficient on high-productivity sectors is *negative* and statistically significant, while that on low-productivity sectors is positive but not statistically significant. In other words, their results show that growth of high-productivity sectors is inimical to employment growth, while growth in low-productivity sectors has no influence on employment growth.

Figure 2.4. Youth unemployment rates and manufacturing share in LICs, 1990–2013

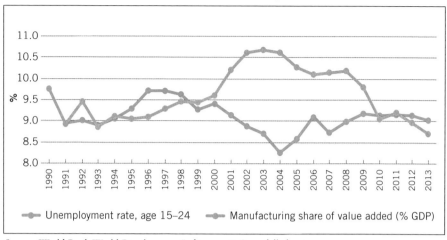

Source: World Bank World Development Indicators, ILO modelled estimates.

In a similar vein, Junankar (2013) finds a trade-off between productivity growth and employment growth: countries with faster-growing productivity have slower employment growth. For many less developed countries, agriculture is a dominant sector in terms of both share of GDP and share of employment. Research on poverty reduction by Loayza and Raddatz (2010) suggests that growth in the agriculture, construction and manufacturing sectors is more likely to reduce poverty by increasing employment. McMillan and Rodrik (2011) find that many LMICs suffer from a "resource curse", such that although the economy is growing, employment is not. Thus, countries that discovered, for example, oil reserves (such as Brazil) had disappointing employment growth.

Are there, then, specific links between youth labour markets and sectoral growth? An examination of the relationship between the share of manufacturing employment and youth unemployment rates is suggestive (see figures 2.2–2.4). Although the relationship is not entirely straightforward in HICs (figure 2.2), there does appear to be a fairly strong negative association between the two in MICs (figure 2.3) and LICs (figure 2.4); for the most part, as the manufacturing share of GDP declines, youth unemployment rates increase, and vice versa.

2.3.1. Econometric analysis

Estimating the determinants of youth labour market outcomes across a range of countries, including terms to control for sectoral output shares, supports the notion that sectoral development, particularly in agriculture, may play an important role in promoting youth employment (table 2.2). The table reports the estimated coefficients for aggregate output shares in agriculture and industry from more general models, also including terms to control for investment, GDP per capita and GDP growth,

Table 2.2. Summary of econometric estimates of the role of sectoral employment shares in determining youth labour market outcomes

		Youth labour force participation rate	Youth employment rate	Youth unemployment rate
Agricultural employment share	Full sample	0.19***	0.18***	−0.10***
	EU	1.08***	1.63***	−1.99***
	HICs	0.51	0.68	−0.88*
	ECA	0.29*	0.30***	−0.25***
	MICs	0.21**	0.19**	−0.06
Industrial employment share	Full sample	0.17***	0.16***	−0.08**
	EU	0.29**	0.45***	−0.51**
	HICs	0.21*	0.32***	−0.29**
	ECA	0.30***	0.27***	−0.14**
	MICs	0.18**	0.13**	−0.01

Note: Statistical significance is indicated by asterisks (* denoting $p < .10$, ** denoting $p < .05$ and *** denoting $p < .01$).

Source: Based on results reported in Junankar, 2016.

as well as country fixed effects. The models were estimated for a variety of country groupings, namely Europe and Central Asia (ECA), the EU, HICs and MICs.[13]

Agricultural output is always associated positively with youth labour force participation and youth employment, and negatively with youth unemployment. Similar associations apply between youth labour market indicators and the industrial output share, although in this case they are a little weaker. The effect of agricultural share on youth labour market indicators is greatest in HICs, and above all in the EU countries, as is the difference between the effects of agricultural and industrial output. These results are largely in line with recent work by the World Bank and others who have suggested that developing agricultural production and especially productivity may be a fruitful way to promote youth employment. Increased productivity will lead, among other things, to higher incomes, which in turn, through multiplier effects, will induce the further development of incomes and economic activity in addition to the direct employment effects of expanded production.

The McKinsey report (MGI, 2012) on youth employment and the *World Development Report 2008* (World Bank, 2007) both emphasized the positive contribution that agriculture can play in a strategy to increase employment. Although agriculture has traditionally been a source of vulnerable employment, the McKinsey report estimated that employment growth in this sector is likely to produce 8 million

---

[13]   Although LICs were included in the full sample, there were too few of them for separate estimates for this group of countries to be derived.

(i.e. 14 per cent of all) new stable jobs by 2020, and that this could be almost doubled to 14 million (or 19 per cent) in an optimistic scenario with appropriate development of the sector. Specifically, the report argues that enhanced employment growth in Africa could be generated by large-scale commercial farming on uncultivated land – the continent currently accounts for around 60 per cent of the world's uncultivated arable land – and through a shift from low value added grain production to more labour-intensive and higher value added horticultural and biofuel crops (MGI, 2012). The example of Burkina Faso is a case in point. Agricultural production here grew by 4 per cent annually between 1995 and 2009, largely driven by productivity gains in the cultivation of cotton, the country's main crop. The growth arose from both land and labour productivity gains, as well as from an expansion of the cultivated land area. Largely as a consequence of this agricultural expansion, real per capita GDP doubled in Burkina Faso between 1995 and 2006 (IMF, 2012).

However, the analysis remains only partially convincing. At a purely arithmetic level there is a direct connection between GDP, productivity and employment.[14] However, this does not necessarily imply causal relations between these variables. At least since Kaldor's seminal analysis which identified manufacturing as the engine of growth (Kaldor, 1967), a substantial literature has emerged centred on the importance of different sectors in generating employment growth. The econometric analysis identifies association, but does not in itself prove causation. Recently Kucera and Roncolato (2016) have compared the roles of manufacturing and services as sources of employment and productivity in 18 Asian and Latin American countries. Although not the main focus of their paper, the key message emerging from their analysis that is of relevance here is that there are different paths to growth, and the existence of a productivity–employment trade-off is by no means a foregone conclusion. One of the tables from Kucera and Roncolato (2016), reproduced here in slightly adapted form as table 2.3, neatly illustrates of the point. The table groups the 18 countries covered by the study according to whether they experienced strong or weak productivity growth and positive or negative employment growth over the period 1990–2005. In the presence of a strong trade-off between productivity and employment growth one would expect countries to be grouped primarily in cells (2) and (3), where strong productivity growth is accompanied by negative employment growth and vice versa. In fact, most of the countries (13 out of 18) are found in either cell (1) or cell (4), where strong employment growth is accompanied by strong productivity growth, and vice versa. Of course, in this case too there is no demonstration of causality; however, the finding is consistent with employment growth and productivity growth being complementary rather than mutually exclusive alternative sources of economic growth.

The analysis then goes on to decompose industry-level contributions to aggregate labour productivity and employment growth. Particularly within the more

---

[14]   Expressed in well-known terms as $Y/_P \equiv Y/_N \times N/_P$ (where Y = GDP, P = population and N = employment). That is, GDP per capita is, by definition, the product of productivity and the employment rate. Hence, growth in GDP per capita arises with growth in either productivity, the employment rate or both.

Table 2.3. Labour productivity growth vs employment growth in 18 Latin American and Asian countries, 1990–2005

	Positive employment rate growth	Negative employment rate growth
Strong productivity growth	(1) Hong Kong (China), Republic of Korea, Singapore, Taiwan (China), Thailand	(2) India, Malaysia
Weak productivity growth	(3) Bolivia, Chile, Costa Rica	(4) Argentina, Brazil, Colombia, Indonesia, Mexico, Peru, Philippines, Bolivarian Rep. of Venezuela

Note: Positive and negative employment growth are defined by whether employment growth is greater or less than the growth of the working-age population and labour force. Strong and weak labour productivity growth are defined by whether such growth is greater or less than 3 per cent. All data are based on annual averages.

Source: Adapted from Kucera and Roncolato, 2016, table 3, p. 184.

populated cells ((1) and (4)), where productivity is shown to be complementary to employment growth, there is a wide variety of patterns in the contributions of specific industries and services to both labour productivity and employment growth. Thus, for example, Kucera and Roncolato found that in India and Peru employment growth was primarily due to agriculture; however, these were exceptions rather than the rule, and moreover, both these countries experienced negative employment growth over the period. The more general lesson emerging is that there appear to be many possible "sectoral" paths to growth.

Furthermore, the econometric analysis above took no account of employment quality. An employment promotion strategy based on the expansion of agricultural employment runs the risk of perpetuating low-quality, low-productivity employment. As Kucera and Roncolato amply illustrate, there are roads to growth which incorporate both employment and productivity growth; this implies that it is possible to raise both the quality and quantity of employment, which surely constitutes a preferable strategy.

2.3.2. Policy-related conclusions

As yet, little research has been done into the potential for sectoral development policies to promote employment specifically for young people. The analysis reported here, as well as the previous studies cited which were undertaken at a more aggregated level, suggest that sectoral development policies may well be useful in supporting the development of jobs for youth; however, analyses to date have undoubtedly only scratched the surface.

A number of studies – including the current analysis – have identified the potential for the development of agriculture to act as a spur to improving youth employment rates and reducing youth unemployment. However, such a strategy runs the risk of promoting youth employment at the expense of the quality of work. In order to avoid this outcome, any strategy based on the development of agricultural employment should be based on improving agricultural productivity as well as developing domestic value chains, so as to increase the value added created by local producers.

In his analysis of the role of agriculture in promoting youth employment in Africa, Losch suggests that "the idea of being able to 'pick' one specific policy option to speed up SSA's structural transformation is pure fallacy: there is no 'sectoral silver bullet' to deal with Africa's structural change challenges in the twenty-first century" (2016, p. 27). It is hard not to concur; indeed, the evidence presented here suggests that this finding can reasonably be generalized to the world as a whole. There are no clear and general lessons to be learned as to which specific sector or sectors is or are the best choice for promoting the quantity and quality of jobs for young people. Rather, while there is much evidence that sectoral development strategies can play a useful role in promoting youth employment, which is the best specific strategy to use will depend on the circumstances of, and opportunities available to, different countries.

2.4. Conclusions and policy recommendations

This chapter has sought to take the discussion of macroeconomic and sectoral policies beyond the now well-established empirical observation that conditions in the youth labour market are heavily dependent on conditions in the aggregate economy as a whole. Of course, this is not the whole story, and both labour market institutions – whether intended to or not – and specific policies and programmes to promote youth employment have key roles to play; these will be discussed in subsequent chapters. Here, however, attention has been directed at ways in which macroeconomic and sectoral policies may actively be engaged to promote more and better jobs for young people. In particular, this chapter has discussed the potential for discretionary fiscal policy and sectoral development policies to improve conditions in youth labour markets and above all to promote youth employment.

Although the findings on discretionary fiscal policy reported here were the result of an econometric analysis of high-income OECD countries, there is no reason to suppose that their relevance is limited to such countries. The choice of sample examined here was dictated by the availability of reliable quarterly data on the main aggregates, and while there are of course important differences concerning relevant structural characteristics as well as available fiscal space, there is no particular a priori reason to suppose that results would be substantially different when analysing LMICs. Indeed, analyses of the determinants of youth unemployment and employment that have been extended to LMICs have found similar impacts of macroeconomic factors in determining youth labour market outcomes.[15]

---

[15] See e.g. Matsumoto et al. (2012), who estimated the effects of (primarily) macroeconomic variables on youth unemployment. They found rather similar effects for the main macroeconomic aggregates such as investment, aggregate demand (proxied by the adult unemployment rate) and public debt. The interested reader is referred also to Choudhry et al. (2012), who looked at debt crises, and Afonso et al. (2010), who examined fiscal policy in both developing and developed countries. In neither case did the authors find significant differences across country income levels.

The central policy-related conclusions arising from the analysis are as follows:

Discretionary fiscal policy

There is clearly a role for expansionary fiscal policy to promote youth employment and to reduce youth unemployment when the economy is in recession.

Expansionary fiscal policy is even more effective – albeit slightly – in promoting employment for young people than for adults, although clearly a discretionary fiscal expansion during a recession can reduce the deleterious labour market consequences of recession for both groups. Such an expansionary fiscal policy is far more effective where the government finances have been well managed and are consequently in surplus (or at least above trend) during pre-recession times. However, perhaps owing to its effects on expectations of necessary future tax increases, as suggested by Alesina and others discussed above, an expansion which is financed by deepening an already established annual deficit may well be counterproductive and actually lead to a deterioration of youth labour market conditions. A related point is that when recessions hit – as they are bound to – the fiscal policy reaction needs to be swift and decisive, implemented before the recession itself worsens the budget balance. In this respect, extensive automatic stabilizers are likely to play an important role in the effectiveness of the response, since by their very nature these do not require specific policy decisions.

Expansionary fiscal policy can also lead to employment growth during boom periods; however, in these conditions the beneficial effects are much less pronounced than during recessions. The beneficial effects of discretionary expansion are conditional on the preceding budget balance being in good condition. Such effects are dramatically reduced once the budget balance drops below trend, as it will tend to do during a recession by virtue of reduced economic activity lowering tax receipts and increasing (non-discretionary) expenditure. Thus, discretionary fiscal policy should be relatively conservative during periods of economic expansion, so as to maintain a budget surplus, while the response to recession needs to be prompt and decisive, with a rapid expansion of, in particular, discretionary government spending to counteract the deleterious effects of the economic downturn on youth (and adult) employment and unemployment.

Sectoral strategies to promote youth employment

There is strong evidence to support the notion that the goal of promoting youth employment can be effectively supported through country-specific sectoral development strategies.

Moreover, the empirical evidence presented above suggests that the effects of economic growth on youth employment vary according to where growth occurs, and in particular that a focus on lower-productivity sectors, and above all on the development of the agricultural sector, can be an effective sector-specific strategy for promoting youth employment, particularly in MICs.

However, the main policy message emerging is that there are many possible sector-specific strategies to promoting youth employment, and it is by no means obvious that a focus on agriculture and/or other low-productivity sectors is the best approach. Such a focus runs the risk of encouraging low-wage, low-quality employment growth.

More detailed recommendations would depend on the specifics of national circumstances. While there are specific country examples which reinforce these rather general findings, there is clearly much heterogeneity across countries, both in the nature of the development process and in the effectiveness of specific strategies adopted. Clearly more evidence is needed, and specific national strategies need to be tailored to the specific situation facing each country.

3. Labour market institutions and youth labour markets: Minimum wages and youth employment revisited

3.1. Introduction

Boeri defines a labour market institution as "a system of laws, norms or conventions resulting from a collective choice, and providing constraints or incentives which alter individual choices over labor and pay" (2010, p. 1182). For the most part, labour market institutions serve to protect the more vulnerable participants in the labour market, typically guaranteeing certain rights and providing workers with some basic protections from harm and/or loss of income. But labour market institutions themselves are just part of the larger institutional setting which determines what actually goes on in labour markets. Berg and Kucera (2008) make the further distinction between labour institutions, which comprise formal and informal rules, practices and policies affecting how the labour market works, and a subset of these, labour *market* institutions, which includes EPL but explicitly excludes "non-market" institutions such as trade unions and the work ethic. The relevant point here is that all these factors have important implications for the quality and quantity of work available to, and performed by, young people. In this chapter, the concern is primarily with the quantitative youth employment effects of labour market institutions, in particular the systems of rules and regulations governing labour markets – as encapsulated in, for example, EPL, statutory minimum wages and organizational arrangements concerning collective bargaining. This is because it is often argued, with or without evidence, that there is a trade-off between the protections offered to (young) workers by legislative provisions and the disincentive effects of such provisions on potential employers.

Many labour market institutions are likely to influence the labour market experiences of young people more than those of other groups. For example, young people are usually, by virtue of their age, either new or relatively recent labour market entrants, and are consequently more likely to be affected by EPL *inasmuch as* this has an effect on the newly employed. Similarly, they are likely to be disproportionately represented among the low paid, and are thus more likely than other age groups to be employed or seeking employment in jobs directly affected by minimum wage legislation.

The influence of specific labour market institutions on labour market outcomes is likely to depend inter alia on the characteristics of other institutions that are present as well as on broader contextual characteristics.[1] The broader approach to labour institutions mentioned above leads naturally to the explicit recognition that labour (market) institutions are endogenous and evolve over time, interacting with each other as well as with the economic environment; there is a rich literature taking this approach which focuses on groups of institutional "regimes". Among others, the volume on *Varieties of capitalism* edited by Hall and Soskice (2001) has given rise to a large body of literature in its own right, as has Esping-Andersen's earlier (1990) analysis in the *Three worlds of welfare capitalism*.

In the context of the school-to-work transition and integration of youth into the labour market, a number of authors have proposed groupings of countries unified by similar combinations of institutional arrangements relevant to youth labour markets.[2] One such classification has been suggested by Eichhorst et al. (2009), whose analysis provides an analytical and empirical basis for the identification of country groupings according to a variety of explicit forms of labour market flexibility. Specifically, they distinguish between internal (to companies) and external (labour market level) flexibility on the one hand, and between numerical (variation of the workload) and functional (organizational adaptability) flexibility on the other; wage flexibility is further considered as a separate category. In their empirical application of this model, the authors use factor and cluster analyses to divide European countries into four groups according to the external and wage flexibility criteria. O'Higgins (2014) uses these country groupings to look in detail at the reactions of a variety of youth labour market indicators to variations in economic conditions, allowing for a structural break before and after the Great Recession.

This chapter seeks to offer a contribution on the effects of interactions between labour market institutions on the youth labour market, focusing on the employment effects of the minimum wage. Recognizing that youth employment programmes and policies are not implemented in a void, it is reasonable to suppose that outcomes arising as a consequence of any specific policy or programme choice will be influenced by existing institutional arrangements. Specific complementarities among labour market institutions have arguably received *relatively* little attention in the literature, notwithstanding the contributions mentioned above. Notable exceptions are the papers by Bassanini and Duval (2006, 2009) which examine in some detail the role of interactions in aggregate labour markets.[3] Estimating empirical panel models of

---

[1]   Such as the state of a country's economy and its level of development, to name just two among many other factors.

[2]   Perhaps the most well known of these is the classification proposed by Pohl and Walther (2007). Hadjivassiliou et al. (2016) present a recent application of this classification, while Raffe (2011) provides a review and overview of the main issues.

[3]   Boeri et al. (2012) also explicitly treat interactions among labour market institutions, although they are primarily concerned with the trade-off between two such institutions (unemployment benefits and EPL) as an *outcome* of the political process, rather than its effects per se. The impact of labour market institutions themselves has been the subject of an extensive literature. In addition to the papers cited in the text, see also de Serres et al. (2012) and OECD (2007, ch. 4), among many others.

aggregate unemployment, they find that labour market institutions are complementary in that the effects of specific institutions such as EPL and unemployment benefits reinforce one another. This contrasts with a more recent analysis from O'Higgins and Pica (2017) which, looking explicitly at young people, finds that in both a theoretical matching model and its empirical counterpart, ALMPs mitigate the effects of stronger (or weaker) EPL, dampening the positive (negative) stimulus to youth employment arising from weaker (stronger) legislation.

Here the emphasis is on the contribution of specific institutional interactions to the substantial heterogeneity of youth employment effects associated with the introduction of, or increases in, the minimum wage. In this respect, the chapter is close in spirit, albeit not methodology, to the analysis of Bassanini and Duval (2009). The meta-analysis of the youth employment effects of minimum wages undertaken in the following section shows that any negative (positive) employment effects of minimum wage legislation are reduced (increased), or even the sign inverted, in the presence of strong EPL. The finding is plausible in that EPL makes it more costly for firms to fire workers, such that they may be less likely to react to a rise in the minimum wage by laying off workers. On the other hand, firms may well adjust to changes in EPL by reducing hiring – in anticipation of higher firing costs in the event of a reduction in the workforce – and hence there is also a potential impetus in the opposite direction.[4]

As regards the analysis of the specific institutional determinants of youth employment, Bassanini and Duval (2006) find a strong negative effect of EPL on youth employment, but a positive and statistically significant effect of minimum wages on youth employment rates. On the other hand, neither Jimeno-Serrano and Rodriguez-Palenzuela (2002) nor Bertola et al. (2007) find a statistically significant role for EPL in depressing youth employment; but the former do report a negative impact of minimum wages on youth employment.

Thus there is little agreement on the effects of labour market institutions on youth employment and unemployment, and estimates of the impact of specific labour market institutions on youth employment either are highly heterogeneous in size and direction (as with minimum wages and youth employment) or have thus far produced no unequivocal theoretical or empirical conclusions as to the direction of possible effects (as with EPL).[5] Precisely because this is the case, it is important to develop our understanding of the effects of different labour market institutions in different circumstances.

The purpose of this chapter, then, is to provide some clear and specific policy-relevant results on the impact of specific complementarities on the youth labour market effects of minimum wages, so as to provide concrete indications on

---

[4]   This double effect on both the firing and hiring practices of firms is the main reason why the net effect of the strength of EPL on employment levels is indeterminate in principle (and, as it turns out in many analyses, also in practice).

[5]   Although it may be argued that the case in favour of negative employment effects of EPL is stronger – both theoretically and empirically – for young people than for workers as a whole, since the former constitute a high proportion of new labour market entrants.

the implications of different policy and programme choices. The next section reports the results of a meta-analysis of the youth employment effects of minimum wage legislation. A number of possible institutional and economic complementarities are considered, and the main finding is that across a broad range of high- and middle-income countries[6] minimum wages and EPL are mutually supportive institutions. That is, the minimum wage is less likely to have a negative impact on youth employment in countries with strong EPL.

3.2. Minimum wages and youth employment: A meta-analysis[7]

A minimum wage establishes a price floor below which wages cannot – legally – fall. Thus, the purpose of the minimum wage is to increase the incomes of especially low-wage workers and hence reduce inequality and poverty (Eyraud and Saget, 2008; Berg, 2015). Since young people are disproportionately represented among the low-paid, given their lack of experience and perceived lack of job-related skills, they are also likely to be disproportionately affected by the establishment of a minimum wage. There is much evidence to support the idea that the minimum wage increases firm-level training, productivity and wages, and reduces wage inequality.[8] However, this may come at a cost. Specifically, it is often argued that minimum wages are likely to "price young people out of jobs". Analyses of the effects of minimum wages on youth employment have produced a wide range of estimates, from strongly negative to moderately positive. The determinants of this heterogeneity are the focus of this section, which reports the results of a meta-analysis of the effects of minimum wages on the employment of young people, focusing on the role of interactions between labour market institutions in determining the size and direction of the effects of minimum wages.

Despite the apparent plausibility of the argument that high levels of minimum wages tend to discourage the employment of (in particular) young people, the available evidence is rather mixed. The comprehensive review undertaken by Neumark and Wascher (2007) found estimates of teenage employment elasticity with respect to the minimum wage ranging from below −1 to above zero. The authors concluded that the existing evidence points towards negative employment effects of minimum wages for young people. Of 102 studies considered, nearly two-thirds found negative (albeit often not statistically significant) estimated employment effects of minimum

---

[6] For fairly obvious reasons, minimum wage legislation is not common in LICs, and we found no studies of the impact of minimum wages on youth employment in such countries.

[7] This section is largely based on Moscariello and O'Higgins, 2017, to which the reader is referred for further details on the meta-analysis.

[8] Recent evidence on minimum wages and productivity is provided by Riley and Bondibene, 2017. Acemoglu and Pischke (1999, 2003) have shown that minimum wages stimulate training, and the positive effects on wages and negative effects on wage inequality have been dealt with by, among others, DiNardo et al. (1996) and, more recently, Autor et al. (2016).

wages, while only eight found "convincing" positive effects. However, an emphasis on demonstrating that the effects are generally negative rather than positive rather misses the central point, which is that in the vast majority of cases the effects are found to be small. In this sense, these results are in line with the review of evidence presented by O'Higgins (2001, ch. 6), which found small or zero (i.e. not statistically significant) employment effects of minimum wages for young people.[9] Furthermore, Neumark and Wascher (2004) suggested that the effects of minimum wages on aggregate employment vary considerably (from negative to positive) according to the presence of other labour market institutions (EPL, ALMPs, etc.); and, in particular, that the negative effects are most pronounced in unregulated labour markets. Allegretto et al. (2011) and Dube et al. (2010) have argued, however, that the methodologies typically employed to identify minimum wage effects are downward biased – hence more likely to find a negative employment effect even where none exists – because they ignore unobserved heterogeneity which, once controlled for, produces no negative employment effect of minimum wages on young people.[10]

Over the past two decades, a number of meta-analyses of the aggregate employment effects of minimum wages have been produced. The first of these, by Card and Krueger (1995a), undertook a meta-analysis of published time series papers. Their main conclusion was that the time series literature had been affected by a combination of specification searching and publication bias, leading to a tendency for statistically significant results to be over-represented in the published literature. Doucouliagos and Stanley (2009) reported the results of a meta-analysis of the employment elasticity of the minimum wage; in their opinion, once publication bias had been corrected, little or no evidence of a negative association between minimum wage and employment remained. They concluded that the minimum wage had either no effect or only a very small effect on employment; on the basis of the 64 studies and 1,500 estimates in their sample, they judged that they had "reason to believe that if there is some adverse employment effect from minimum-wage rises, it must be of a small and policy-irrelevant magnitude" (Doucouliagos and Stanley, 2009, p. 423).

Boockmann (2010) reported the results of a meta-analysis of 55 empirical studies estimating the employment effects of minimum wages in 15 industrialized countries. Two-thirds of the estimates in the sample indicated negative effects; however, the findings also strongly supported the notion of heterogeneous effects of minimum wages across countries. The paper was a rare example of the approach – also adopted here – in which the source of heterogeneity is sought in labour market institutions; in Boockman's case, with particular attention to the unemployment benefit replacement ratio, employment protection and the collective bargaining system.

---

[9]   Similar findings are reported also by Kolev and Saget (2005). Thus, it is not unreasonable to suggest that two further decades of research have confirmed the enduring veracity of Richard Freeman's assertion that "the debate over the employment effects of the minimum wage is a debate of values around zero" (Freeman, 1996, p. 647).

[10]   On the other hand, Neumark et al. (2013) have argued that the approach of these two papers essentially takes *too much* account of heterogeneity, hence leading to insignificant coefficients.

His study is also of interest in that it included analyses from several countries, in contrast to its predecessors, which had looked exclusively at the United States.

More recently, meta-analyses of the employment effects of minimum wages have been undertaken by Belman and Wolfson (2014) and Leonard et al. (2014) in HICs, and by Chletsos and Giotis (2015) in both HICs and LICs, while Nataraj et al. (2014) have examined two LICs (India and Indonesia) and Broecke et al. (2017) a broader range of countries. In none of these cases do the results lead to a substantial modification of the conclusion arising from previous studies that the effect of minimum wages on aggregate employment is small or zero.

Almost all of the evidence cited above was collected in higher-income, industrialized countries. In LICs there is relatively little evidence on the impact of minimum wages on young people; however, in the new millennium there have been a number of studies looking more generally at the effects of minimum wages, above all in Latin America.[11] For the most part the estimated size of the employment effect is in the −1/0 range; mostly smaller rather than larger (in absolute terms).

Few studies have looked at the interactions between the effects of the minimum wage and other labour market institutions. One notable exception is the analysis by Neumark and Wascher (2004), mentioned above. Although this is not its main focus, the paper includes a specification with interactions between minimum wages and other labour market institutions. It finds that the two institutions which consistently have statistically significant interactions with minimum wages are strong EPL and expenditure on ALMPs, both of which offset the estimated negative employment effects of minimum wages on young people as a whole (15–24) and on teenagers (15–19). That is, increasing employment protection and increasing expenditure on ALMPs tend to reduce any negative employment effects for young people arising as a consequence of an increase in the minimum wage.

Boockmann's (2010) meta-analysis also looks explicitly at the role of labour market institutions in determining cross-country differences in the estimated employment effects of minimum wages. His analysis differs from that of Neumark and Wascher (2004) in that the dependent variable is the effect of the minimum wage on labour market outcomes, rather than the labour market outcome itself. In this respect it is closer to the meta-analysis presented in this chapter.[12] He finds that more generous unemployment benefits reduce any negative employment effects of minimum wages, as does, albeit to a lesser extent, centralized collective bargaining; on the other hand, in direct contrast to the findings of Neumark and Wascher (2004), Boockmann's results suggest that strong EPL increases the negative employment

---

[11]   See e.g. the review by Freeman (2010) and the studies cited therein.

[12]   Boockmann's analysis differs from the current approach, however, in that he includes many different types of analysis and outcome. In particular, Boockmann includes studies which look at the effects of minimum wages on unemployment as well as on employment. Including the impact on unemployment means implicitly also incorporating supply-side effects – that is, if raising the minimum wage encourages some people to actively search for work, then unemployment will rise even if the demand for labour and hence employment is unaffected by the minimum wage.

effects of minimum wages. He suggests that a possible explanation lies in a difference between short- and long-run complementarities – or substitutability – between EPL and the minimum wage. Boockmann (2010) argues that Neumark and Wascher (2004) are concerned with short-run effects, in respect of which, he argues, it is plausible that strong EPL primarily reduces dismissals (more than appointments) and hence impedes the operation of any negative employment effects, whereas his own analysis covers both short- and long-run effects, in which any EPL-based obstacles to dismissal are weaker.[13] One might also note, however, that the negative effect found by Boockmann is not very robust; it emerges only when other institutional variables are included in the model,[14] disappearing completely when the strength of employment protection is the only institutional influence considered. Hence, it is sensible to agree with Boockmann himself when he says that the institutional variables "taken together may describe the countries' regulation system but it is unclear [from this analysis] whether they have a separate impact on the estimated minimum wage effects" (Boockmann, 2010, p. 178).

3.2.1. What are the mechanisms underlying the effects – or their absence?

In their seminal study on minimum wages in the fast-food industry in New Jersey, Card and Krueger (1995b) found that minimum wages had positive effects on employment. How can this be explained? A simple competitive model of the labour market suggests unequivocally that increasing minimum wages will lead to employment losses. If the demand for labour equals its supply and firms compete to hire young people from a large pool of homogeneous potential workers, raising minimum wages above the market equilibrium will unequivocally lead to a reduction in employment and an increase in unemployment. The only possible alternative is that the minimum wage is set below the market clearing rate and will thus be irrelevant since market equilibrium will in any case lead to a wage which is above the legal minimum.

If, however, employers have some market power in setting wages – a rather more realistic scenario in practice – they may well be able to set wages at below the market clearing rate. In this situation, increasing minimum wages may actually lead to an increase in employment, as was found by Card and Krueger. So long as the minimum wage is set below the competitive market clearing rate, raising minimum wages will

---

[13] An alternative explanation could be that while the analysis of Neumark and Wascher (2004) includes a variable representing countries' adoption of labour standards, that of Boockmann (2010) does not. If the adoption of labour standards and the strictness of EPL are strongly correlated across countries, as is plausible, then this might explain the divergence in results. Another source of the divergence might be the countries and/or time period covered; Neumark and Wascher (2004) consider a slightly different group of countries and a completely different time period (1975–2000 as opposed to post-1995) from Boockmann (2010), which would also have implications for the quality of the EPL (and other) explanatory variables, as noted by Howell et al. (2007).

[14] Specifically, a measure of the generosity of unemployment benefits (the benefit replacement ratio) and a measure of the degree of coordination of collective bargaining systems.

increase employment by eliciting a positive labour supply response; above the market clearing rate, further increases in the minimum wage will lead to employment losses. A further reason why higher minimum wages may not necessarily reduce employment – even in an otherwise competitive setting – lies in arguments of the "efficiency wage" type which suggest that productivity may be positively related to the wage paid for a variety of reasons: for example, because higher wages allow employers to hire more productive workers (sorting), or because higher wages induce greater effort from existing employees (gift exchange and/or less shirking).

In fact, then, the employment effects of a minimum wage may be positive or negative; however, the higher the level at which the minimum wage is set – relative to some benchmark such as the average wage – the more likely there is to be a negative effect on employment. Following a similar reasoning, workers on low earnings are more likely to be negatively affected by minimum wage provisions; and since young people tend to earn less than older workers on average, they too are more likely to be negatively affected. Indeed, studies that have considered the issue (e.g. Broecke et al., 2017) have found that the employment effects for young people are more strongly negative (or more weakly positive) than for older workers.

3.2.2. Main findings

Our meta-analysis is based on 328 effects from 43 papers published since 1990. In this sample, a range of effects of minimum wages on employment were found, ranging from small and positive at one end to substantial and negative at the other. We found, in common with reviews undertaken over the years, that on average the effects were small and negative; moreover, there is little variation in the estimates according to the methodology employed in arriving at them.

A substantial portion of the studies used in the meta-analysis were concerned with the United States, which accounts for a little under half (around 45 per cent) of the papers and estimates. The United Kingdom and Canada account for another 10 per cent each. Although more studies these days look at the effects of labour market institutions in general, and minimum wages in particular, in LMICs, still relatively few look at the employment effects specifically for young people; hence the number of estimates drawn from MICs is relatively small.[15] Only 43 (13 per cent) of the 328 estimates fall into this category.

In order to be able to compare the results of studies employing different methodologies, we divided estimates of the effects of minimum wages on youth employment into four possible outcomes: (1) negative and statistically significant; (2) negative but not statistically significant; (3) positive but not statistically significant; and (4) positive and statistically significant (table 3.1).[16] We then applied an ordered probit model to the resultant integer dependent variable (taking values from 1 to 4). This approach is similar to that adopted by, inter alia, Card and Krueger (1995a)

---

[15] We did not find any studies at all of the youth employment effects of minimum wages in LICs.

[16] We employ a 5 per cent level of statistical significance.

Table 3.1. Distribution of estimates of the effects of minimum wages on youth employment across outcomes

	No. of estimates	%
Negative; statistically significant	133	40.6
Negative; not statistically significant	132	40.2
Positive; not statistically significant	52	15.9
Positive; statistically significant	11	3.4
Total	328	100

and Boockmann (2010). Organizing the estimates in this way leads to a straightforward intuitive interpretation of the results. Also, where necessary, the explanatory variables were rescaled to lie between zero and 1 so as to make the reported coefficients broadly comparable in size. Given the large variability in the number of estimates in each paper, following usual practice we also weighted the estimates by the reciprocal of the number of estimates in each paper.

The distribution of the four outcomes is in line with those reported in the literature, in both reviews and meta-analyses.[17] That is, the estimates are primarily negative but the majority (around 57 per cent) of them are not significantly different from zero.

To put this finding another way, around four out of five of the estimates are negative, two out of five being both negative and statistically significant; and around one in five of the estimates are positive, although only 11 (or just over 3 per cent of all estimates) are positive and statistically significant.

The explanatory variables included are:

The Kaitz index: This is the ratio of the minimum wage to the "average" (mean or median; we use the median) wage of full-time workers. As noted above, whether labour markets are monopsonistic or closer to perfect competition, one would expect the likelihood of a negative employment effect of the minimum wage to increase with the level of the minimum in relation to the average wage.

Employment protection: We employ the ILO's EPLex summary index of EPL.[18] This is a composite index which takes into account various aspects of legal protection of employees in the event of dismissal at the initiative of the employer. We prefer this index over the analogous OECD index for several reasons. In particular, it covers some additional relevant areas of employment protection; it has also been consistently calculated by the ILO for a wider range of countries. One possible

---

[17] In addition to the meta-analyses mentioned already in the text, the reviews in O'Higgins, 2001, and Neumark and Wascher, 2007, are also worth mentioning. Although interpreted somewhat differently, the distribution of estimates is similar to those reported here; specifically, mostly negative but small and/or not statistically significant.

[18] http://www.ilo.org/dyn/eplex/termmain.home. For further details on the index, including a comparison with the OECD's index of employment protection, see ILO, 2015b.

drawback is that it has only been calculated for recent years, while some of the studies in the meta-analysis include estimates of effects going back three or four decades. However, the difficulty is more apparent than real. EPL – with the partial exception of recent years in the EU (explicitly covered by the EPLex index) – tends to change rarely and incrementally. For example, the OECD index value for the United States, which accounts for 45 per cent of the estimates and which has the broadest time span of estimates, has not changed during the period 1985–2013.[19] It has also remained unchanged over the period of interest for four other countries in our study, and such changes as have occurred for other countries over the period of study have for the most part been very minor.[20] As to the direction of the effect, this is not determined a priori. A higher level of employment protection would make it harder for employers to react to the introduction or raising of minimum wages by firing workers; however, it has been argued that an anticipation effect associated with stronger employment protection (and higher minimum wages) might discourage hiring.[21] If such an effect is present at all, it is likely to be particularly pronounced among young people. The two papers which explicitly include consideration of this point – Neumark and Wascher (2004) and Boockmann (2010) – find opposing effects; as noted above, the former finds a positive "mitigating" effect of stronger EPL, while the latter finds a negative "reinforcement" effect. We argued, however, that Boockmann's results suggested the existence of interactions between EPL and other labour market institutions in determining the employment impact of minimum wage legislation, rather than a negative reinforcement effect of EPL per se.

Prevalence of vulnerable employment: This is defined as the sum of own-account workers and unpaid family workers as a proportion of the employed. It was suggested by the ILO as a simple proxy for informal employment (ILO, 2010), which is rather harder to calculate or indeed define in an agreed fashion.

To these three key variables we also report specifications to which further economic and institutional factors were added. In the first place:

Gross national income (GNI) per capita: expressed in purchasing power parity (PPP) constant US dollars. This is included to capture the level of development of a country.[22]

Gini index: We include Gini indices of income inequality calculated by Branko Milanovic of the World Bank[23] from household surveys. Here the expectation is

---

[19] The period for which historical OECD data are available.

[20] It might also be observed that the EPLex and OECD indices have a correlation coefficient of 0.8 for the period 2009–13 and, in support of the relative lack of change of the index, the 1985/2013 correlation for the OECD index is over 0.9.

[21] This, of course, is the intuition underlying the indeterminacy of the employment effects of EPL in general, since greater protection provided by EPL will tend to discourage both hires and fires.

[22] Taken from the IMF World Economic Outlook database, http://www.imf.org/external/ns/cs.aspx?id=28.

[23] Available at: http://econ.worldbank.org/WBSITE/EXTERNAL/EXTDEC/EXTRESEARCH/0,,contentMDK:22301380~pagePK:64214825~piPK:64214943~theSitePK:469382,00.html

of a negative – or null – interaction between the Gini index and the employment effects of minimum wages. Broadly speaking, the more unequal the incomes, other things being equal, the more low-wage/low-productivity jobs there will be in an economy, and hence the larger the number of jobs that will be affected by an increase in (or introduction of) the minimum wage. Simply stated, any negative employment effects associated with minimum wage increases are likely to be stronger where more people are directly affected by it. Hence we would expect a negative coefficient on this variable and a higher Gini rating (and hence a greater degree of inequality) to be associated with a more negative youth employment effect.

The third set of three indicators represent the structures related to collective bargaining; although important, these variables are available for only a relatively limited number of countries and, in particular, limit the number of LMICs included in the estimates. The specific variables included are:

Trade union density: The proportion of workers who are members of trade unions (data provided by OECD).

Coordination: This is a dummy variable taking the value of 1 for highly co-ordinated wage-setting systems. It is derived from a categorical variable (taking five possible values) calculated by the Amsterdam Institute for Advanced Labour Studies.

Degree of centralization: This is a summary index (varying between zero and 1) capturing the degree of centralization of collective bargaining, taking into account both union authority and union concentration at multiple levels.[24]

We focus here on the results of applying the ordered probit model to the estimates as described above (table 3.2).[25] The table displays four sets of results on the basis of three different specifications, with the second and third columns reporting the same specification but on a different sample. This is for illustrative purposes to reflect the different samples used. A complete set of collective bargaining indicators is available only for a more limited set of countries, so that the model is estimated using 285 – as opposed to 328 – observations. Specifications 2a and 2b differ only in the number of observations included, and are reported to enable observation of any differences arising from the different samples.[26] We return to this point below.

As is usual in meta-analyses, not very much is strongly statistically significant, which makes the key result all the more striking. This is that the EPLex index has a consistently statistically significant positive interaction with minimum wages. That is, stronger EPL reduces the negative impact (or, as the case may be, increases the

---

[24] Data for the creation of the centralization and coordination variables are from Visser, 2016.

[25] Tests for publication bias were undertaken (see Moscariello and O'Higgins, 2017), but it was found that this did not affect the estimates. Also, various controls were experimented with, such as the timing of the publication of studies, timing of estimates, type of estimates, age, skill level and gender of young people under consideration, as well as explicit dummy controls for level of development of countries. In general, these did not appear to be significant in determining the results, nor did they alter the sign or (greatly) the size of the other coefficient estimates.

[26] Specifically, the larger sample includes more MICs, so that the smaller sample used in the last two columns is dominated by HICs.

Table 3.2. Results of the ordered probit model

Variables	Spec. 1	Spec. 2a	Spec. 2b	Spec. 3
Kaitz index	−0.88	−1.28	−0.30	−0.70
	(0.93)	(0.92)	(1.17)	(1.40)
EPLex	2.07***	2.18***	2.28***	2.15***
	(0.72)	(0.78)	(0.80)	(0.82)
Vulnerability	1.03*	1.56**	0.32	−0.02
	(0.61)	(0.63)	(1.09)	(1.46)
GNI per capita (PPP)		1.21	3.10	3.65*
		(1.06)	(2.06)	(2.10)
Gini index		−1.58	−2.58	−3.36
		(1.36)	(2.64)	(3.03)
Centralization				−2.66**
				(1.07)
Trade union density				3.19**
				(1.31)
Coordination dummy				1.12**
				(0.53)
(Pseudo) R^2	0.04	0.04	0.04	0.06
(Pseudo) log likelihood	−53.62	−53.40	−48.03	−46.86
Observations	328	328	285	285

Note: Standard errors in parentheses. Statistical significance indicated as follows: * = p <.10; ** = p < .05; *** = p < .01.

positive impact) of increased minimum wages on youth employment. This is in line with the findings of Neumark and Wascher (2004) cited above; and, in contrast to the negative impacts found by Boockmann (2010), the effect is statistically significant for all the specifications and is resistant to the inclusion of control variables. Moreover, the value of the coefficient changes relatively little across specifications. This provides strong evidence to support the idea that in countries with stronger EPL, employers are less prone to reducing their workforce in reaction to higher minimum wages.

The Kaitz index, on the other hand, is not statistically significant in any of the results; however, it too has a consistently negative sign, and its value does not vary greatly across specifications. Income per capita and the Gini index also have the expected signs, although again they are not typically statistically significant. Income per capita becomes marginally statistically significant (at 10 per cent) only in the last specification with the inclusion of variables related to collective bargaining. Our interpretation is that variations in per capita income are more influential for HICs.

Finally, the last three variables appear to have an interesting role. It would appear that the role of trade unions and collective bargaining more generally is more nuanced than has been captured in other analyses (e.g. Boockmann, 2010). Inserting only one of these variables at a time produces coefficients which are not singly statistically significant.[27] Taken together, however, they suggest that while coordination and high union membership tend to mitigate any negative employment effects of minimum wages for young people, highly centralized wage bargaining systems seem to reinforce any such negative effects. This would be consistent with the notion that strong coordination and strong unions compress the wage schedule from below – in other words, reduce wage inequality. A reduction in the numbers of (young) employees on low wages would, other things being equal, reduce any negative effects of a minimum wage since it would be binding for fewer workers. On the other hand, highly centralized wage bargaining systems are likely to be associated with less geographical variation in wages to take into account local conditions; this, in turn, is likely to lead to a greater (negative) impact of minimum wages.

3.2.3. Conclusions

Although it is true that the vast majority of estimates included in the analysis here find negative employment effects associated with the introduction or raising of minimum wages, around half of these estimates are not significantly different from zero, and the vast majority of the statistically significant effects are small; hence, the evidence presented here provides no reason to modify the viewpoint expressed 15 years ago that the impact of minimum wages on youth employment seems to be either small or not statistically significant, or both.[28]

There is wide variation in the estimates of the effects of minimum wages on youth employment, and the analysis presented here shows that this variation can, to some extent, be accounted for by differences in labour market institutions. Specifically, evidence supports the notion that strong EPL mitigates any negative youth employment effects associated with raising young people's minimum wages. There is also somewhat weaker evidence to support the notion that strong and coordinated, but decentralized, collective bargaining also mitigates any negative youth employment effects of minimum wage rises; clearly this second point deserves further investigation.

The fact that both of these key findings can be related to plausible underlying mechanisms, as well as their persistence across specifications, tends to strengthen the conviction that the meta-analysis presented here has indeed identified important complementarities between minimum wages and other labour market institutions which should be taken into account when designing legislation.

---

[27] This result is analogous to that found by Boockmann (2010) regarding labour market institutions as a whole, where EPL (or indeed either of the two other labour market institutions included), when considered separately, does not have a statistically significant impact on the employment effects of minimum wages; the negative impact of EPL arises when the institutions are considered together, strongly suggesting complementarity between labour market institutions.

[28] O'Higgins, 2001, ch. 5.

3.3. Conclusions and policy recommendations

This chapter has focused on the impact of labour market institutions on youth labour market outcomes, concentrating on the youth employment effects of minimum wage changes. It has also taken into account, in particular, the role of interactions between different labour market institutions in affecting the labour market outcomes of young people. The specific implications for policy are as follows:

Employment effects of minimum wages

The analysis reported in this chapter has confirmed earlier findings[29] that, on average, minimum wages slightly reduce the employment of young people. In the overwhelming majority of cases, however, the estimated youth employment effects of minimum wages are either zero (i.e. not statistically significant) or very small: in cases where the elasticity of youth employment with respect to the level of the minimum wage could be estimated, this was almost always well below 1. In some situations, raising minimum wages may even increase the employment of young people.

The implications for policy are:

The introduction of, or an increase in, minimum wages is unlikely to harm youth employment to any significant degree. Even where the minimum wage does have a negative impact on the employment of young people, this is typically small in percentage terms compared to the increase in minimum wages.

Similarly, reducing or removing the minimum wage is unlikely to have a significant positive impact on youth employment.

Moreover, although few studies have looked explicitly at the effects of setting minimum wages for young people at a lower rate than for older workers, reasoning analogous to that applied above suggests that lowering minimum wages for young people is unlikely to be an effective tool for improving the employment prospects of the young.

Interactions and complementarities

Minimum wages and average wages

The effects of minimum wages do tend to increase as they approach the level of average wages. Hence, there is a case to be made for not setting the minimum wage at excessively high levels compared to average wages.

Minimum wages and levels of development

The analysis here suggests that the disemployment effects of minimum wages fall with the level of GDP per capita. A point to which we shall return below is that although evidence on the youth employment effects of minimum wages in MICs is limited and for LICs practically absent, taken at face value the meta-analysis

---

[29] See e.g. O'Higgins, 2001.

suggests that minimum wages are *more* likely to have negative youth employment effects in MICs than in HICs.

Complementarities

The meta-analysis in this chapter has confirmed the presence of strong complementarities between minimum wages and other labour market institutions. It is important to take these into account when designing an appropriate policy framework to promote the integration of young people into employment.

Minimum wages and employment protection legislation

The effects of minimum wages on youth employment in HICs and MICs are very heterogeneous and depend inter alia on the strength of EPL: the stronger the EPL, the smaller the negative effects (if any) on youth employment.

Minimum wages and EPL are mutually supportive institutions and the introduction or raising of minimum wages will have less of a negative impact on youth employment in the presence of strong EPL. *It is advisable to use EPL and minimum wage legislation as complementary labour market measures to improve the quality of work for young people.*

Minimum wages and collective bargaining

For HICs, the analysis suggests that minimum wages will have a smaller disemployment effect in the presence of the appropriate collective bargaining arrangements – specifically in the presence of strong worker representation, accompanied by co-ordinated but decentralized collective bargaining arrangements.

More generally, the findings on the importance of other labour market institutions in determining the youth employment effects of minimum wages, coupled with the finding that minimum wages tend to have more detrimental effects on youth labour markets in LICs where, inter alia, labour market institutions are weaker, suggests that the minimum wage is best established where other effective protective labour market institutions are already in place.

This provides a plausible explanation for the finding referred to above that the youth disemployment effects of minimum wages decrease with a country's average per capita income (and hence level of development). That is, minimum wages work best (and have fewest disemployment effects) in the presence of a well-developed system of labour market institutions. This is consistent with the findings of, for example, Rani et al. (2013), who document the lower compliance with minimum wages observable in LMICs. Hence, the development of a minimum wage needs to take account of the existence and functioning of other labour market institutions in the country.

4. Active labour market programmes: The role of wage subsidies

This chapter focuses primarily on the role and impact of wage subsidies in promoting the employment and employability of young people. Wage subsidy programmes – involving reducing the costs for firms of employing young people – have become a mainstay of active labour market programmes (ALMPs) in high-income countries (HICs), above all since the onset of the global recession. Such programmes are less common in low- and middle-income countries (LMICs), where the emphasis tends to be more on skills training and entrepreneurship promotion. At the same time, interest in wage subsidy programmes is growing in the developing world. In Latin America there are numerous examples of such programmes, many of which have been subject to impact evaluation. In 2014, South Africa introduced a large-scale wage subsidy programme for young people, and several such programmes have been implemented and evaluated in recent years in the Middle East and North Africa (MENA) region, for example in Jordan and Tunisia. It is not unreasonable to expect such interest to grow as countries implement development strategies based on the growth of private sector manufacturing and services.[1]

The next section briefly reviews the more general findings on ALMPs for young people as a whole, before looking in more detail at the usefulness of specific design features of wage subsidy programmes. In this regard, section 4.2 considers the definition, purpose and possible pitfalls of wage subsidies for young people. Section 4.3 then discusses theoretical and practical considerations in the design of such subsidies. Section 4.4 provides an overview of specific wage subsidy programmes implemented in countries at differing levels of economic development, and section 4.5 reviews the evidence from impact evaluation studies. The chapter concludes with a number of explicit policy recommendations on the design features of effective programmes.

---

[1]   In Asia and the Pacific, although wage subsidy programmes do exist, training programmes (and internships) are more common; however, impact evaluations of such interventions appear to be lacking. See e.g. the discussions in Divald, 2015; ILO, 2015c, 2015d; Kring and Breglia, 2015; and Wang et al., 2016.

4.1. ALMPs for young people

4.1.1. What are ALMPs?

ALMPs are typically publicly funded programmes which aim to improve the employment prospects of participants. Usually these involve one or more of the following elements:[2]

Employment services and job search assistance (ESJSA). This typically takes the form of public employment services playing a mediating role between jobseekers and firms seeking workers.

Subsidized employment. This takes two primary forms:

(a) employment on public projects (public employment programmes or PEPs) such as infrastructure construction, socially useful work, etc.;

(b) employment with private employers via wage subsidies.

Skills training. This typically involves training on or off the job with the purpose of providing young people with job-related skills.

Often, single programmes offer a range of support measures covering more than one of these elements. This may mean that individual participants receive a combination of forms of support – e.g. ESJSA combined with a wage subsidy with a private employer on condition that the employer provides training. Table 4.1 provides a summary of the strengths and weaknesses of different types of programme.

4.1.2. What purpose do ALMPs serve?

ALMPs serve a variety of functions under the general aim of promoting the employment prospects – or, more generally, the employability – of participants. It is of some importance in assessing ALMPs to bear in mind that different programmes serve rather different specific functions, although they are typically evaluated using similar criteria. ALMPs generally serve one or more of the following purposes:

- increasing the skills of participants;
- increasing the employability of participants;
- creating new short-term employment opportunities;
- providing immediate income support;
- increasing the chances of finding employment in the longer term – as a consequence of enhanced employability of participants and/or profitability of firms;
- increasing the wages/incomes of participants in the longer term – primarily as a consequence of the greater (long-term) productivity of participants.

---

[2] A further category comprises programmes supporting the start-up and development of new businesses. Although these may reasonably be, and often are, considered as a type of ALMP, given the ILO call for action's separate emphasis on this type of support and the rather different issues it raises, it is here dealt with separately in the following chapter on self-employment and entrepreneurship.

Table 4.1. The main types of ALMP for young people: Advantages and disadvantages

Type of programme	Strengths	Weaknesses
Employment services and job search assistance	Can help youth make realistic choices and match their aspirations with employment and training opportunities; improve information on job prospects as well as efficiency, effectiveness and relevance of initiatives.	May create unrealistic expectations if not linked to labour market needs and often cover only urban areas and the formal economy.
Public employment programmes	Help young people gain labour market attachment and, at the same time, improve physical and social infrastructure and the environment – especially if combined with development and sectoral strategies – and enhance employability, if combined with training.	Low capacity for labour market integration; young workers may become trapped in a carousel of public works programmes; often gender-biased; displacement of private sector companies.
Wage subsidies	Can create employment if targeted to specific needs (e.g. to compensate for initial lower productivity and training) and to groups of disadvantaged young people.	Potentially high deadweight losses and substitution effects (if not targeted); employment may last only as long as the subsidy.
Skills training	Works better with broader vocational and employability skills that are in demand and includes work-based learning as well as employment services; positive effects of training on labour market outcomes. Can enhance the skills of young people, promoting their longer-term employability.	May produce temporary rather than sustainable solutions and, if not well targeted, may benefit those who are already "better off". Training alone may not be sufficient to increase youth employment prospects.

In the present context, the general aim of such programmes is to raise the quantity and quality of employment among young people as a whole, whether in the short or the longer term.[3]

With these ends in view, evaluations of ALMPs aimed at young people (or indeed at others) typically pose one or more of the following questions:

---

[3] Particularly in LMICs, such programmes may also have as their focus the goal of poverty reduction and community development as well as the construction of local infrastructure useful for development. This in part explains why public works type programmes which do not tend to lead to substantial longer-run employment and income gains for participants are relatively popular in LICs.

- Does the programme improve the short-run employment prospects of programme participants?

- Does the programme improve the long-run employment prospects of programme participants?

- Does the programme have impacts on the wages of programme participants?

- Does the programme raise the likelihood of programme participants finding "good" jobs[4] once the programme has been completed?

- Do ALMPs lead to stable jobs?

- Which types of ALMPs for young people are the most effective, and in which contexts?

- What about the programmes' aggregate effects: do they raise the levels of employment and/or wages of the target group as a whole?

There tends to be much more emphasis on evaluating the effects of programmes on individuals than on their aggregate impact, and recent research work in this area has focused primarily on evaluating the extent to which programmes raise the probability of participants subsequently obtaining employment, or on evaluating the post-programme wages of participants compared to a control group of non-participants.[5]

4.1.3. Evaluation evidence: What does it tell us?

Before entering into discussion of the specific design features of wage subsidy programmes, it is worth briefly summarizing the findings on youth employment interventions. These have focused on the effects of programmes at the individual level.

An enormous number of primarily microeconomic evaluations of ALMPs have been undertaken.[6] There are a number of common features in the findings of these studies; however, here as elsewhere a growing literature has often given rise to con-

---

[4]   Of course, this also raises the question of what constitutes a "good" job. The quality of jobs for young people is a major issue which underlies the discussions in Chapters 6 and 7 and to some extent also Chapter 5 below.

[5]   There is an extensive literature on methods for the evaluation of ALMPs. A simple introduction is provided in O'Higgins, 2001, ch. 5 sec. 3 and the discussion below also provides a very brief overview of issues. However, there are many excellent and much more extensive methodological treatments of impact evaluation. Kluve et al. (2016a) also present an overview of the different methodologies and Khandker et al. (2010) provide a more comprehensive review.

[6]   There are correspondingly a number of overviews and meta-analyses which summarize the findings in one way or another. These include Betcherman et al., 2004, 2007; Card et al., 2010, 2015; Fay, 1996; Grubb and Ryan, 1999; Heckman et al., 1999; Kluve, 2010; Kluve et al., 2016a, 2016b; Martin and Grubb, 2001; and Quintini and Martin, 2006. Apart from Betcherman et al. (2007) and Kluve et al. (2016a, 2016b), these reviews cover ALMPs as a whole with – usually – separate consideration of programmes for young people.

flicting results – or at least a greater ambiguity as to the role played by different fac-tors. Some of the main findings of the evaluation literature are summarized here.

Comprehensive interventions for young people: Comprehensive programmes in-volve some combination of subsidized employment, training, self-employment sup-port, guidance and counselling, and possibly other elements. They have a long history in OECD countries and above all in the United States. In Europe, as well as in Latin America and the Caribbean, such programmes have achieved substantial success. For example, the United Kingdom's New Deal for Young People has proved to be a rel-atively cost-effective programme.[7] In the United States, the Job Corps programme offering multiple interventions for disadvantaged young people has proved so successful that it has remained in operation since 1964.

ESJSA: Going back to the early study of Fay (1996), measures to improve job search efficiency have been found to be the most cost-effective form of active labour market intervention. Having said this, once again, ESJSA are likely to be of great-est value when there are sufficient jobs available, so the problem is one of matching workers to jobs. In times of recession, this type of intervention, of itself, is likely to be less effective. Indeed, the recent meta-analysis of Kluve et al. (2016a) finds such forms of intervention to be of limited effectiveness.

Training plus employment subsidies: In general, programmes which impart some training, especially those based with private employers, seem to be more effective than subsidized employment per se. This is one of the more robust findings in the literature, although, as noted below, the relative usefulness of the elements may depend on the business cycle. Recent research has suggested a more nuanced picture, with wage subsidies being more effective in the short run and training programmes – of sufficient duration and quality – tending to have a more significant impact over the longer run (Card et al., 2010, 2015).

Programme duration: A finding which is increasingly emerging – and to which we shall return below – is that programmes need to be of sufficient duration to have a significant effect. This seems to be a key factor in driving the effectiveness of ALMPs in Latin America and the Caribbean (ILO, 2016c).

On-the-job training: This appears to be more effective than *off-the-job training,* possibly in part because by its very nature on-the-job training involves direct contact with employers.

---

[7]   Although the effectiveness of the programme seems to have varied significantly across the different options available. Consistent with other findings in the evaluation literature reported below, Dorsett (2006), for example, found substantial differences in the effectiveness of the New Deal according to the (post-gateway) option adopted. The most effective channel was, unsur-prisingly, subsidized employment with a (private) employer, which proved to have a much more significant impact on post-programme employment and income than did the education, training or voluntary work options. This mirrors findings by others, such as Sianesi (2008), who found that wage subsidies – as opposed to labour market training or public employment programmes – were the most effective programme type in the Swedish context.

On- and off-the-job training: Also consistent with the hypothesis above, training programmes that combine off- and on-the-job training have universally been found to be more effective than exclusively off-the-job training (e.g. Kluve et al., 2016a).

Business cycle: There is general agreement that training programmes appear to be less useful in times of recession, particularly when compared with other ALMPs such as employment subsidies. Training programmes perform better when they are instituted during periods of economic expansion (Betcherman et al., 2004; Røed and Raum, 2006; McVicar and Podivinsky, 2010). The suggestion is that during a recession, more emphasis should be put on employment subsidies and other measures aimed at creating temporary employment opportunities and providing income support. This view has been supported by the analyses of the OECD (2009). Once economies start to return to positive economic growth, then training and other policies (such as appropriate educational policy) may also play a more constructive role in supporting recovery.

However, work by Kluve (2010)[8] and Card et al. (2015) partially contradicts this finding. These meta-analyses find that ALMPs as a whole work better when unemployment is higher; although the marginal effect is fairly small, it is larger and more statistically significant when attention is restricted to training programmes. On the other hand, there the effect disappears (but does not become negative, as implied by the previous results) when youth programmes are considered on their own. The authors' suggested explanation for this surprising result is that in times of recession, the pool of potential candidates for programmes – which, de facto or de jure, are for the unemployed – will be of a higher average quality. Thus, the authors conclude that it is not that programmes are more effective during recessions, but rather that the composition of the unemployed changes and, in particular, that the average quality of programme participants tends to rise during such periods, leaving the basic conclusion outlined above unchallenged.

Microeconomic and (meta-analysis) findings have also been complemented by more general macroeconomic studies which tend to support the idea that ALMPs as a whole can mitigate the negative employment effects of a recession (Bassanini and Duval, 2006).

Targeting: In general, evaluations have found discouraging results as regards their impact on young people compared to interventions targeting other groups. Indeed, one of the central findings of the study by Card et al. (2010) confirms this result. However, the analyses of Betcherman et al. (2007) and Kluve et al. (2016a) find that programmes which target *disadvantaged* youth seem to be more effective than programmes targeting youth as a whole. The result confirms the more general

---

8   Similarly, an earlier meta-analysis by the same author (Kluve and Schmidt, 2002) found a negative effect of GDP growth on ALMP effectiveness; however, in this case – and with a smaller sample size – the effect was not statistically significant. Lechner and Wunsch (2009) also found a positive relationship between programme effectiveness and the national unemployment rate in Germany, although the relationship disappeared when they controlled for regional (rather than national) unemployment rates. Since it is the local labour market which is likely to have a more direct impact on post-programme outcomes, it is not clear how to interpret this result.

finding of several reviews – going back to the relatively early analysis of Fay (1996) – that targeted programmes are more effective.

Timing of the evaluation: The meta-analyses conducted by Card et al. (2010, 2015) and by Kluve et al. (2016a) look specifically at the issue of when evaluations are undertaken, and find that this is an important characteristic in determining estimated effects. In particular, over the medium term (two to three years after programme participation), job training programmes are found to be particularly successful; and longer programmes, which appear to be less effective than short programmes when looking at immediate impacts, are found to have significant positive effects in the medium term.

Social partner involvement: Although there is little systematic evidence on this question, there is a general consensus that the involvement of social partners in the formulation and implementation of ALMPs is likely to increase the effectiveness of such policies for several reasons, including the following:[9]

- The involvement of employers and workers implies a commitment on their part to the success of policies and programmes. This joint commitment, in itself, will tend to enhance the effectiveness of policy.

- The quality of programmes is likely to be higher if the social partners are involved. Numerous studies have demonstrated that programmes which are more closely linked to private employers are likely to be more effective. Employers may use programmes as a recruitment and/or screening device. Also, the relevance of training is probably greater in the context of private employer involvement. The skills acquired are likely to be closer to those required by the labour market than those taught on programmes without such direct labour market links. In addition, the involvement of workers' organizations can help avoid some of the pitfalls of work experience and training programmes. In promoting the training content (and, through careful monitoring, ensuring the effective implementation) of programmes, workers' organizations can guard against the exploitation of programme participants, at the same time helping to promote their long-term prospects of good quality employment. They can also ensure that programme participants are not substituted for other categories of worker.

4.2. Wage subsidies: What are they and how do they work?[10]

Typically, in the context of youth employment, wage subsidies are viewed as a means to stimulate the demand for young workers, whereas training programmes are viewed as mechanisms to improve the quality of the supply of young workers by enhancing skills. In practice, as is discussed further below, the distinction can be blurred; in particular, wage subsidy programmes can impart skills to participants whether an explicit

---

[9]   O'Higgins (2001, ch. 9) provides a more detailed discussion.
[10] Sections 4.2–4.5 are largely based on Bördős et al., 2015.

training component is included or not. Subsidized employment of one kind or another has become increasingly popular in the context of the global recession, where the key problem was clearly the lack of adequate aggregate output demand and hence of demand for labour, leading to a lack of opportunities which was particularly severe for new entrants to the labour market.

As noted above, a distinction is usually made between: (a) *public employment programmes*,[11] involving subsidized employment on public projects of some benefit to the community as a whole; and (b) *wage subsidies*, which reduce the costs to private employers of employing young people. The ILO has long been involved in the implementation of the former type of project, particularly as regards the development of a country's infrastructure. Such programmes are often used to provide temporary work to those who are very hard to employ – the long-term unemployed, for example – and much of their value lies in their ability to create something of value, and thereby indirectly also employment opportunities, for the broader community, as well as in their role as a (temporary) income support mechanism for participants. This distinguishes them from other forms of ALMP, which typically aim at enhancing the longer-term employment prospects of participants. The difference is one of emphasis, but many of the early impact evaluation studies viewed PEPs as counterproductive precisely for this reason. However, it is worth recalling that: (a) there is no reason why PEPs cannot be integrated with skills development in order to provide more lasting enhancement of the employment prospects of participants; (b) one of the main functions of such programmes is often precisely its income support function; and, perhaps most importantly, (c) the major impact of such programmes on employment comes through their indirect multiplier effects throughout the community rather than through their direct impact on participating individuals, which is typically the focus of microeconometric evaluations.

Analysis by the ILO (2015e) suggests that such programmes can indeed be useful in providing income support and skills training for young people, although the paper does not present evidence on the impact of PEPs on the post-programme employment prospects of young participants.

4.2.1. What are wage subsidies?

Wage (and hiring) subsidy programmes have been part of the ALMP toolbox for over 30 years, and have been shown to produce moderately positive results. Almeida et al. (2014) stress that the success of these programmes depends to a large extent on the specificities of the design (including the amount of the subsidy, the target group and any attached conditions for employers). In the context of the rapidly increasing youth unemployment and NEET rates as a consequence of the recent economic crisis, a number of European countries have introduced hiring subsidies as a means of fighting youth unemployment.

---

[11]   Also referred to as public works programmes in the literature.

Wage (or hiring) subsidies are transfers to employers or employees that cover at least part of the eligible individual's wage and/or non-wage employment costs. Their main goal is to provide incentives for firms to employ members of the target group by lowering the cost of doing so. Those considered here involve direct transfers to either firms (through subsidies or payroll tax reductions) or workers (through wage supplements or, potentially at least, tax reductions on income from dependent employment), conditional on the worker to whom the subsidy relates being in formal employment. These programmes may include an on-the-job training component, so long as they also entail significant subsidized employment, meaning that at least two-thirds of the young person's time is devoted to "actual work".

Wage subsidy programmes are intended to increase employment both in the short term and in the longer term, once programme support has expired. In the short term, these programmes provide significant work experience and income support; in the longer term, they may also improve young people's "employability" and hence employment prospects by two key mechanisms.

First, they may raise the level of the individual's human capital, in the form of skills and productivity. In this regard, wage subsidy programmes often include an explicit training component. Even where they do not, subsidized employment typically involves the acquisition of some skills through learning-by-doing on the job. This may increase a young person's productivity and hence their employment prospects over a significant period (Heckman et al., 2002), and thus lead to employability benefits which extend, potentially at least, well beyond the period during which a subsidy is paid.

Second, such programmes may address an information problem whereby firms may be reluctant to hire young people if they lack adequate indication of their skills. Hiring a young person in this context involves some risk to the firm, since there are inevitably some costs involved with both hiring and (if the appointment does not work out) firing new employees. Typically, contractual arrangements allow for a probationary period for new employees which reduces these costs, but wage subsidy programmes, and more explicitly hiring subsidies, may reduce such costs further, thus encouraging firms to override any such reluctance.

4.2.2. How do (or can) wage subsidies enhance the employment and employability of young people?

The basic rationale for introducing a wage subsidy is that it will lead to a rise in employment for the groups targeted; the subsidy reduces the cost of labour for employers, and as a result increases the demand for labour services.[12] There are several alternative mechanisms that can contribute to better labour market outcomes for the targeted group(s), and there are also several indirect effects that can undermine the success of these programmes. There is a general consensus that the effectiveness

---

[12] A worker-side subsidy increases potential employees' take-home wages, encouraging more workers to enter the labour market. Owing to this expansion of labour supply, employment rates will rise.

of wage subsidy programmes depends crucially on the specific design (and economic context) of these policies,[13] which is the main focus of this chapter.

The first reason why employers might be reluctant to hire prospective employees is that they lack information on their productivity and skills, a situation which is especially relevant for young people, most of whom are new labour market entrants with limited or no work experience. In other words, employers are likely to ask for a "risk discount", and be willing to hire young and inexperienced workers only at a wage that is significantly below their (expected) marginal productivity of labour. Additionally, employers may perceive low levels of educational qualifications or extended periods of non-employment as signals of low productivity. Wage subsidies can compensate employers – by reducing wage costs – for the (supposed or real) lower productivity or other perceived risks, making it worth their while to hire young people with little work experience or low levels of education.

This positive effect on the target group's employability will persist in principle only as long as the subsidy is paid. However, two factors can lead to longer-term integration effects even after the subsidy has expired. First, if the main barrier to youth employment is the risk associated with recruiting a person with no work experience, then the period of subsidized work can act as a screening device, providing direct information on the young person's productivity. Second, the subsidized employment can promote skill formation through "learning-by-doing", leading to increased productivity and subsequent improvement in employment prospects over the longer term Heckman et al., 2002).[14]

Researchers use various measures of success to assess the different mechanisms through which wage subsidies may increase young people's employment prospects. In order to ascertain the short-term effect of subsidies, the proportion of young people who have found a subsidized job among those eligible (relative to the job-finding rate of those who are not eligible) is commonly measured. To determine whether long-term integration goals are met, researchers examine the employment probability (or wages) of those who participated in the programmes during the period after the subsidy has ended (for a more comprehensive overview of evaluation methods, see subsection 4.1.3 above).

Employer wage subsidies can also have supply-side effects, in both the short and the longer term. First, awareness of their eligibility for a wage subsidy may change job-seekers' perceptions of success rates in the labour market. Better prospects of finding employment might prompt eligible workers to increase their job search efforts, which might in turn lead to greater success. In this sense, wage subsidies increase effective labour supply. Second, wage subsidies can also – by offering the opportunity to gain work experience – influence workers' preferences for certain work or careers, thus

---

[13]   See e.g. Neumark and Grijalva, 2013; Almeida et al., 2014; Brown, 2015.

[14]   The relative importance of these two mechanisms depends on the target group of the subsidy: while the first (overcoming employers' reluctance to hire where evidence of productivity is lacking) might be relevant for all young persons, the second (promoting skill formation) is of particular importance for disadvantaged (low-skilled) young jobseekers.

enabling young people to target more "suitable" opportunities in their subsequent search for work. Through this so-called "job ladder effect", the subsidy can improve the quality of future job matches (Kluve, 2014). In contrast, if workers accept less skilled or informal jobs in the absence of the subsidy, this can create a trap and harm their career paths in terms of future employment prospects or earnings (Viollaz et al., 2012). An effective wage subsidy may therefore have long-term positive effects on both employment probability and job quality.

4.2.3. Potential problems

Wage subsidy programmes are subject to several potential shortcomings which can reduce the net benefits of schemes. Specifically, indirect effects may offset any potential impacts on overall employment. Although not exclusive to wage subsidy programmes, such effects can be particularly pronounced for these schemes.

First, the subsidy may support some eligible workers who would have been hired in any case, regardless of whether the subsidy were offered – this is known as *deadweight costs*.

A second concern is that firms may not raise the numbers of their workforce in response to the subsidy but, instead, hire a member of the target group only to fire an ineligible worker with similar characteristics (this is called the *substitution effect*). Thus, in the extreme case, the subsidy may not raise overall employment, but simply "reshuffle" the pool of non-employed. Whether or not this is desirable then becomes a policy choice. For example, it might be argued that if there are long-lasting scarring effects from youth non-employment, then perhaps shifting the composition of employment across age groups may be desirable.

Finally, increases in employment in firms that use subsidized labour may come at the expense of job losses in firms that do not have eligible workers, as the first type of firm gains a cost advantage enabling it to out-compete the second type; this is called the *displacement effect*.

Wage subsidy measures targeted at young people can also have perverse effects: for example, increasing young people's incentives to leave education. Subsidies which target disadvantaged youths (e.g. those with a lower level of education or on low wages) might be especially prone to these disincentives, as acquiring the skills that would lead to increases in productivity and wages implies losing eligibility for the subsidy (Oskamp and Snower, 2006; O'Leary et al., 2011). For example, the model for skill formation developed by Heckman et al. (2002) suggests that, in some circumstances, a wage subsidy can reduce incentives to invest in skills development, as eligible candidates consider the subsidy too attractive to "waste time" on schooling or training. If this is the case, wage subsidies may promote positive labour market outcomes among young people in the short run, but be detrimental in the longer term.

Finally, stigma effects can occur when firms view the targeted subsidy as an indication of the potential employee's low productivity and so, contrary to the intention of the policy, they avoid hiring from the group of those eligible. Alternatively, the targeted workers themselves may feel that eligibility is stigmatizing and degrading, and may try to conceal their eligible status.

4.3. Designing effective subsidies: Theoretical and practical considerations

4.3.1. The recipient

The first issue to consider is the extent to which the potential employment gain depends on the direct recipient of the subsidy. According to standard economic theory, whether the payee is the employer or the employee should not matter in terms of employment and wage outcomes in a flexible labour market,[15] since the extent to which the employer and employee each benefit from the subsidy will depend only on the elasticity of labour demand and supply.[16] However, if there is no downward flexibility in wages, it is preferable that the employer receives the subsidy. For example, if the amount of the subsidy is just equal to the difference between the legislated minimum wage and the marginal productivity of the worker (which, by assumption, is lower than the minimum wage), and the subsidy is paid to the employer, the worker can be hired at the minimum wage, the subsidy leads to a large increase in employment and the whole amount of the subsidy is captured by the employer as compensation for the lower productivity. On the other hand, if the subsidy goes to the worker (for example, in the form of an income tax credit), it raises employment by increasing workers' take-home pay while reducing negotiated wages.[17] If there are (binding) minimum wage laws in force, then negotiated wages cannot decrease and therefore the wage supplement (paid to workers) is likely to have no effect on formal employment.

4.3.2. The target group

Regarding the targeting of subsidies, the first question is whether the subsidy should apply to both incumbents and new hires, or only to the latter. General wage subsidies are likely to be more costly, as they apply to a wider group of workers and may lead to large deadweight effects. Hiring subsidies, applying only to new employees, on the other hand, require more complex administration and monitoring, which can reduce the take-up of the subsidy (and therefore its impact) as well as increasing costs.

The issue of targeting is of course broader than this. For hiring subsidies, a further issue is whether they should apply to all new youth hires or only to a specific group of (say, disadvantaged) young persons. The first option is likely to lead to larger deadweight costs as it is more likely to subsidize the employment of young people who would in any case find employment. If a lack of signals of young people's productivity is a major factor influencing the level of youth unemployment, then

---

[15] This is referred to as the "invariance of incidence" or the "equivalence hypothesis".

[16] The more elastic the labour supply (relative to labour demand), the larger will be the employment increase and the smaller will be the rise in wages.

[17] Thus, the take-home pay is equal to the worker's marginal product.

making first-time jobseekers the target of hiring subsidies would be the most effective policy. In contrast, targeting subsidies at disadvantaged youth (e.g. those who have been unemployed for more than six months, or those with low skill levels[18]) is sensible if it is believed that, for these groups, there is a gap between the market (minimum) wage rate and their productivity, and that subsidized jobs could lead to skill formation through learning-by-doing. In general, carefully focused targeting can contribute to higher cost-effectiveness by limiting deadweight effects, but it can also lead to a higher risk of substitution and stigma effects.

4.3.3. Generosity of subsidies

The generosity of the subsidy, which is determined by the reduction in employers' wage costs as a result of the programme and the duration of the subsidy, is the main determinant of employers' willingness to recruit young people, and of the increased demand for young workers as a result of the subsidy.

The subsidy clearly needs to be sufficiently high to make it profitable for the employer to hire an eligible young person; however, theory offers little guidance on what the optimal subsidy amount might be. For subsidies that aim to promote the employment of all young people, it is sensible to define the subsidy as a percentage of the total wage. However, if the goal of the programme is the integration of disadvantaged youth into jobs, then it may be preferable to set a maximum threshold for the subsidy or define it as a fixed amount, since this design naturally predisposes employers towards hiring low-skilled (and hence low-paid) young people, given that subsidies of fixed amount cover a larger proportion of wage costs for low-paid workers than for other groups.

Furthermore, if policy-makers seek to close the gap between young people's productivity and the minimum wage, then higher subsidies should be given for hiring those with greater disadvantages (such as longer unemployment duration or lower qualifications).[19] Finally, there is an argument in favour of front-loading the wage subsidy (so that the size of the subsidy falls over time during the subsidy period), since productivity will increase with experience, and hence the need to subsidize wages will fall as the young person's length of employment increases.

The duration of the subsidy should depend on the type(s) of problem that it is intended to overcome. Subsidies of short duration (six months or less) are useful for overcoming employers' initial reluctance to hire owing to the absence of informative signals on young people's productivity. Medium-term and longer subsidy periods (from nine months up to two years) can allow young workers to develop

---

[18] Or, in certain contexts, young women.

[19] Note, however, that this can create perverse incentives for both the young person and the firm to "wait" until they become eligible for higher subsidies. Higher subsidies for lower-skilled individuals can also result in a reduced incentive to invest in education in the medium to long term.

necessary skills, and as a result increase their productivity, which in turn means that, in the end, there is no further need for the subsidy. Subsidization beyond this learning-by-doing period is likely to lead to greater deadweight loss and hence be less cost-effective. Long-term subsidies are therefore extremely rarely used – typically only in the case of target groups with multiple disadvantages (for example, the low-skilled, long-term unemployed and health-impaired).

4.3.4. Conditionalities

Imposing conditions on employers can help to limit unintended behavioural responses that reduce the effectiveness of hiring subsidies. First, in the absence of a rule that obliges employers to pay back the subsidy if the hired worker is dismissed during the subsidy period, it is likely that the basic integration goals of the policy will not be met. Second, in order to prevent employers from "churning" their workers to exploit hiring subsidies, as well as to ensure longer-term integration, employers can be obliged to extend the contract of the subsidized worker after the expiry of the subsidy. Third, restrictions can be imposed on subsidized employers to reduce substitution effects and to promote net job creation (for example, by stipulating that a firm is eligible to be granted the subsidy only if it has not previously dismissed any of its workers in a given period).

In order to ensure that subsidies contribute to the long-term integration of youth into work, further rules can make it compulsory for employers to provide training or other forms of skills development to the subsidized worker, which may further enhance the effectiveness of these programmes and at the same time reduce indirect – and in particular deadweight – costs.

4.3.5. Implementation issues

The effectiveness of wage or hiring subsidies depends to a degree on how they are implemented, specifically through the selection of participants, indirect (administration) costs and take-up. Unlike training programmes, hiring subsidies involve a two-way matching process. It is therefore impossible to rule out positive selection – where the most employable individuals are recruited from the pool of eligible candidates – leading to deadweight losses. This tendency can be counteracted by the presence of an implementing agency, such as the public employment service (PES), which pre-screens participants for eligibility. This process, however, increases both administration costs and the risk of stigma effects. Requirements governing employers' conduct will not be satisfied unless the funding agency monitors compliance regularly and effectively; this requires additional capacity in terms of both agency staff and data sources, making these programmes more expensive.

Imposing conditionalities on employers reduces negative indirect effects, but increases the administrative burden and compliance costs for firms, thereby reducing the potential benefits of the subsidy for employers. The extent of these costs is difficult to quantify, as different types of employers might weight them differently, according to their subjective valuation of the burden. Furthermore, in order to avoid very low take-up rates, stricter compliance rules need to be counterbalanced by more generous subsidies. There is a trade-off between the additional costs incurred owing to dead-weight and substitution effects, and reduced effectiveness due to low take-up.[20]

The form of the wage subsidy – the "payment vehicle", as Almeida et al. (2014) refer to it – is the way in which the subsidy is paid to the beneficiaries. This may be a reduction in social security contribution or payroll tax (targeted at youth), a tax refund (where the subsidy is paid through the tax system, in the form of a refund-able tax credit) or a direct payment to the employer or the worker covering at least part of the worker's wage. Both evidence and theory are sparse on the significance of the payment vehicle considered in isolation, although some implications and inherent features of the way in which the subsidy is granted that can affect its take-up and success rate have been identified. Naturally, payroll tax reductions can only be as large as the tax element of the wage itself, whereas direct transfers and tax credits can also cover part of the wage in addition to non-wage costs. Payroll tax cuts therefore imply less generous support than may be made through direct subsidies to firms. The administrative burden on payees also varies with the form of subsidy: direct payments usually entail more time and administration costs, hence poten-tially limiting take-up.

4.4. An overview of recently implemented wage subsidy programmes

4.4.1. The European Union

In Europe, wage subsidies for various target groups are relatively widespread and have been implemented since the early 1980s. In France and Germany, these programmes were introduced partially in response to rising youth unemployment following the re-cessions caused by the oil crises of the 1970s (for France, see box 4.1). Most of these early programmes offered generous hiring subsidies (up to 50 per cent of youth wages) for a limited period of time (up to 12 months), and were targeted at disadvantaged (low-skilled) jobseekers. Firms had to meet several behavioural conditions, including an embargo on dismissals during, and for a limited period after, the subsidy period, demonstrable growth in the number of persons on a firm's payroll and limits on the number of subsidized hires per firm.

The unemployment crisis of the early 1990s saw the implementation of a new wave of hiring subsidies, for example those in Denmark and Sweden, which were more limited in duration (typically six months), while new, specifically youth-focused

---

[20]   On the one hand, subsidies with very light conditions for employers might have high costs and only a modest net employment effect, owing to deadweight and substitution effects. On the other hand, programmes which impose strict conditions on employers – while avoiding in-direct effects and thus leading to the creation of new jobs – can only ensure employer take-up if the subsidy amount is high. Furthermore, while programmes with strict conditions may be highly beneficial for those who actually participate in them, they may contribute to the creation of very few employment opportunities overall (due to low take-up rates).

Box 4.1. The evolution of youth hiring subsidies in France

Hiring and wage subsidies for employers in the private sector targeted at young people have a long history in France, dating back to 1977. We focus here on the evolution of these types of programme over the past 20 years. Where earlier programmes were short-lived and consisted mainly of a cut in payroll taxes for the hiring of young (unqualified) persons, in 1996 a generous hiring programme (the Employment Initiative Contract) was initiated for long-term unemployed youth (aged 16–25) without higher education. Within this programme, in addition to being granted an exemption from paying social security contributions, employers were entitled to a subsidy amounting to up to 47 per cent of the minimum wage for two years. The targeting of this programme became increasingly strict, and in 2002 the hiring subsidy was restricted to those individuals who had been unemployed for at least two years. At the same time, a new programme (the Youth-in-Business Contract) entitled employers who hired low-skilled youths (aged 16–22) on open-ended contracts to subsidies amounting to roughly 20 per cent of labour costs for two years and half this amount for a third year. Dismissals of young workers were prohibited during the subsidy period. In 2006 the programme was extended to include young people with low levels of education up to the age of 25, but the subsidy duration was cut to two years. In 2008, the hiring subsidy for low-skilled youth was abolished and integrated into the new version of the Employment Initiative Contract.

In 2010, hiring subsidy programmes were streamlined and the Unique Inclusion Contract was introduced. This offers a subsidy on the hiring of disadvantaged jobseekers on fixed-term contracts. The contracts can run from six months to two years, and the subsidy amount is regulated by the regional PES offices, but cannot exceed 47 per cent of the minimum wage. In order to claim the subsidy, employers must not have dismissed any regular employees in the six months prior to recruiting a person eligible for the subsidy.

Between 2010 and 2012, in the aftermath of the recent financial crisis, youth unemployment continued to grow in France, resulting in the introduction of new hiring programmes specifically targeting youth. During 2013 two programmes, which were primarily oriented towards non-profit organizations but were also open to the private sector, were launched. The first, Jobs of the Future, is targeted at young people (aged 16–25) without qualifications who have been out of work for at least six months. It offers subsidies amounting to 35 per cent of the minimum wage (€500 per month) for a period lasting up to two years; and, in principle, a complementary mentoring/training plan should be drawn up. The second programme, Generation Contract, offers lump-sum payments of €4,000 per year for three years upon hiring a young person (aged 16–25) on a permanent contract, along with the obligation to keep (or hire) older employees (aged 55 and over) and to assign an older "mentor" to newly appointed young employees.

Source: Aeberhardt et al., 2011; Gineste, 2014.

programmes were introduced in the late 1990s in Germany and the United Kingdom. The novel feature of some of these programmes was that they combined on-the-job training and counselling with wage subsidies. The Youth Practice (Ungdomsprakt) programme, launched in 1992 in Sweden, aimed to provide work experience for youths (aged 18–24) who had completed high-school education and had been unemployed for four months. The placements lasted six months; participants received an "allowance" (which was below the market wage) partly financed by the PES, and were also obliged to participate in training as well as counselling and job search assistance provided by the PES; however, in practice these obligations were not strictly enforced (Larsson, 2003; Costa Dias et al., 2013). Under the terms of the United Kingdom's New Deal – rolled out in 1998 – young people (aged 18–24) who had been unemployed for at least six months could be placed, following a mandatory four-month job search programme, in subsidized jobs, whereby a flat-rate hiring subsidy (equivalent to about 40 per cent of the starting wage) was paid to the employer over a 26-week period and the employer was obliged to offer at least one day's training per week to the young person (for which the employer received a flat-rate reimbursement).

In several continental European countries, wage subsidy programmes aiming to promote the reintegration of long-term unemployed, those at risk of long-term unemployment and disadvantaged (low-skilled) people have been in use for more than 15 years. In some cases, young people were given preferential access to these programmes, for example through a shorter qualifying period of unemployment than that applicable to adults or by other means; in others, these programmes were complemented by programmes specifically targeting youth. In Germany, the Immediate Action Programme for Lowering Youth Unemployment, a federal ALMP aimed at reducing youth unemployment, was in place between 1999 and 2004. Under this programme, firms hiring young people (under the age of 25) had the opportunity to choose between a subsidy that covered 40 per cent of the worker's wage for two years and an alternative that covered 60 per cent of the wage but lasted for only one year (Caliendo et al., 2011). In accordance with other hiring subsidy programmes in Germany, strict conditions were imposed on employers: if they dismissed the worker during the subsidy period, or within a period equal to half the length of the subsidized period after the subsidy expired, they were obliged to pay back half of the subsidy.

A hiring subsidy programme instituted in 1999 in Austria (Eingliederungsbeihilfe) was similarly generous, with subsidies lasting for up to two years covering up to 60 per cent of the gross wage. While adults became eligible for this subsidy after 12 months of unemployment, young people (aged 16–24) qualified after only six months of registration as unemployed. In both the Austrian and German programmes, selection for participation depended to a certain extent on soft profiling by PES caseworkers.[21]

The ACTIVA programme, rolled out in 2002 in Belgium, offered employers flat-rate reductions in payroll taxes and direct wage subsidies for hiring long-term

---

[21] That is, caseworkers have a degree of discretion in the choice of participants and selection is not just an issue of meeting eligibility criteria.

unemployed people. Low-skilled young people (those who have not graduated from upper secondary school) qualified for the subsidy after six months of unemployment, and employers of this group of beneficiaries benefited from a reduction in payroll taxes 50 per cent higher than, and for a period (two years) twice as long as, those applicable to employers of adults or young people with higher skills.[22]

The number of wage subsidy programmes for young people in Europe has grown since the early years of the millennium, largely in response to rising youth unemployment in the wake of the recent economic crisis. These take a variety of forms. In Sweden, youth employment was promoted by a reduction in payroll taxes for *all* young workers, introduced in two successive steps between 2007 and 2009, effectively resulting in the halving of payroll taxes for young employees between the ages of 18 and 26.[23] Since 2010, policy-makers in Finland have taken the path of simplifying administrative procedures and promoting hiring subsidies for young people by issuing vouchers to eligible jobseekers. In the United Kingdom, a new hiring subsidy (forming part of the Youth Contract) targeted at young people who have been unemployed for six months was introduced in 2012. This subsidy, which is set at a flat rate and paid in arrears, covers around 40 per cent of a young person's wages for a six-month period. In Belgium, the existing hiring subsidy, ACTIVA, was temporarily (for appointments made during 2010) rendered more generous for young people under the age of 19, with complete exemption from payroll taxes, higher direct subsidies and longer subsidy periods.

In countries particularly badly affected by the recent crisis, many different incentives were introduced to promote youth employment. In Portugal, the initial response (in 2009) took the form of a lump-sum subsidy for hiring and a two-year exemption from social security contributions. In 2012, a new combined hiring subsidy and vocational education programme was introduced for those already unemployed for six months, including a wage subsidy covering 60 per cent of the wage for a period of 18 months for young workers hired on open-ended contracts. In Greece, a number of different temporary hiring subsidies (including subsidized internship programmes followed by hiring subsidies) have been implemented since 2010.

In countries with strict EPL and a *two-tier labour market* (in Europe, mainly France, Italy and Spain),[24] wage subsidies addressing youth employment issues have certain notable common aspects. In the 1980s, they aimed to lower youth unemploy-

---

[22] The main conditionality for employers was that they could not hire an individual eligible for a subsidy (a) if another worker in the same line of work had been made redundant within the previous six months or (b) if the person hired had worked at the same company in the previous six months.

[23] A hiring subsidy (New Start Jobs) targeting long-term non-employed was also introduced in 2007. This entitled employers to a subsidy equal to the level of payroll tax; young people (aged 18–25) were eligible for the subsidy after a six-month period of non-employment, and their employers were entitled to the subsidy for one year. The rate of the subsidy was doubled in 2009.

[24] A "two-tier labour market" is characterized by a primary labour market comprising jobs subject to permanent labour contracts and a secondary labour market comprising relatively unstable, precarious jobs under fixed-term labour contracts.

ment by introducing subsidized fixed-term contract jobs. For example, the Job Training Program in Italy (effective between 1984 and 1991) introduced a two-year fixed-term contract, complemented by a generous reduction in employers' social security contributions (coupled with the requirement to offer on-the-job training). More recently, with increasing numbers of young people in precarious employment (characterized by a cycle of fixed-term jobs and unemployment), programmes in these countries have aimed specifically at increasing the number of young people working on permanent contracts. Policy-makers in Spain introduced payroll tax cuts for hiring young people on open-ended contracts, along with a reduction in firing costs for open-ended contracts (between 1997 and 2001) and lump-sum payments for hiring young people on permanent contracts (between 2006 and 2010). In Italy, temporary tax credits for firms hiring workers on open-ended contracts (between 2001 and 2003), similar programmes for young people (starting in 2011) and lump-sum payments for converting fixed-term contracts into permanent contracts for young employees (in 2012) were used. In order to enable these measures to contribute to overall employment growth, policy-makers have introduced conditionalities for employers that curtail the churning of workers[25] or tie subsidies to an expanding workforce.

In Central and Eastern European countries, hiring subsidies for disadvantaged unemployed (including youth and first-time jobseekers) have been used since the mid-1990s (for example, in Hungary and Poland) or early 2000s (in Bulgaria, Croatia, Estonia and Romania). Most of these programmes largely followed the lead of Western European countries, offering employers generous subsidies (up to 50 per cent of wages) for, typically, a year, with conditions similar to those applying to programmes in Germany. In the immediate aftermath of the financial crisis, a number of these countries introduced new programmes, which took a wide variety of forms. For example, in 2009 Slovenia introduced a hiring subsidy in the form of a lump-sum payment (corresponding to roughly 55 per cent of the minimum wage) for employment contracts that lasted for at least one year. In Hungary, a hiring subsidy in the form of reductions in payroll taxes targeting first-time jobseekers had been introduced in 2005 in the form of a voucher issued to the eligible jobseeker, which entitled the employer to a reduction in labour costs for a two-year period. In 2011 this measure was replaced by an employment subsidy programme targeting young people (under the age of 25), also for two years. Most recently, in the context of the Youth Guarantee, and with financial support from the European Social Fund, new youth hiring subsidy programmes have been implemented (in Croatia, Latvia and Lithuania) or extended (in Bulgaria) since 2012. These initiatives have some common features: they target first-time jobseekers and youth (aged 16–29) and provide a generous subsidy (between 25 and 50 per cent of youth wages) for a fixed amount of time (nine to 12 months).

---

[25]   In Spain, firms that had wrongfully dismissed any of their workers eligible for the payroll tax cut in 1997 were not allowed to hire another worker eligible for the subsidy within one year; also, the subsidized worker could not have been an employee of the firm in the previous 24 months (Elias, 2014; Kugler et al., 2002).

4.4.2. Anglo-Saxon countries outside the EU

In English-speaking OECD countries outside Europe, subsidies either are aimed at disadvantaged youth, often linked with on-the-job training, or cover all youth hires and take the form of tax credits. In the United States, two large-scale federal programmes included disadvantaged youth among the targeted groups, while a wealth of state-level hiring subsidy programmes exist which are rarely targeted (Neumark and Grijalva, 2013). The Targeted Jobs Tax Credit (between 1979 and 1994) provided relatively generous hiring incentives through tax credits (primarily for low-wage jobs), initially for a two-year period.[26] The Job Training Partnership Act (between 1983 and 1988) provided temporary hiring subsidies (for six months) to employers who recruited disadvantaged jobseekers and offered on-the-job training programmes. In Canada, while direct payments to employers in apprenticeship programmes are widespread at the regional level, at the federal level the Youth Hires Programme briefly (in 1999 and 2000) provided a small payroll tax reimbursement for increasing the number of young employees on the payroll (Webb et al., 2012). The Australian Special Youth Employment Training Programme (SYETP) was a large-scale measure that ran from 1976 to 1985, targeting disadvantaged youth, which provided a short-term flat-rate wage subsidy for employers; despite its name, there was little emphasis on actual training (Richardson, 1998). The subsequent Job Start programme was a hiring subsidy targeting long-term unemployed, irrespective of age, with the rate and duration of subsidy varying according to age and length of unemployment.

4.4.3. Low- and middle-income countries

Despite a growing tendency in many LMICs towards the adoption of employment subsidy measures (Almeida et al., 2014), wage subsidies for young people are still much less common outside the OECD. Impact evaluation studies of youth wage subsidy programmes are still scarcer in these countries. This can be explained partly by the "evidence gap" relating to labour market programmes in developing countries, where both data and research capacities are widely lacking, and partly by the comparative rarity of youth wage subsidy programmes in developing countries.

This situation may be explained by two principal factors. First, in developing countries training programmes can be more effective than subsidies alone, as young people here tend to have fewer skills, owing to the lower quality of education. Notably, in Latin America and the Caribbean, youth-targeted training programmes tend to have a greater impact on employment rates than in Europe (Corseuil et al., 2013; Kluve, 2014). These programmes are not included in our analysis; however, box 4.2 provides an overview of some typical large-scale on-the-job training programmes in Latin America.

Second, as has already been observed above, the scope of formal wage employment is often limited in developing countries, where the majority of workers are

---

[26]   The duration of the subsidy was later halved to one year.

> **Box 4.2. Evaluation of combined on-the-job training programmes in Latin America**
>
> A number of large-scale, work-based training programmes have been implemented in Latin America, for example in Colombia, the Dominican Republic and Mexico.
>
> In **Colombia**, the Jóvenes en Acción was introduced as a randomized controlled trial (RCT) in 2001, and ran until 2005. The programme provided three months of classroom training and three months of on-the-job training to disadvantaged young people between the ages of 18 and 25. Participants worked five hours per day on average during their unpaid internship, and received a food and transportation allowance. The impact evaluation of this programme yielded positive estimated impacts on both employment probability and earnings (Attanasio et al., 2011).
>
> In the **Dominican Republic**, a combined classroom training and internship programme of experimental design (Juventud y Empleo) was implemented from 1999 to 2007. The target group comprised low-income youth (aged 18–29) with less than secondary education; participants were enrolled on a three-month off-the-job training course followed by a two-month internship at a private firm, during which they received a stipend. Several impact evaluations (Ibarrarán et al., 2006; Card et al., 2011; Ibarrarán et al., 2014) were conducted on programme effects; no evidence of positive overall impact on employment was found, although the evaluations did find some small positive effects on earnings.
>
> In **Mexico**, the PROBECAT training programme (renamed SICAT in 2001 and Bécate in 2005) started in 1984 and had expanded dramatically by the second half of the 1990s. Participation was not limited to youth (though most participants were under 25) and comprised a mixture of classroom and on-the-job training for a three-month period, during which participants received a scholarship. Participating firms were obliged to hire at least 70 per cent of the trainees at the end of the three-month period. According to the impact evaluation by Delajara et al. (2006), the programme had a small but positive impact on the employment probability of participants, but no effect on wages.
>
> Further Latin American examples of combined wage subsidy and training measures for unemployed youth are provided by programmes in Chile (Chile Joven, from 1991), Argentina (Proyecto Joven, from 1993) and Uruguay during the early to mid-1990s; the impact of these programmes, however, was never evaluated (Smith, 2006).

self-employed and/or in informal employment. In view of the limited possibilities for formal job growth, encouraging (formal) self-employment of young people through entrepreneurship subsidies tends to be seen as a more fruitful way of promoting youth employment (Kluve et al., 2016a).[27] Start-up subsidies can thus take over the role of hiring subsidies in some countries, and are particularly popular in the

---

[27]   See also, however, the discussion in Chapter 5 below.

> ### Box 4.3. A shared subsidy: The Subsidio al Empleo Joven
> ### programme in Chile
>
> In order to tackle persistently high youth unemployment rates and to increase formal youth employment, two wage subsidies were instituted in Chile. The 2008 pension reform* incorporated a small cut in payroll taxes for employers hiring young persons (aged 18–35) in low-wage jobs for up to two years. In 2009, a new programme offered wage subsidies targeting vulnerable youth between the ages of 18 and 25. This programme had a number of interesting features. Eligibility was based on a "vulnerability score" (Ficha de Protección Social), and hence it effectively targeted young people in the poorest 40 per cent of the population, with eligibility running out one month after the individual's 25th birthday. The subsidy was shared between the employer and the worker, each of whom had to apply separately. Workers were entitled to a direct subsidy (a wage bonus) which amounted to 20 per cent of their wages, paid either annually as a lump sum or in monthly instalments. Employers received a monthly payment of up to 10 per cent of the eligible worker's wage. The exact amount of the subsidy depended on the worker's wage, with a higher percentage allowed for lower wage earners. In the event that the employer's social security contribution payments were not up to date, the claim for the subsidy could be rejected (which happened in approximately 11 per cent of cases), although this condition did not apply to workers. Therefore, a case could arise in which only the employee received the benefit.
>
> Evaluations of the measure (Bravo and Rau, 2013; Gersdorff and Benavides, 2012) revealed that take-up by firms was relatively low (at about 3–5 per cent), and about half of the firms which took advantage of the subsidy were micro-enterprises with fewer than ten employees. Considering all the eligibility criteria, approximately 20–30 per cent of workers were covered by the subsidy.
>
> * The pension reform also included a 50 per cent cut in employees' pension contributions for low-wage earners (defined according to slightly different terms from those in the SEJ) aged between 18 and 35, which applied for 24 months. Either this subsidy or the SEJ could be applied for (it was not possible to take up both). The employment impacts of this part of the reform have not been evaluated.

Middle East and Africa. We found very few examples of large-scale wage subsidy programmes in Latin America and the Caribbean, where youth-oriented measures primarily focus on the training element. The most notable example comes from Chile, where the Subsidio al Empleo Joven (SEJ) was initiated in 2009 targeting vulnerable youth aged between 18 and 24 (for details, see box 4.3). This was a rare example of a "pure" large-scale wage subsidy programme where training was not a compulsory element. In North Africa and the Middle East, high unemployment rates among young people present a serious problem. Spending on ALMPs for youth is relatively high in this region, and hiring subsidies are common.

In North Africa, hiring subsidy programmes often target higher education graduates, among whom the unemployment rate is relatively high, in an attempt to achieve their long-term labour market integration. Such programmes for graduates

Box 4.4. The youth wage subsidy pilot and subsequent debates in South Africa

South Africa is characterized by extremely high youth unemployment rates, especially among black Africans: close to two-thirds of non-white South Africans aged 20–24 were unemployed in 2012 (Levinsohn et al., 2014). To tackle this problem, a committee of experts came up with a proposal for a youth wage subsidy in 2006, and a pilot programme was launched in 2010. The programme had an RCT design: vouchers were handed out to randomly selected unemployed young people between the ages of 20 and 24. Each voucher entitled its holder to a subsidy with a total value of 5,000 South African rand (ZAR), which could be claimed in instalments over a minimum of six months until the total amount was exhausted. The maximum monthly amount of the subsidy was half the wage or ZAR833 (whichever was lower). This monthly cap corresponded to about 40 per cent of the median wage in the target group. The subsidy was also transferable between companies before exhaustion.

After the pilot, which reported significant gains in the post-programme employment probability of participants, plans for national implementation were worked out and debated. A simulation based on a structural search model (Levinsohn and Pugatch, 2014) estimated that a wage subsidy of ZAR1,000 per month would lead to a fall in the proportion of long-term unemployed youth of 12 percentage points.[*] A firm-level survey conducted in 2011 (Schöer and Rankin, 2011) investigated employers' reactions to a hypothetical youth wage subsidy. Their results indicated that the majority of the surveyed firms would have considered hiring more young workers, although they also suggested that they would not necessarily increase their labour force but would substitute younger workers for older ones.

After several round-table discussions and background studies, in 2013 President Jacob Zuma signed the Employment Tax Incentive Act, which introduced the wage subsidy nationwide. In contrast to the original scheme, which offered direct payments at a relatively high level, the new scheme offered tax incentives for up to two years to employers who, after 1 October 2014, hired low- to middle-level wage earners (those earning below ZAR6,000) aged between 18 and 29 years.

This measure has received substantial media attention ever since its first planning phase. The Congress of South African Trade Unions has opposed the wage subsidy, fearing the displacement of older workers and rising levels of unemployment, with demonstrations and the threat of strikes.

Evaluations of the full programme are disappointing and suggest that it has not had any appreciable impact on youth employment rates (Ranhhod and Finn, 2014, 2015).

[*] The assumption of the model was that the subsidy would be passed to jobseekers in its entirety in the form of wage offers, thus presenting a very optimistic best-case scenario.

seeking their first jobs have been used in Tunisia since the late 1980s. The Introduction to Professional Life (Stage d'Initiation à la Vie Professionnelle: SVIP) programme included a combination of reductions in payroll taxes and direct hiring subsidies for a period of 12 months; the subsidies varied according to the level and subject of graduate degree, on average covering one-third of starting wages. Employers had to repay subsidies (and payroll taxes) in the event that they broke the contract, and they were allowed to recruit a new subsidized graduate only if they could prove that they had hired at least one-quarter of their subsidized workers over the previous three years under permanent contracts.

A similar programme has been in place since 1999 in Algeria, providing subsidies of 12 months' duration to employers who hire graduates from higher education. A new and more generous hiring subsidy programme (Contrat de Travail Aidé) started in 2008, under which subsidies were made available for the hiring of all first-time jobseekers. The amount and duration of the wage subsidy are dependent on the young person's level of qualification, and employers also benefit from a reduction of payroll taxes during the period of the subsidy.

Another similar programme (Idmaj) was established in Morocco in 2006: this is the country's largest ALMP targeted at young people, with an average of 50,000 participants each year during the period 2006–13. This programme targets young university graduates, baccalaureate holders, and young people with equivalent levels of education who have graduated from vocational-type programmes who are registered as unemployed. The programme offers payroll tax reductions for firms who employ young workers in these groups on a fixed-term paid internship programme lasting between 18 and 24 months, as well as a reduction in personal income tax for young people participating in the programme. An employer who recruits the participant at the end of the internship period may benefit from a tax exemption for a further 12 months (Ibourk, 2012).

In Jordan an experimental programme, New Opportunities for Women, targeted recent female college graduates. Randomly selected participants received a voucher that entitled their potential employers to a six-month flat-rate wage subsidy with a value equal to the minimum wage.

The reduction in payroll taxes for new recruits in 2008–09 in Turkey had the dual aim of (a) reducing informal employment and (b) favouring the integration of relatively disadvantaged groups into the labour market. The Employment Package waived all employers' social security payments – which constitute approximately 15 per cent of labour costs – for hiring women (of any age) and young men (aged 18–29) who had not been formally employed during the previous six months and on the condition that the new appointments would increase the size of the firm's workforce. The subsidy was designed to last for five years, covering all social security payments in the first year of hiring and subsequently decreasing annually in four steps. While this programme was originally intended as a temporary measure, it has been extended several times, most recently in 2011.

In sub-Saharan Africa youth wage subsidy programmes are rare. With the exception of South Africa (which is a richly documented case: see box 4.4), none of these measures has been subject to impact evaluation. The inventories surveyed suggest that most measures which offer subsidized work for youth are similar to PEPs, offering temporary employment on the secondary labour market in areas such as construction, maintaining public infrastructure and agriculture.

4.5. Evidence on the impact of wage subsidies

In this section, after a brief overview of the evaluation strategies for wage subsidies, we provide an in-depth analysis of the empirical studies assessing programme effectiveness. Throughout, studies are reviewed by category of programmes; a summary of the typical features of these stylized categories is provided in table 4.2.

4.5.1. Impact of wage subsidies: Methodology

The main objective of evaluation studies is to assess the impact of a programme, that is, to compare what actually happened to programme participants with an estimate of what would have happened to them in the absence of the programme (i.e. the counterfactual). This is done in order to distinguish between factors that have little to do with the intervention (stemming, for example, from the composition of programme participants or more favourable economic conditions in programme areas) and factors arising from the programme itself. The primary challenge, then, is to find a suitable "control group", composed of individuals who possess characteristics that may influence their labour market opportunities similar to those of programme participants (the "treatment group"), but who do not participate in the wage subsidy under study. Here we will provide a brief overview of the methods used in microeconometric evaluation studies, specifically calling attention to some of the pitfalls, as well as providing some insights into whether substitution and deadweight effects can be addressed.

We should note one very specific empirical issue that arises when evaluating wage subsidy programmes (rather than other ALMPs): namely, while some studies aim to identify the effect of *being eligible* for a wage subsidy, others examine the impact of *actually receiving* a wage subsidy. Which approach is taken is often determined by the design of the programme under review, as well as the specificities of the data at hand.

Looking at all those eligible to receive a subsidy (but who do not necessarily receive it) is useful for estimating whether the "offer" of a subsidy increases the (re-)employment probability of the target group,[28] as well as for evaluating the take-up of the subsidy. This type of study is primarily used for programmes with relatively simple eligibility rules (say, a young person who has been registered as unemployed for six months is entitled to a wage subsidy) or those which are both comprehensive

---

[28] This is what is called in the evaluation literature the "intention to treat" parameter.

Table 4.2. Main features of wage subsidy programmes for young people

Programme type	Targeting	Target group	Generosity (% of wage costs)	Duration	Conditionality	Payment vehicle
Payroll tax reduction	All eligible	All youth	Low (maximum 10%)	Temporary or permanent	Weak, mostly for hiring	Payroll taxes
Hiring subsidies for disadvantaged youth	Finely targeted, caseworker selection	Disadvantaged (LTU, low education)	High (50%)	12–24 months	Strict (no dismissal; no direct substitution)	Direct payment
Work experience programmes	Broad	Unemployed	High (50% or more)	3–6 months	Weak	Direct payment
Subsidies in two-tier labour markets	Broad	Unemployed	Low (10–15%)	24 months	Recruitment on permanent contract	Varies
Combined hiring subsidy and on-the-job training	Finely targeted, profiling	Unemployed (LTU)	Medium (20–40%)	6–12 months	Provision of training	Direct payment
Experimental programmes in developing countries	Broad	Varies	High (40–50%)	6 months	Weak (hiring in formal job)	Vouchers, direct payment

Note: LTU = long-term unemployment.

and extensive, such as the Youth Guarantee.[29] The areas of interest are eligible individuals' labour market outcomes both during the subsidy period and in the longer run. However, the latter can only be estimated if researchers have access to administrative data (and hence know whether a particular job was subsidized) and if the programme provided only a temporary subsidy.

In contrast, for programmes where eligibility is (partially) dependent on the decision of a PES caseworker, the "offer" of a subsidy is typically not recorded in (administrative) data sets used by researchers; as a result, they can only know whether the individual participated or not. In this context, the treatment group is composed of individuals who were recruited with a subsidy, and the outcome of interest is primarily whether participants are able to retain jobs after the subsidy is exhausted.[30]

Experimental evaluation studies are often deemed the most reliable (in that they have the highest degree of internal validity), since in this case the offer of a wage subsidy is randomized, which guarantees that the members of the "treatment" and of the "control" group do not systematically differ in their productive characteristics. The drawback is that it is not easy to estimate what the effects of a scaled-up programme would be, since many of the indirect effects might not materialize during the experiment, and only simply designed programmes can be evaluated, as the researchers often do not have the tools to monitor and enforce behavioural conditions.

A second fruitful approach is often applied when the eligibility for subsidies is determined by a cut-off value of some observable characteristic (for example, age or months of prior unemployment).[31] Since determinants of potential outcomes are not expected to exhibit a jump at these points, a comparison of persons just below and just above the threshold value can produce reliable estimates of the effect of eligibility for the subsidy. However, the risk that the potential positive impact of the programme is due to substitution effects is pronounced in this case.[32] It should also be noted that this method relies on a comparison with those individuals close to the threshold, and so extrapolation to the whole population can only be achieved using strong assumptions.

A third commonly used method examines the trends in labour market outcomes of those eligible and ineligible for the programme around the time of introduction of the subsidy.[33] Specifically, it compares the change in outcomes between

---

[29]   Since the Youth Guarantee is intended to cover *all* young people before they are NEET for four months, a control group would tend to be drawn from outside these eligibility rules. An obvious control group in this case is those of similar age, but (just) outside the age range for the programme. The size of programme means that it is reasonable to consider all young people as the "treated".

[30]   Since, in this type of analysis, by definition all "treated" individuals have taken up the subsidy, looking at employment rates during the subsidy period can only inform researchers whether any of those recruited with the subsidy were fired "early".

[31]   This is the so-called "regression discontinuity" method.

[32]   Since individuals just above and just below the cut-off value for eligibility can be assumed to be otherwise identical, and hence easily substitutable.

[33]   This is the so-called "difference-in-difference" method.

the participant group and the selected comparison group – who typically come from similar (but ineligible) age groups, or from those who live in similar locations where the programme was unavailable – before and after the introduction of the programme. The idea behind this method is that the trend in labour market outcomes of the comparison group yields an accurate representation of what would have happened to the participant group in the absence of the programme. This relies on the assumption that there were no other changes (for example, owing to legislation or labour market shocks) corresponding to the introduction of the programme that might have affected the outcomes of the two groups *differentially*.[34]

Finally, there are methods which rely on the assumption that, given a sufficiently rich data set, if those who are ineligible but otherwise possess the same observable characteristics (relevant to determining labour market outcomes) are "matched" to participants, then the only difference between the two groups in their employment chances will be due to the programme. This method has most frequently been used in cases where no data about the offer (only the take-up) of a wage subsidy are recorded, and requires very careful consideration of how the pool of ineligible comparators is selected.[35]

Studies based on individual (worker) level data typically do not provide evidence regarding the indirect substitution effects of subsidies on other groups.[36] This requires further information;[37] hence most of the studies reviewed provide estimates of the individual level impact on the employment probability of the targeted youth without taking this into consideration.

4.5.2. Impact of wage subsidies: Payroll tax reductions

The evidence on payroll tax reductions targeted at youth is scarce and analyses report mixed results. The common feature of the programmes reviewed is that they did not explicitly target disadvantaged young people, that they led to modest reductions in labour costs and that their aim was to increase the employment rate of youth in general.

Egebark and Kaunitz (2014) estimated the impact of the payroll tax changes enacted in 2007 in Sweden on young people (aged 18–24).[38] This change led to a

---

[34] This is the so-called "parallel trends" assumption.

[35] Researchers typically use two groups, selected from among those whose spell of unemployment began at the same time as the wage subsidy recipients: those who – in the period during which the subsidy beneficiaries started their jobs – found jobs without a subsidy, and those who were still unemployed at that time.

[36] This is true of the microeconometric impact evaluation of all types of ALMPs, not just wage subsidies.

[37] Researchers relying on worker data mainly use circumstantial evidence to determine indirect effects. For example, to establish the substitution effects of youth wage subsidies, they compare the outcomes for a slightly older age group – who are likely to be those most easily substituted for youth – with those of even older groups.

[38] Note that the effects of the financial crisis became evident in the Swedish labour market only in 2009, so this analysis concerns a relative boom period.

reduction of 11 percentage points in payroll taxes (representing approximately a 9 per cent decrease in total labour costs) and applied *unconditionally* to all young employed people.[39] The authors showed that this decrease in payroll taxes resulted in a very modest increase in the employment probability of the target group, of around 2 per cent, relative to slightly older individuals. Moreover, when substitution effects were taken into account, the net impact of the tax reduction on the absolute employment rate of young people was shown to be only about 1 per cent. Due to this very small effect on employment, the payroll tax reduction is unlikely to have been particularly cost-effective: the total costs of additional jobs created for young people were close to four times the total hiring costs of these individuals.[40]

Evidence of a more effective payroll tax reduction policy emerges from the work of Webb et al. (2012) on the Canadian Youth Hires programme, which temporarily reduced the labour costs of hiring young persons (aged 18–24) by about 3.5 per cent in 1999–2000. This subsidy came in the form of an automatic refund of employers' contributions to the unemployment insurance fund and led to an *increase* in the aggregate insurable payroll for those in the relevant age group relative to the base year of 1998. The authors found a 3.5 per cent increase in the number of weeks spent in employment for the target group, relative to a slightly older comparison group (aged 25–29). However, they also presented evidence that the increase in young people's employment came partially at the expense of these slightly older persons – hence, the net impact of the tax reduction was probably closer to 2.5 per cent.

The Employment Package of 2008 in Turkey included a generous subsidy, in the form of a reduction of employers' payroll taxes, for hiring women (of all ages) and young men (aged 18–29) who had not been formally employed during the preceding six months. The subsidy applied exclusively to new hires that increased firms' total employment, and lasted for five years, covering all payroll taxes initially – equivalent to about 15 per cent of labour costs – and subsequently decreasing in four annual steps to zero. Barza (2011) evaluated the short-term impact of the subsidy on the outcomes of young men (aged 25–29).[41] Her results showed a very small positive impact on formal employment, in the region of a 4 per cent increase in employment probability for eligible young men. The author also showed that this increase is mainly due to young people moving from unemployment and inactivity into formal employment, and that only about one-quarter of the impact is due to employers formalizing the employment contracts of previously informal workers. This policy was originally available for hires over a one-year period, but was prolonged for

---

[39] The authors use a difference-in-difference type of methodology, with slightly older (non-eligible) individuals constituting the control group.

[40] The total costs of additional jobs created equate to the total payroll tax revenues forgone relative to the (estimated) number of additional jobs created through the programme. The total hiring costs equate to total labour costs less payroll taxes.

[41] This analysis is carried out using a difference-in-difference methodology, by contrasting the change in outcomes between 2007 and 2008 for young men aged 25–29 with that for men aged 30–34.

an additional year. Ayhan (2013), who examined the impact of the policy over a two-year period, presented positive results, showing that the policy increased the hiring rate of young men (aged 25–29) by 1.3 percentage points, relative to slightly older men.

These studies highlight some important aspects of payroll tax reductions. First, it is evident that hiring subsidies are more effective than wage subsidies in increasing the employment probability of the target group. Second, the institutional context and labour supply incentives play an important role in influencing the employment effects. In countries where the supply of young workers is more responsive to potential wage increases (either because the welfare system is less generous,[42] or because there is significant informal employment), hiring subsidies lead to larger increases in formal employment.

4.5.3. Impact of wage subsidies: Targeted hiring subsidies for the disadvantaged

The main features of these programmes are that they cover a substantial fraction (typically 40 per cent or more) of the young person's wage costs; they can be claimed for a limited, but relatively long period (typically for one to two years); and the offer of the subsidy is often partially dependent on a PES caseworker's decision. The aim of these programmes is to provide subsidized jobs for sufficiently long periods to enable the young participants to develop skills and improve their long-term employment opportunities.

Caliendo et al. (2011) studied the impacts of two wage subsidy programmes – the standard wage subsidy available for insured unemployed and a youth-targeted wage subsidy – on the long-term outcomes of unemployed youth (aged 18–24) in Germany, specifically those who entered unemployment in 2002. The "standard" wage subsidy covered up to 50 per cent of the participant's wages (paid to the employer) for up to one year; the youth wage subsidy ran for two years, covering 40 per cent of the young person's wages. Employing workers with a subsidy entailed some strict conditionalities for employers: if they dismissed the worker during the subsidy period or within a period equal to half the length of the subsidy after the subsidy expired, they were obliged to pay back half of the subsidy. The authors – comparing the outcomes of wage subsidy beneficiaries with those of young people who did not participate in an ALMP but who otherwise had similar observable characteristics – found very large post-programme employment effects in respect of unsubsidized jobs for both programmes. Moreover, not only was the employment probability of participant youth substantially higher immediately after the subsidy period; the effect of the programme – although it decreased over time – persisted for up to five years after entry into the programme. In other words, even two to three years after the subsidy had run out, young people who had participated in a wage subsidy programme had

---

[42]   The net replacement rate of unemployment benefits for low-wage single people is more than 20 percentage points higher in Sweden than in Canada or Turkey.

employment rates approximately 10–15 per cent higher than non-participants.[43] Unsurprisingly, the impact of the youth-targeted wage subsidy was higher than that of the general one, since the value of the targeted subsidy was higher for the employer. Finally, it is worth noting that the beneficial effects of the subsidies were higher in the eastern part of the country, where the labour market was more depressed, and that highly skilled youth obtained the greatest benefit from the subsidies.

Eppel and Mahringer (2013) evaluated a similarly generous wage subsidy in Austria – lasting for up to two years and covering up to 60 per cent of gross wages (but without strict non-dismissal clauses) – targeting the long-term unemployed.[44] Their results point to somewhat more muted effects for this programme: young people accumulated approximately nine to nine-and-a-half months' more employment and about four months' more unsubsidized employment than similar non-participants (which equates to a 10 per cent increase) five years after the start of programme participation.[45] However, it is worth noting that, according to the authors' estimates, approximately 60 per cent of those who found a job with the help of the subsidy would also have been employed in its absence.[46]

This type of wage subsidy has also been used in Eastern Europe; however, reliable impact evaluations are very scarce – indeed, the only study that examined the outcomes for young people is that by O'Leary (1998). He evaluated a programme implemented in 1996 in Hungary, which targeted young people who had been unemployed for at least six months. The subsidy lasted for up to one year, covering 50 per cent of wage costs, and entailed penalties for any employer who dismissed a subsidized worker either during the period of the subsidy or afterwards for a period at least as long as the subsidy's duration. Comparing the outcomes of wage subsidy beneficiaries with similar non-participants one year after the subsidy ended showed a small positive impact of the programme for young people (aged 16–29), whose employment probability was estimated at about 15 per cent higher than that of non-participants.[47] However, much of this success is attributable to participation in (further) subsidized employment, as employment in non-subsidized jobs in the primary labour market was only slightly higher for wage subsidy beneficiaries.[48]

---

[43] This means that subsidized workers had accumulated approximately eight-and-a-half to nine months' more unsubsidized employment over a period of five years than non-participants.

[44] For young people, this meant having been unemployed for at least six months.

[45] However, for prime-age (25–44) and older (45–54) unemployed people, the effects are more pronounced.

[46] As a result, a simple cost–benefit analysis reveals that the programme would break even after five years. However, this analysis is restricted to the direct labour market effects of the programme and only considers the gains accruing to the public budget.

[47] It should be noted that the author's data set contained a limited number of background variables, casting some doubt on the reliability of the estimates.

[48] It must be noted that a raw comparison of employment outcomes for participants and non-participants (without adjusting for differences across the two groups in observable characteristics) yields differences that are three times as large. This is a clear indication that employers were selecting individuals who would have been able to find a job in any event; hence the deadweight effect of the programme may have been large.

While the results of these studies are mixed, they point out that: (a) generous hiring subsidies with substantial durations can be conducive to improving the long-term employment outcomes of youth; (b) it is likely that imposing non-dismissal obligations on employers is beneficial for the long-term employment prospects of subsidized youth; (c) fine-tuning the targeting of these subsidies is important, since they can have substantial deadweight effects.

4.5.4. Work experience programmes

These are programmes that aim to provide short-term work experience to young people, with the primary objective of providing firms with concrete evidence of participants' productivity and therefore increasing their employability.

Australia's SYETP, which was in place until 1985, offered a flat-rate subsidy for young people (aged 16–24) who had been unemployed for at least four months in the previous year. The subsidy lasted for only 14 weeks and covered about 50 per cent of typical youth wages. Richardson (1998) and Knight (2002) examined the impact of the programme roughly one year after participation, and found a small positive effect of around 10 per cent on participants' employment probability. A similar programme, which provided subsidized work experience for young people (aged 18–24) with a high-school education who had been unemployed for four months, existed in Sweden between 1992 and 1995. The placements, which lasted six months, were heavily subsidized, paid below market wages and intended to be supplementary in nature (i.e. not displacing existing jobs).[49] Evaluations of the short-term (Larsson, 2003) and medium-term (Costa Dias et al., 2013) impacts of the programme on participants' employment probability showed small *negative* results.

Although the evidence on short-term work experience programmes is very limited, it appears that those in which young people are recruited in the market sector and are paid wages are more successful than programmes that create explicitly "additional" subsidized positions. A potential explanation for this latter result is that the work performed in these positions neither builds human capital nor is sufficient to provide evidence of productivity in the workplace for potential future employers.

4.5.5. Hiring subsidies in developing countries

Wage subsidies in MICs outside Europe have seldom been evaluated, and the existing evidence is mainly based on pilot programmes.

In North Africa, the expansion of higher education and a contraction of work opportunities in the public sector have led to an increase in graduate unemployment. In response, Tunisia introduced the SVIP programme, targeted at recent graduates who had been looking for their first jobs and had been unemployed for three months;

---

[49] In principle, participants were intended to undertake regular job search activities and were to be provided with on-the-job training; however, neither of these intentions was strictly enforced.

this provided a subsidy covering approximately one-third of wages as well as employers' social security contributions for up to one year. The programme has been popular, with about one-quarter of the target group participating. Broecke (2013) evaluated the impacts of the programme up to one-and-a-half years after the expiration of the subsidy, by contrasting the outcomes of participants and non-participants with similar observable characteristics. He found that joblessness among programme participants was reduced by about 25 per cent compared to non-participants, and that participants were more likely to be employed in private firms, but less likely to have permanent contracts.[50] However, owing to the design of the programme, which was applied on a first-come first-served basis, it is likely to have had large deadweight effects.

Two recent experiments have explored the effects of wage subsidies in MICs. In Jordan, participants in the New Opportunities for Women programme targeting recent female college graduates, were randomly selected to receive vouchers entitling their potential employers to a six-month flat-rate wage subsidy with a value equal to the minimum wage. Groh et al. (2012) reported that the receipt of the voucher more than tripled young women's employment probability during the period of the subsidy, and that this effect was particularly pronounced outside the capital, where the labour market for female graduates is especially weak. However, while the employment probability was 10 per cent higher among those who received a subsidy voucher than among those in the control group, the positive impact of the wage subsidy was much dampened four months after the subsidy ran out, at which point the difference was no longer significant. The most likely explanation for this short-lived positive effect of the wage subsidy is that most of the jobs created were temporary (and unregistered),[51] and it is very probable that they arose from the displacement of other graduates.

An experimental wage subsidy programme in South Africa, where young people (aged 20–24) were allocated vouchers entitling their employers to a refund of 50 per cent of their wages for a six-month period, proved to be more successful. In their evaluation of the pilot programme, Levinsohn et al. (2014) showed that the short-term impact of the subsidy (one year after allocation) was close to a 25 per cent increase in employment probability; and, while the medium term effect (two years after allocation) was more modest, those allocated the voucher were still 10 per cent more likely to be employed. The authors provided some evidence that this positive result was attributable not only to firms' behaviour (as the take-up rate of the subsidy was low), but also to a decrease in young people's reservation wages. They further pointed out that, owing to the role of networks in information flows, young people with family members in formal employment might have gained greater benefit from the vouchers.

---

[50]   The effect of the programme was found to be more pronounced in areas outside greater Tunis where the participation probability of youth in the programme was lower – an indication of ineffective targeting.

[51]   The effect of receiving the subsidy voucher was around 50 per cent lower on employment in jobs that were registered with the social security authorities. In fact, it is likely that almost 90 per cent of additional jobs were unregistered.

More recently, the full-scale wage subsidy in South Africa has been evaluated with more disappointing results. Ranhhod and Finn (2014, 2015) evaluated the first six months and one year (respectively) of the programme and found that the subsidy had no effect on the employment rates of young people. Several reasons may underlie the difference in results between the pilot and the fully fledged subsidy. Of necessity, different methodologies were used for the evaluation of the pilot and full schemes;[52] so, in principle, in the presence of substitution between subsidized and unsubsidized young workers during the pilot which was not possible under the full subsidy (since all unemployed young people were eligible), the two sets of results may be consistent. If this is so, then it implies that the (pilot) subsidy helped those who received it at the expense of those who did not, while the subsidy, once extended to all young people, did not help young people as a whole. This analysis is also consistent with the tapering off of the effect (in the pilot evaluation) once the subsidy was removed. There appears to be evidence of substantial deadweight loss, as well as difficulties with take-up by (in particular small) firms which may have impeded the programme's success. In any event, the experience raises several issues concerning both the design of programmes, to which we will return below (see section 4.6), and the care needed in moving from pilot programmes to large-scale interventions.

A similar experimental wage subsidy programme in Argentina was rolled out in 1998. The programme entitled firms to a direct wage subsidy, with a value equal to roughly 40 per cent of the wage costs of a minimum-wage worker, for employing randomly selected individuals for up to 18 months, on the condition that they formally register the worker. Galasso et al. (2004) found that rates of wage employment for younger (below age 30) voucher recipients almost doubled.[53] However, this increase was primarily in temporary informal jobs, as very few employers actually claimed the subsidy.[54] This suggests both that voucher beneficiaries changed their job search behaviour and that potential employers may have interpreted the voucher as a positive signal of young workers' potential productivity and/or attitudes towards work.

In Chile, wage subsidies provided to both employees and employers for disadvantaged youth since 2009 have been shown by Bravo and Rau (2013) to lead to a significant labour supply response. This programme entitles disadvantaged young people up to age 25 to an income subsidy which amounts to 20 per cent of earned

---

[52]   For the pilot, the evaluation estimated the *average treatment effect* on the treated, comparing eligible young people who were and were not allocated the subsidy; evaluation of the full programme estimated the *intention to treat*, using a difference-in-difference approach comparing eligible young people (aged 20–24) with those who were a little older.

[53]   This was measured immediately after the subsidy period ran out. Note that the effect of the subsidy seemed to fluctuate over the follow-up period, which is probably due to the seasonal variation in labour demand.

[54]   This is probably due to the fact that at the time a large number of employers operated in the informal sector, and registration of workers was probably seen as too costly (as it might have led to legal action against the firm by the government).

income for low wages (wages less than 1.5 times the minimum wage), while their employers are eligible for a subsidy equal to 10 per cent of the young person's wages. However, the employee and the employer had to claim independently, and the take-up of the employee subsidy was much higher than that of the employer component.[55] Using a regression discontinuity design applied to the index of youth disadvantage used for programme qualification,[56] the authors found that the programme led to a 9 per cent (4.5 percentage point) increase in the labour force participation rate of eligible disadvantaged youths during the programme's first year of operation, compared to the control group; the difference fell to 2 per cent (2 percentage points) in the programme's second year. Similarly, the programme led to an increase in (formal) employment of 13 per cent (5 percentage points) in the first year of operation which then fell to 3 per cent (1.3 percentage points). No discernible effect was found on wages. The reduced effectiveness of the programme in the second year is attributable to the recovery of the Chilean economy following the recession of 2009; indeed, the month-by-month effectiveness of the programme is clearly and closely correlated with the macroeconomy as measured by the overall youth unemployment rate. The authors also provided evidence that the positive response was not due to displacement of older workers.

Several common findings are worth noting in respect of the programmes reviewed above. First, employer take-up of the subsidies was generally low,[57] which could have been due to insufficient information being available to employers, or to high administration costs. Second, much of the impact of these programmes comes from labour supply reactions, indicating that eligibility for a subsidy may influence young people's job search behaviour. Third, it is important to disentangle the conditions under which vouchers change employers' perceptions of those eligible for subsidy; in particular, under which conditions do vouchers act as a signal of positive qualities valuable to employers independently of the subsidy itself? Fourth, the design of existing hiring subsidy programmes in developing countries, possibly due to the lack of both statistical and soft profiling by PES staff, is likely to lead to large deadweight losses. This points to a fundamental design issue for hiring subsidies: how to design programmes that are sufficiently simple (in terms of their administrative burden) to encourage employers to recruit young people into registered jobs, but in which the targeting is sufficiently sophisticated to avoid large deadweight costs.

---

[55] In three-quarters of the employment relationships where subsidies were claimed, only the employee received the subsidy.

[56] In order to qualify for the programme, young people had to belong to the poorest 40 per cent of the population measured by the Ficha de Protección Social. The effect of the programme was evaluated comparing eligible young people just below the 40 per cent threshold to ineligible young people just above it.

[57] However, it is difficult to judge, purely on the basis of pilot schemes, whether a national roll-out coupled with publicity campaigns would lead to higher take-up rates.

4.5.6. Wage subsidies in two-tier labour markets

In labour markets with strong EPL for jobs within the primary labour market (those with permanent labour contracts) and relatively unstable, precarious jobs in the secondary labour market (those with fixed-term labour contracts), one aim of hiring subsidies for permanent contracts can be to provide an entry point for young people otherwise excluded from the primary labour market.

In France, a hiring subsidy for recruiting young (under age 22), low-skilled people on open-ended contracts was initiated in 2002. Employers received the subsidy for three years; the value corresponded to roughly 14 per cent of total labour costs for a minimum-wage worker for the first two years, and to 7 per cent in the third year. The employer was not allowed to dismiss the young person during the first three years of the employment relationship. Roger and Zamora (2011) evaluated this policy by comparing eligible young people's probability of being employed with a permanent contract to similar ineligible young people's employment outcomes at the time of the introduction of the policy, and found no discernible impacts. They pointed out that only about half of all eligible firms claimed the subsidy, which might be an indication that the protection awarded to workers by the policy was potentially too costly for firms.

In 1997, a reduction of payroll taxes for the hiring of young people below the age of 30 on open-ended contracts was implemented in Spain. This hiring subsidy represented approximately a 7.5 per cent reduction in labour costs and lasted for two years. During this period, employers were not allowed to dismiss the newly hired young workers. At the same time, dismissal costs for workers on permanent contracts were reduced by 25 per cent. Kugler et al. (2002) evaluated the impact of this change and found an increase in the probability of employment of young people in permanent contracts of 2.5 per cent for young men and 6 per cent for young women, which was attributable to a rise in transitions from non-employment and temporary contracts to permanent contracts. Elias (2014) found slightly smaller positive impacts, estimating that about 46 per cent of appointments under the new programme were due to deadweight effects. However, he presented evidence to show that there was no displacement of older workers.

A comparison of the results of these studies suggests that (a) hiring subsidies for permanent contracts will be successful only if they are coupled with reductions in dismissal costs; and (b) employers need to be offered substantial wage cost reductions to promote the employment of low-skilled young people on permanent contracts.

4.5.7. Wage subsidy programmes with on-the-job training

While there are numerous programmes around the world that either subsidize the employment of young persons in the form of apprenticeships or combine formal classroom training with work experience programmes, the number of wage subsidy programmes with a substantial on-the-job training element is limited.

The primary example of this type of programme was the wage subsidy option within the UK New Deal. For young people (aged 18–24) who had been un-employed for at least six months, following a mandatory four-month job search programme, this programme guaranteed a flat-rate wage subsidy (equivalent to about 40 per cent of starting wages) for employers over a 26-week period; participating employers were obliged to offer the young person training for at least one day per week, for which they received a flat-rate reimbursement. Blundell et al. (2004) examined the short-term employment prospects of young people who had taken up the wage subsidy option, and found that it led to a 20 per cent increase in outflows to jobs, and that only about one-fifth of this impact was due to the job search programme element of the policy. Dorsett (2006) examined the medium-term effects of the wage subsidy option and found that, 18 months after the start of the programme, participants were about 20 per cent less likely to be unemployed than non-participants, indicating that employers had retained previously subsidized workers on completion of the programme.

The use of subsidized on-the-job training for young people has a long tradition in France, where the operation of a two-tiered apprenticeship system means that a large number of firms are certified as training providers. A series of alternative programmes since the middle of the 1980s all had a similar structure: young people were hired on fixed-term employment contracts for at least six months and up to two years, during which period firms were obliged to provide training for at least 15–20 per cent of the young people's time; in return, the employers were exempted from payroll taxes and training costs were reimbursed by the state. Brodaty (2007) evaluated a version of this programme from the end of the 1980s which provided shorter (six-month) contracts, and found a significant positive impact (20 per cent) on the re-employment probability of participants in the short term, especially for those who had previous labour market experience (and hence were probably more employable in any event). Looking at a programme that entailed longer contracts (of at least one year's duration) and estimating the impact up to five years after participation, Pessoa e Costa and Robin (2009) also found a small increase (of 5 per cent) in both employment probability and wages.

These studies suggest that a combination of on-the-job training and subsidized work is particularly effective for reintegrating low-skilled, disadvantaged young people into the labour market and can lead to long-lasting benefits.

4.6. Conclusions and policy recommendations

The evaluation studies reviewed above yield a number of specific recommendations on programme design:

Targeting

More precise targeting tends to lead to more cost-effective programmes with lower deadweight loss; above all, recent evidence tends to support the notion that programmes targeted at disadvantaged young people tend to be more effective than programmes aimed at youth as a whole. On the other hand, it is important to make programmes attractive to young people, and to avoid participants being (or feeling) heavily stigmatized by participation, which is likely to damage the effectiveness of programmes. Hence there may be a trade-off between efficiency gains to be had by more precisely targeted programmes on the one hand and efficiency losses arising from generalized belief by participants themselves and/or prospective employers that programme participants are "no-hopers" on the other. Such stigma effects can be largely avoided through programme quality and results; however, they are an issue to be aware of in programme design.

Programmes subsidizing new hires are more cost-effective than general wage subsidies which include incumbent young workers; the latter, by their nature, run far higher risks of incurring deadweight losses. This is particularly evident in labour markets with less generous welfare systems, where the labour supply of young people is more responsive to potential wage increases.

Both general wage subsidies and those limited to new hires are liable to substitution costs – the employment of the eligible group at the expense of similar non-eligible individuals. Since they do not exclude incumbent workers, general wage subsidies are more prone to this type of problem. The evidence reviewed above suggests that at least one-quarter of the employment impact of broad payroll tax cuts for employing young people comes at the expense of employment losses among slightly older workers.

General wage subsidies are much simpler administratively than those targeted at new hires. This leads to the more general point that targeting, in any shape or form, requires more complex administrative procedures and is reliant on a relatively well-developed, and sufficiently resourced, PES adequately fulfilling its job mediation function and capable of effectively monitoring implementation.

In MICs with a relatively large formal sector, targeted payroll cuts for the hiring of young people lead to modest (formal) employment gains, provided that there is sufficient administrative capacity to ensure that subsidies are granted only for newly recruited young workers.

Programme duration and generosity

The most effective programmes are those that have a medium duration, that is, between six months and two years. Although shorter programmes provide an opportunity for employers to gain information about young workers, they are too short to bring about any appreciable difference in young people's skills; and the evaluation evidence suggests that, overall, this is what matters most to employers.

For low-skilled youth who have been unemployed for longer spells, heavily subsidized jobs (in which up to half of the labour costs are covered) with medium-term subsidy periods (of between six months and two years) have been found to promote longer-term employment gains in Europe. Human capital formation gained through learning-by-doing during these longer subsidized employment spells can enable these young people to be integrated into unsubsidized employment in the long run. It is essential, however, that these programmes are carefully targeted to avoid deadweight losses (see above); under selection procedures currently in place in European PES, more than half of the available subsidies go to individuals who would have been likely to find a job in the absence of the subsidy.

Programmes which are too long can be unnecessarily expensive. Although effects vary according to the precise nature of the programme, at some point programmes start to display decreasing marginal returns to duration; in other words, as programme duration rises, the longer-term employment prospects of participants also increase but, after a certain point, at a decreasing rate. In the end, these marginal returns may even become negative.

Programmes need to be sufficiently generous to encourage participation; this may require them to be quite substantial, depending on the target group and context. In this regard, although payroll tax reductions have been found to have unequivocally positive employment effects, the size of these effects is often small – mainly, it appears, because their generosity is intrinsically limited by the level of payroll taxes themselves. Wage subsidies, by contrast, naturally have a much higher upper limit.

In line with the decreasing returns to duration, the optimal structure of a wage subsidy includes a reduction over time – particularly if it has a significant duration (say, more than one year). That is, the percentage of the wage subsidized should (tend to) decrease over time, as the benefits of work experience for productivity start to make themselves felt.

Conditionalities

Conditionalities on firms claiming subsidies have a number of benefits. In particular, they tend to reduce deadweight and/or substitution effects, for fairly obvious reasons. There are some obvious instances: for example, outlawing or limiting the substitution of subsidized workers for non-subsidized workers, whether at the programme's inception or when previously subsidized workers are fired in favour of new workers eligible for subsidization, helps to reduce substitution effects.

Substantial medium-length (six months to two years) wage subsidy programmes are particularly effective if they are coupled with non-dismissal clauses that remain in force after the subsidy has expired, although the enforcement of these rules requires significant administrative capacity on the part of the funding agency.

Some programmes have the explicit aim of promoting the hiring of young people on permanent contracts – particularly in countries with a two-tier labour market, where insiders are employed on strongly protected permanent contracts and outsiders on precarious temporary ones. However, such measures do not seem to have been very successful to date in achieving their aims.

Conditionality has also been introduced in some cases regarding the provision of training; in general, the combination of training and subsidized employment has consistently been found to be more effective for the longer-term labour market integration of young people than subsidies on their own. Conditionality on training also naturally tends to reduce substitution and deadweight effects.

Complementarities

Complementarities across labour market institutions featured strongly in Chapter 3 above. The issue also arises in discussing wage subsidy programmes. For example, it was noted above that a smaller payroll tax reduction for young workers in Canada increased youth employment by a greater degree than a more generous – but otherwise similar – reduction in Sweden. It is plausible that the difference in effectiveness is attributable in this case to the existence of more extensive welfare benefits for the young in the latter country, which meant that the labour supply effect of the subsidy was more substantial in the former.

More generally, it is clearly important to bear in mind potential complementarities across labour market institutions in the design of subsidy programmes.

Labour supply effects

This review of wage subsidy programmes has also made clear that such programmes are not purely about labour demand; there may be – indeed, are likely to be – some labour supply effects as well. These have been observed not only in the reaction of the labour supply of young people to wage subsidy programmes, but also as a consequence of increases in the quality of young people's labour supply due to increases in their human capital, arising either explicitly through the incorporation of training components in wage subsidy programmes, or through learning-by-doing on the job, which is an intrinsic part of even (nominally) unskilled jobs.

5. Self-employment and entrepreneurship[1]

In recent years, supporting the growth of self-employment and entrepreneurship has become a key element of international organizations' proposed strategies for promoting youth employment, particularly in lower-income countries. This chapter specifically explores self-employment and entrepreneurship interventions that have been adopted in various contexts (from low-income to high-income countries) in order to help facilitate the integration of young people into the labour market and encourage inclusive development.

Throughout academic research, policy literature and the media, self-employment has come to be seen as synonymous with entrepreneurship.[2] The two concepts have been conflated, and both appear in connection with interventions and policies promoting training and leadership, coaching and mentoring, microcredit schemes and business start-up loans (Sheehan and McNamara, 2015, pp. 11–13). For the purposes of the research presented here, the focus is on self-employment and associated interventions, which are referred to as "entrepreneurship programmes" within particular evaluation studies. For clarity, it is proposed that self-employment and entrepreneurship possess different motivating and contextual factors. According to Sheehan and McNamara, this differentiation may have significant effects in terms of job creation and sustainability,

---

[1]   This chapter is largely based on Burchell et al., 2015.

[2]   Economists have used self-employment as a measure of entrepreneurship as people in self-employed positions "fulfil the entrepreneurial function of riskbearing" (see Parker, 2004; Sheehan and McNamara, 2015, pp. 11–13). Davidsson (2004) has examined 20 definitions of entrepreneurship. The recent Eurofound report on youth entrepreneurship identifies definitional differences along academic lines. Within sociology, entrepreneurship may be seen as "the creation of a new organization and the analysis takes place at the individual level or firm level, focusing especially on the role of networks". Within psychology, entrepreneurship may be framed "in terms of cognitive processes, or psychological traits such as creativity, motivation or the mental process generating the intention of starting a business". Economists are mostly interested in firms and the processes underlying job creation and growth. See Eurofound, 2015a, pp. 10–11.

5.1. Self-employment: An overview

The self-employed include all those who,

working on their own account or with one or a few partners or in a co-operative, hold the type of jobs defined as "self-employment jobs", i.e. jobs where the remuneration is directly dependent upon the profits derived from the goods and services produced. Self-employed workers include four subcategories of employers, own-account workers, members of producers' cooperatives, and contributing family workers.[3]

The level of self-employment in a country can provide an indication of the overall "health" of the labour market and economy. Rising rates of self-employment may reflect "hidden" unemployment where it acts as a "temporary option for individuals to work a limited number of hours as an alternative to unemployment but who would prefer jobs in companies" (Tatomir, 2015, p. 58). Self-employment may also indicate that people are underemployed, e.g. in the case of persons who are receiving some income from formal employment but wish to work additional hours to increase their income. This may be particularly apparent among the recently self-employed, those wishing to establish a customer base or individuals approaching retirement who wish to save more money. Increases in self-employment may also reflect long-term demographic trends, technological developments or institutional regulations that prompt individuals to set up independent freelance businesses (ibid.).

In considering self-employment as a potential policy mechanism to address youth unemployment, it is important to note that, for the large majority of young people, self-employment is not the dynamic and highly profitable venture that is widely reported by the mainstream media, government, intergovernmental organizations and think-tanks (RSA, 2014; O'Leary, 2014). Within HICs, start-ups, especially in sectors such as information technology, have tended to be viewed as policy solutions for returning young people to work and reducing unemployment (Poschke, 2013). However, as the available evidence from a variety of economic contexts demonstrates, self-employment, particularly for young people, is often a highly vulnerable employment status in terms of the levels of pay and job security that it offers (Fields, 2014).[4] There is also the problem of "bogus" or false

---

[3]   ILO, Key Indicators of the Labour Market (KILM) database. Further, the International Standard Classification of Occupations defines self-employed jobs as "those jobs where the remuneration is directly dependent upon the profits (or the potential for profits) derived from the goods and services produced (where own consumption is considered to be part of profits). The incumbents make the operational decisions affecting the enterprises, or delegate such decisions while retaining responsibility for the welfare of the enterprise". See http://www.ilo.org/public/english/bureau/stat/isco/docs/intro2.htm.

[4]   Indeed, the ILO defines it as such: "Vulnerable employment – that is, either self-employment or work by contributing family workers – accounts for almost 48 per cent of total employment. Persons in vulnerable employment are more likely than wage and salaried workers to have limited or no access to social security or secure income. The number of people in vulnerable employment expanded by around 1 per cent in 2013, which is five times higher than during the years prior to the financial crisis" (ILO, 2014b, p. 12). See also: http://mdgs.un.org/unsd/mdg/Metadata.aspx?IndicatorId=0&SeriesId=772.

self-employment practices (Sheehan and McNamara, 2015, p. 13), concerning "individuals who call themselves self-employed but who, in reality, only work for a single client" (Eurofound, 2015a, p. 18).

5.1.1. Self-employment in LMICs

The prevalence of self-employment is closely – and inversely – related to the level of per capita income in a country. In LMICs a clear majority of the economically active population are self-employed, concentrated in sectors such as construction, agriculture and street trades (Gindling and Newhouse, 2014, p. 318). These authors go on to comment that "in all regions men are more likely than women to be self-employed (employers or own account workers). The proportion of both men and women who are own account workers increases sharply with age until the late 30s, levels off, and then begins to fall from 40 on" (ibid.). Within LMICs, self-employment often means undertaking work within the informal sector with low wages and limited access to social protection or social insurance coverage (Fields, 2014; Cho et al., 2012, pp. 8–9). The majority of self-employed jobs within LMICs are "not productive and generate low earnings, and as a result many of these workers and their families remain poor" (World Bank, 2012a, 2012b). The other side to this coin is, of course, that the push factors towards self-employment are all the stronger where there are limited opportunities for wage employment, as is the case particularly in LICs. This and other issues are analysed in more detail in section 5.2 below using evidence on LMICs drawn from the ILO's SWTS.

5.1.2. Self-employment in HICs

Self-employed workers in HICs also enjoy few rights to paid sick leave, holidays, maternity or paternity leave, redundancy pay or protection against unfair dismissal. Within the EU, the self-employed generally work longer hours and have lower earnings compared to full-time contract employees (Eurofound, 2010; D'Arcy and Gardiner, 2014; TUC, 2014a).

The precarious situation of self-employed workers is further compounded by recent policy proposals made by a number of European governments, including that of the United Kingdom, "to exempt most self-employed workers from basic health and safety protections" (TUC, 2014b). The potential for young people who take up self-employment to be "scarred" by the transition is a major policy concern, as it is likely to have negative effects on their future career trajectories and job search motivation (OECD, 2014a).

According to the recent Eurofound report (Eurofound, 2015a), there were 2.67 million self-employed 15–29-year-olds in the 28 EU Member States, which amounts to 6.5 per cent of their total youth population. The report showed that self-employment is most common among youth in Greece and Italy (16 and 15.3 per cent respectively), followed by the Czech Republic, Poland, Romania and Slovakia (between 8.7 and 11 per cent). In the United States and the Republic of Korea, self-employment rates are also high. In other European States, such as Austria,

Denmark, Germany and Luxembourg, self-employed young people comprise less than 3.5 per cent of all working youth. The available data show that older individuals are more likely to be self-employed than younger, and men are more likely to be in self-employment than women (within the EU context this is supported by Green, 2013; Storey and Greene, 2010; OECD, 2014a; Marcén, 2014).

The Eurofound report also stated that "young people are interested and enthusiastic about becoming entrepreneurs, with almost half of them stating that self-employment would be a desirable career option. Unfortunately, the share of young people who find this option to be feasible is low" (Eurofound, 2015a, p. 99). Overall, Europe tends to be perceived as an unfavourable environment for the development of entrepreneurship and self-employment for young people. The primary barriers cited pertained to access to finance and administrative procedures for developing small businesses.

5.1.3. Determinants of self-employment

Existing evidence relating to the determinants of self-employment within the OECD demonstrates the importance of taxation regulations for self-employed "and the replacement rates offered by unemployment, as well as the female labour force participation rate". The same research also suggests that "there is a positive relationship between unemployment and self-employment rates" (D'Arcy and Gardiner, 2014, p. 12): self-employment tends to be more common in labour markets where unemployment is high. This also relates to the levels of assistance the self-employed can access in terms of tax code regulations, credits and/or benefits, or support from government agencies such as advice on business creation and financial management (see box 5.1). Variations in self-employment rates reflect existing differences in terms of barriers to or opportunities for establishing new businesses, as well as cultural norms and labour market conditions at the macroeconomic level (D'Arcy and Gardiner, 2014, p. 12; Eurofound, 2015a).

Employment decisions, including the transition to self-employment, are influenced by both micro- and macro-level factors in the labour market (Dawson et al., 2009). The overall "health" of the economy, along with social and individual attitudes, shape the perception and feasibility of entrepreneurship as a career option within particular contexts (Gilad and Levine, 1986). Research by Gindling and Newhouse (2014, p. 326) suggests that as the per capita income of a country increases, "the proportion of the self-employed who are either successful or have high potential for success increases rapidly". It is also the case that as per capita incomes increase, workers move out of agriculture-based employment into wage and salaried work. The authors found that the proportion of the self-employed in LICs who are successful or have a high potential for success in the labour market is between 17 and 33 per cent. In HICs the proportion of successful self-employed increases to between 66 and 94 per cent. They conclude that "as per capita income increases those who remain self-employed are more likely to be self-employed by choice rather than necessity" (ibid.). The more economically buoyant a country is, the fewer are the contextual "push" factors into self-employment

> **Box 5.1. Legislation affecting self-employment: The United Kingdom**
>
> In 1995 the Inland Revenue altered the taxation rules in the construction indus-
> try in an attempt to reduce tax avoidance. It is estimated that this may have
> led to 200,000 self-employed workers reclassifying themselves as employees,
> lowering the self-employment rate by around 0.7 per cent by 1997.
>
> In April 2002 a change in corporation tax eliminated liability on the first
> £10,000 of company profits. This allowed directors of small companies to save
> income tax by taking their salaries as profits, which may have increased the
> incentives to become self-employed.
>
> Source: Tatomir, 2015.

(Cho et al., 2012). Similarly, labour markets with high levels of NEETs have also
been found to have higher levels of young people in positions of self-employment
(Eurofound, 2015a).

At the individual level, self-employed young people in the European context
possess a different set of values and personality traits in comparison with non-self-
employed young people: "the entrepreneurial personality seems to be characterised
by stronger creativity and innovative tendencies, relatively low risk aversion and more
freedom and independence and autonomy" (Eurofound, 2015a, p. 99), although Gilad
and Levine (1986) suggest that personality is relatively unimportant compared to
other factors. Consequently, as suggested by Cho and colleagues among others, policies aimed at stimulating youth entrepreneurship might be best tailored to the target groups with the complementary skill sets and values in a way that addresses
their main constraints (Cho et al., 2012; Peprah et al., 2015). In an analysis of the
Quarterly Labour Force Survey in the UK, Dawson et al. (2009) found a significant heterogeneity in the motivation to become self-employed. The authors concluded that the opportunities to start a business, the nature of an individual's
profession, the desire for a particular lifestyle, and the need to balance family commitments with working life interact to increase or decrease the likelihood of becoming self-employed. Gender differences were apparent, with women more likely
than men to report lifestyle and family reasons for choosing self-employment.
Older individuals were also found to be more likely to occupy positions of self-
employment. Little evidence was found of individuals who selected self-employment "out of necessity because of loss of previous paid employment and a lack
of other paid alternatives" (Dawson et al., 2009, p. 28).

Across HICs, "there is little evidence of the relationship between level of
education and self-employment" (Green, 2013, p. 5). "Eurostat data for 2013 show
that 60.0% of the young European self-employed (defined in this case as those aged
15–24 years) have completed an upper secondary/post-secondary non-university
education level (ISCED 3–4), whereas 16.3% have completed a first/second stage
of tertiary education level" (Eurofound, 2015a, p. 16). A number of studies report
both positive (Blackburn, 1997; Storey and Greene, 2010) and negative relationships (Astebro and Bernhardt, 2005; Van der Sluis et al., 2005). The reason for the

lack of association may be that while more highly educated young people are better equipped with the skills and knowledge required to establish and run new businesses (Green, 2013), they are also likely to be more attractive to employers offering high-quality jobs and therefore to enter formal employment before embarking on self-employment (OECD, 2012).

5.2. The nature of self-employment in LMICs: Evidence from the ILO's SWTS

Information from the ILO's SWTS can help clarify a number of issues concerning the nature of self-employment among young people. As a whole, it clearly illustrates the importance of self-employment for young people in LMICs (figure 5.1). As was observed in Chapter 1 above, in sub-Saharan Africa (SSA) self-employment is clearly the dominant employment form; it is much more limited in Eastern Europe and Central Asia (EECA) and in the Middle East and North Africa (MENA), and falls somewhere between these two extremes in Asia and the Pacific (AP) and in Latin America and the Caribbean (LAC). In SSA, around four out of five young working people are self-employed, while the corresponding proportion in EECA and MENA is only around one in five.

5.2.1. Hours of work and underemployment

Long working hours are an accepted feature of self-employment in the EU, in part because working time regulations do not apply to the self-employed. However, data from the SWTS suggest that the exact opposite is the case for developing countries. Only 51 per cent of the self-employed respondents reported working 30 or more hours in the previous week. Family workers were slightly more likely to be working 30 or more hours per week (55 per cent). Employees were the most likely to work 30 or more hours per week (83 per cent), followed by employers (73 per cent).

There was a predictable gender gap, with 73 per cent of men working 30 or more hours per week compared to 61 per cent of women, a gap of 12.3 percentage points. This gap was only 3.94 percentage points for employees, but 11.5 percentage points for employers and self-employed, so slightly less than half of self-employed women were working 30 or more hours a week. Around one-fifth (19 per cent) of men who were employers worked 66 or more hours per week; the figure was around 10 per cent for all other groups. All workers were also asked whether they would have liked to work more paid hours in the last week. One-quarter (25 per cent) of all workers, but 30 per cent of the self-employed, replied that they would have liked to work more hours.[5] Overall, this suggests that some women are drawn to self-employment as a way to work short hours that are compatible with their domestic work, but also that involuntary underemployment is a more serious problem for the self-employed than for employees.

---

[5] This is based on data from the 28 surveys in the first round of the SWTS. The question was not asked in the second round.

Figure 5.1. Status in employment among young people (aged 15–29) in selected LMICs, 2012–15

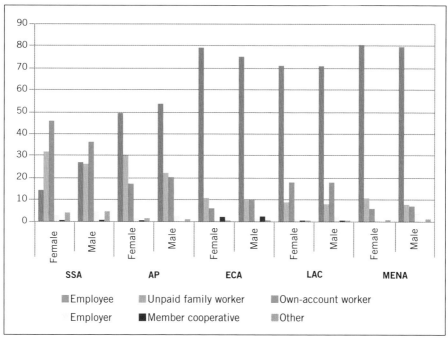

Note: This figure uses all the available data from both rounds of the SWTS made between 2012 and 2015. See the appendix for details on the survey and methods of aggregation. The countries included are, by region: Benin, Liberia, Madagascar, Malawi, United Republic of Tanzania, Togo, Uganda, Zambia; Egypt, Jordan, Occupied Palestinian Territory, Tunisia; Brazil, Colombia, El Salvador, Jamaica, Peru; Armenia, Kyrgyzstan, the former Yugoslav Republic of Macedonia, Republic of Moldova, Russian Federation, Ukraine; Bangladesh, Cambodia, Nepal, Samoa and Viet Nam.

Source: Author's calculations based on ILO-SWTS data.

5.2.2. Job satisfaction

About three-quarters of all workers said that they were very satisfied or somewhat satisfied with their jobs. The differences between groups and genders were relatively small, but employers were the most satisfied (83 per cent), followed by employees (82 per cent), the self-employed (73 per cent), and then family workers who were the least satisfied (64 per cent). This was also reflected in their responses when asked whether they would like to change their current employment situation. Overall, 47 per cent replied positively, and again this was highest for family workers (61 per cent), followed by the self-employed (51 per cent) and employees (44 per cent). Only 34 per cent of employers wanted to change.

When asked why they wanted to change, higher pay was given as a reason by 16 per cent of workers, followed by the temporary nature of their job (10 per cent), "to improve conditions" (7 per cent) and "to make better use of their skills" (5 per cent). Responses were broadly similar for all of the groups, except that "improved conditions" was more important for the self-employed (10 per cent) than for employees (6 per cent).[6]

Levels of job satisfaction were not found to vary greatly between regions, but an interesting pattern was apparent. In the two regions where self-employment was most common (i.e. SSA and AP) the average level of satisfaction was marginally higher among the self-employed than among employees, but where self-employment was less common, the self-employed were less satisfied than employees.

5.2.3. Job search

There were clear differences between the three groups in their means of entry into their current jobs. The most common method for all three groups was through asking friends, relatives or acquaintances (56 per cent for employees, 34 per cent for self-employed, and 30 per cent for employers). Enquiring directly at workplaces was common for employees (18 per cent), but less so for other groups. Seeking financial assistance was the second most important for employers (18 per cent) followed by looking for land, equipment, a building or machinery (14 per cent).[7] Informal entry routes into employment were more common for those with lower levels of education. For those with the highest levels of education becoming employers, seeking finance was more important compared to the informal and family routes used by those with lower levels of education.[8]

Respondents were also asked how long they had actively been looking for work before finding their current position. The majority of all groups reported a search period of less than three months: 66 per cent of employees, 67 per cent of employers and 73 per cent of self-employed. At the other end of the distribution, 16 per cent of employees had been looking for more than one year, compared to 18 per cent of employers and 19 per cent of the self-employed. This suggests that a higher proportion of self-employed individuals than of employees may have been forced into self-employment by lack of alternatives.

5.2.4. Job security

Respondents were asked how likely it was that they would be able to keep their current job if they wanted to.[9] Nearly three-quarters (73 per cent) of employers considered it very likely, as did 64 per cent of self-employed, while the most subjectively insecure group were employees; just 56 per cent of them felt it "very likely" that they would be able to keep their jobs. In a follow-up question, of those who reported that it was "likely but not certain" or "not likely" that they would be able to keep

---

[6]   As before, this question was not included in the second round, so statistics on this question are based on responses to the 28 first-round surveys.

[7]   The specific question was: "How did you get your current job?" (SWTS survey questionnaire).

[8]   Here too, this question was not included in the second round, so statistics on this question are based on responses to the 28 first-round surveys.

[9]   There was an option to respond "I don't want to keep my current job" on this question.

their jobs, all groups were split fairly evenly between those who were troubled by this and those who were not.

These findings are at odds with the norms one might expect to see in developed countries, where self-employed individuals are the most insecure; for young people in developing countries, it is employees who express the highest perceptions of insecurity and threat to employment. Employees, particularly in developed countries, are much more likely to benefit from another source of job security, that is, trade unions, but the proportions of self-employed and employers who are members of unions are much lower.

5.2.5. Starting up and funding

When asked why they were self-employed rather than waged or salaried employees, the most common answer for both self-employed and employers was "to gain greater independence": 43 per cent of employers gave this reason, as did 37 per cent of the self-employed. Not being able to find a waged or salaried job was given as the main reason for 29 per cent of self-employed and 19 per cent of employers. In other responses, the two groups were quite different: higher income was a much more likely motivation for employers (21 per cent) than for the self-employed (11 per cent). Being required by the family to work in that way was given as the main reason by 14 per cent of self-employed, but only 8 per cent of employers.

Over three-quarters (78 per cent) of employers had received help with their economic activity; this was also true, somewhat surprisingly, for 39 per cent of self-employed, for whom the help had presumably come mainly from their families.[10]

The responses to a question about their main source of funding to start up their current activity showed predictable differences between the self-employed and employees, but for both groups informal sources were far more common than more formal sources of financial capital. Over one-quarter (27 per cent) of the self-employed said that they did not need any money, as did 12 per cent of employers. For the rest, money from friends and family was the most common source cited by employers (38 per cent) and the self-employed (31 per cent).

Over a third (36 per cent) of both groups relied on their own savings. A small minority of employers used loans from microfinance institutions (4 per cent) or banks (5 per cent), but this was less common for the self-employed (2 per cent for both sources). Loans from informal financial operators or from government, and remittances from abroad, were used as the main start-up funding for only 1 per cent or less of each group. Unfortunately, the question permitted each respondent to give only one main source of funding, so these figures will underestimate the prevalence of some sources as presumably many start-ups are funded from more than one source. Those with the highest levels of education were about three times as likely

---

[10] Here again, this question was not included in the second round, so statistics on this question are based on responses to the 28 first-round surveys.

to use banks for finance as those with the lowest levels of education, but even for this group the proportion using banks was small compared to those using informal and family funding. The proportion using microfinance institutions was unrelated to education.

Respondents were also asked about sources of funding for "working capital". Over a third (36 per cent) of the self-employed and 21 per cent of employers said that this was not needed. As with start-up capital, money from friends and family was the most common source (27 per cent for both groups), followed by own savings (24 per cent for employers, 19 per cent for the self-employed). Loans from banks, informal sources and microfinance were given as the main source for between 2 per cent and 4 per cent of each group. Again, these are almost certainly underestimates as the question permitted only one source to be given. A puzzling 18 per cent of employers and 9 per cent of self-employed chose the "other" option; perhaps some respondents were not familiar with the concept of "working capital"?[11]

When asked about the most important problem they faced in their economic activity, 7 per cent of both groups said they did not have any problems. A lack of financial resources was the most common response given by 31 per cent of employers and 35 per cent of the self-employed.[12] "Competition in the market" was seen as the most important problem by 21 per cent of employers and 14 per cent of self-employed. Again, there was a puzzling number of "other" responses – 12 per cent of employers and 21 per cent of self-employed. All of the other response categories were used by 4 per cent or less of the respondents; in descending order of importance, these were: insufficient (personal) business expertise; shortages of raw materials (breakdowns in the supply chain); labour shortage; product development; access to technology; insufficient quality of staff; legal regulations; and finally political uncertainties.[13]

5.2.6. Income

The self-employed and employers were asked to consider their income from sales or turnover and their expenses (for example, rent, electricity, water, raw materials, salaries, etc.), and thus to calculate their profit for the past month. A small proportion (0.4 per cent) of both groups claimed to have made a loss in the last month, and 2 per cent of both groups gave their net profit as exactly zero (perhaps showing that a sizeable proportion of these businesses were inactive; many others may have received income only a few times a year, for instance, when selling their harvest).

Employees were asked about their most recent wages. Thus an hourly rate of pay could be calculated for all three categories, employers, employees and the self-employed, although the compatibility of the data across the three groups is ques-

---

[11]   This question was not included in the second round, so statistics on this question are based on responses to the 28 first-round surveys.

[12]   It should be noted that the question did not differentiate between insufficient financial capital to invest in the business and ongoing income being too low.

[13]   This question was not included in the second round, so statistics on this question are based on responses to the 28 first-round surveys.

Figure 5.2. The relationship between employment status, income and age

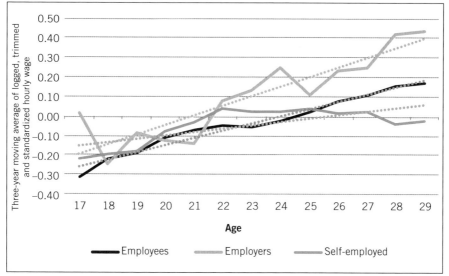

Note: The countries included are, by region: Benin, Congo, Liberia, Madagascar, Malawi, Sierra Leone, United Republic of Tanzania, Togo, Uganda, Zambia; Egypt, Jordan, Lebanon, Occupied Palestinian Territory, Tunisia; Brazil, Colombia, Dominican Republic, El Salvador, Jamaica, Peru; Armenia, Kyrgyzstan, the former Yugoslav Republic of Macedonia, Republic of Moldova, Montenegro, Russian Federation, Serbia, Ukraine; Bangladesh, Cambodia, Nepal, Samoa and Viet Nam. The dotted lines in the figure indicate three-year moving averages in order to smooth the data.
Source: Author's calculations based on ILO-SWTS data.

tionable. Incomes from employment data were standardized,[14] which has the effect of eliminating differences between richer and poorer countries, but permits some interesting insights into the patterns of pay broken down by employment status and age (controlling for the predictable and large gender pay gap).

Employers' incomes, thus measured, were higher than employees' wages, self-employed workers without employees received the lowest incomes, but these varied significantly between regions. Lower pay for the self-employed was particularly marked in MENA countries; the contrast was small in EECA countries and there was little difference in the other regions.

Some caution is advisable when discussing comparisons of hourly income across categories, given the well-known unreliability of self-reported earnings, particularly for the self-employed. Having said that, it may be observed that the gender pay gap is broadly similar across these three categories; on the other hand, a disaggregation

---

[14]   As the amounts were recorded in their local currency, the data had to be manipulated to make them comparable across countries. After negative and zero values were eliminated, the data were trimmed, replacing variables that were in the top 2.5 per cent and bottom 2.5 per cent observations of each country. Afterwards that variable was logged to reduce the skew and then standardized separately for each country to give a mean of zero and a standard deviation (SD) of 1.

of hourly income by age is particularly revealing. Figure 5.2 shows the way in which income increases with age. Employers have the steepest upward trajectory, whereas for self-employed workers without employees, the age-related hourly income profile is much flatter. Indeed, beyond age 22 own-account workers' incomes appear not to rise at all and even to fall slightly, so that by age 26 the hourly income of employees overtakes that of own-account workers. Possible reasons for this could include the limited nature of self-employment businesses, or a lack of opportunity for learning new skills and increasing human capital in own-account work.

Employees were also asked about other benefits they received. Common benefits were sick leave (45 per cent), annual leave (44 per cent), medical insurance (37 per cent), pensions (36 per cent), social security payments (41 per cent), meals (34 per cent) and occupational safety equipment (32 per cent). These questions were not asked of the self-employed, but the levels would certainly be very low, thus further exacerbating the pay gap.

5.2.7. Education

The relationship between education and employment status is particularly strong. For instance, examining the respondents' own status (patterns are similar when using parents' education), 87 per cent of those with a high (post-secondary) level of education are employees, compared to 64 per cent of those with a medium level of education and only 41 per cent of those with low (none or primary) levels of education. The situation is reversed for own-account workers, with high rates of self-employment for those with "low" education (44 per cent), falling through "medium" education (25 per cent) to just 9 per cent of those with "high" education. The gradient for family workers is even more extreme, going from 12 per cent of those with "low" levels of education to only 2 per cent of those with "high" educational levels. Interestingly, the proportion becoming employers was almost identical for the three educational groups.

5.2.8. Work histories

SWTS respondents were asked to list, sequentially, all employment experiences that lasted at least three months up to and including their current situation. They were asked a number of questions about each of these activities, for instance, their economic status, dates of starting and ending that activity, type of contract, job satisfaction, and reason for leaving each job.

The durations of completed activities varied from two months or less (7 per cent) up to over 20 years (because the start date was before the respondent was ten years old and they had been in that same activity ever since). The median duration was 13 months, and the 90th centile was 58 months or just under five years.[15]

---

[15] As the duration data were highly skewed with a long upward straggle, we used medians rather than means to indicate averages.

Table 5.1. Duration of young people's economic activity

Economic activity	Number of spells	Median spell duration (months)
Work for wage/salary with an employer	20 875	13
Own account/employer	3 288	17
Work as unpaid family member (work for family gain)	3 893	33
Engaged in an apprenticeship/internship	1 356	12
Available and actively looking for work	8 180	8
Engaged in training	1 983	12
Engaged in home duties	3 823	20
Did not work or seek work for other reasons than home duties	2 672	20
All activities (months)	46 070	13

Source: Author's calculations based on ILO-SWTS data.

Table 5.1 shows these duration data broken down by type of activity. The most stable form of work, by a large margin, is unpaid work as a family member, with a median duration of 33 months. The statuses of being engaged in home duties (e.g. as a housewife or stay-at-home father) and other forms of economic inactivity are also relatively enduring, both with a median of 20 months. Interestingly, being self-employed[16] is a slightly more stable status (median = 17 months) than being an employee (median = 13 months).

Gender effects were small, although the majority of those working as unpaid family members and "engaged in home duties" were women. They also tended to stay slightly longer than men in these duties. Predictably, having a limited-duration contract shortened average tenure, but only for job contracts for less than 12 months. However, national income (measured as gross national income, GNI) had a marked effect on median durations, such that the poorest countries had a median duration of 24 months, compared to only 12 months for the high- and middle-to-high-income countries. This effect was spread evenly across all economic statuses.

It is not entirely clear how these data on duration should be interpreted. Discussion surrounding precarious employment emphasizes the cost of short-term employment, so by that criterion own-account work is no more precarious than wage employment, and working as an unpaid family member is the least precarious. However, an alternative interpretation of these duration data is that turnover provides an indication of individual progress, so those longer durations typical of the poorest countries, family work and self-employment may represent a lack of opportunities for advancement.

---

[16] In the work histories, there was no separate category for employers.

5.2.9. Transitions

Another useful feature of the work histories data is that they enable us to examine trajectories as a way of understanding which types of economic status are likely to lead to advancement and which are likely to lead to stagnation or even deterioration in young people's working lives. For this set of analyses, adjacent spells in an individual's work history are combined so that the relationship between a source job and a destination job can be determined.

First, who is likely to become an employee in their next transition? Just under half (47 per cent) of destination spells were as employees, making it the most common destination. Those most likely to become employees were unemployed jobseekers (79 per cent), followed by people doing home duties (in most cases, childcare) (53 per cent). The group least likely to become employed were unpaid family workers (33 per cent), followed by the self-employed and apprentices/interns (both 34 per cent).

As for who is likely to become self-employed, 14 per cent of transition destinations were to own-account work; but this proportion was much higher for unpaid family workers, 29 per cent of whom became own-account workers in their next spell. One-fifth (20 per cent) of those doing home duties would also become own-account workers. The people least likely to do so were employees (10 per cent) and the un-employed (9 per cent).

More generally, the transitions data suggest that there are two "clusters" of individuals' trajectories. Some individuals move from one job to another, and if they are not in employment, then they are most likely to be unemployed. Other individuals move between family work, own-account work and being out of paid work.[17] Although self-employment spells are much more common in the lowest-income countries, this same pattern holds in all categories of countries by income group.

5.3. Self-employment programmes and interventions for young people: A review of the evidence

The World Bank youth employment policy primer (World Bank, 2010) proposes five "categories of constraints" that may limit the access of a young person to the labour market and the success of self-employment ventures:

1. job-relevant skills constraints, such as a lack of basic skills, technical and behavioural skills mismatch, or a lack of entrepreneurial skills;

2. low labour market demand at the macro and micro levels through slow job growth and employer discrimination;

3. job search barriers, such as limited access to information about job vacancies or low levels of "soft skills" and ability to present oneself effectively to potential employers;

---

[17] Whether looking for it (i.e. unemployed) or not.

4. start-up constraints, such as lack of access to local business networks and seed funders; and

5. social constraints, such as local peer group and familial social norms that may act as psychological barriers to or sanctions against taking up certain jobs or working in certain business sectors.[18]

Self-employment and entrepreneurship programmes which typically seek to redress some or all of these constraints may be categorized into three types:

1. interventions promoting an entrepreneurial mindset and culture among young people;

2. those providing information, advice, coaching and mentoring to young people who want to become self-employed entrepreneurs; and

3. those aimed at reducing the perceived logistical barriers to self-employment, for example by facilitating access to credit and reducing bureaucracy. (Eurofound, 2015a)

Typically the most effective programmes and interventions combine all three elements.

Until relatively recently, evidence on the effectiveness of self-employment and entrepreneurship programmes tended to be dominated by case studies with little or no attempt at rigorous impact evaluation. Increasingly, however, evidence surrounding the impacts and effects of self-employment programmes is being generated from LMICs. This has come about as a result of the recognition of the importance of impact evaluations and, in particular, RCTs by development practitioners in these contexts as well as in response to calls from donors for better evidence in order to assess aid effectiveness (Banerjee et al., 2015; Blattman et al., 2011, 2014; Betcherman et al., 2007). Since 2014 several meta-analyses as well as some systematic albeit qualitative reviews have been published which include consideration of the effectiveness of entrepreneurship programmes for young people. Perhaps owing to the relative dearth of impact evaluations – at least until recently – none of the studies focus exclusively on this issue.

Cho and Honorati (2014) conducted a meta-analysis of 37 impact evaluation studies of self-employment and entrepreneurship programmes.[19] They found large variations in the types of programmes and interventions used by governments and development agencies to support and promote self-employment among young people. They note that microcredit programmes are by far the most common

---

[18] Adapted from World Bank, 2010, p. 2.

[19] The studies cover 25 countries across sub-Saharan Africa (nine studies), South Asia (ten studies), Latin America and the Caribbean (ten studies), East Asia and the Pacific (four studies), Eastern Europe (two studies) and North Africa (two studies). Two-thirds of the interventions evaluated took place in low-income or lower-middle-income countries. Of the estimates, 80 per cent were based on experimental interventions. The most commonly measured outcomes were labour market income, profits and labour market activities.

form of intervention, followed by business training. In terms of the impacts and outcomes, interventions focus on "hard" economic outcomes, such as job entry rates, business creation, hours of work, earnings, and profits and business performance. A number of "soft" outcomes, such as job search behaviours, motivation, attitudes to work and financial behaviours (borrowing, saving) are increasingly included in evaluations. In terms of labour market outcomes, they report that around one in five programmes have a statistically significant (at 5 per cent) impact on employment or income; however, programmes for young people are much more likely to have a positive impact. They conclude that "entrepreneurship programs have a positive and large impact for youth and on business knowledge and practice, but no immediate translation into business set-up and expansion or increased income" (Cho and Honorati, 2014, p. 111).

Similarly, in their meta-analysis of the employment effects of interventions aimed at micro-, small and medium-sized enterprises in LMICs, Grimm and Paffhausen find that "particularly (micro-) finance and training interventions achieve positive effects only very early in the result chain, improving management practices, skills and investments but without further or lasting results on business performance and, finally, employment" (2015, p. 79).

Two recent meta-analyses have looked at the effects of ALMPs for young people as a whole, including self-employment and entrepreneurship programmes as an explicit separate category. Consistent with other earlier meta-analyses of ALMPs cited in Chapter 4 above (see section 4.1.3), Kluve et al. (2016a) find that ALMPs for young people, on average, have small positive impacts on employment and income. Interestingly, however, they find that entrepreneurship programmes have, on average, by far the biggest impact among all ALMPs for young people. These types of programme are also the ones with the greatest variation in impacts. They appear to be particularly effective in LMICs; indeed, in HICs, self-employment support for young people is found to have negative employment and income effects on average.

Eichhorst and Rinne (2015) conducted a meta-analysis of ALMPs for young people using data drawn from the ILO/World Bank Youth Employment Inventory;[20] they reported that 44 per cent of interventions covered by the inventory possessed an entrepreneurial component. The vast majority (69 per cent) of the interventions studied are reported as having a positive impact. In common with Fay (1996), cited in Chapter 4 above, they found employment services[21] to be the most effective form of intervention; indeed, in common with Betcherman et al. (2007), they did not find statistically significant differences in impact across the other forms of intervention. Having said that, however, consistently with the analysis by Kluve and others, Eichhorst and Rinne did find a numerically larger impact

---

[20] The Youth Employment Inventory is a database of over 1,000 projects across 110 countries aimed at stimulating youth employment.

[21] The terms "employment services" and "job search assistance" are used interchangeably here.

of entrepreneurship programmes compared to training (or indeed subsidized employment).[22] Both studies – in common also with the earlier work of Betcherman et al. (2007) – found that interventions have greater impacts in LMICs than in HICs.

There are also recent review papers worth mentioning in this context. Specifically, McKenzie and Woodruff (2014) reviewed a series of business training programmes and found that while training programmes helped prospective owners launch businesses more quickly, training had relatively modest effects on business survival. They noted that the usefulness of studies is limited by the sample sizes and by the relatively short time horizon – both factors that have been found to be important in other contexts.[23] In addition, they note the importance of seeking to measure spillover effects such as displacement – an issue generally ignored in micro-econometric impact evaluations – and they further suggest that more needs to be understood about the significance of different elements of programme content and how these contribute to determining outcomes.

Eurofound (2016) reviewed nine impact evaluations of start-up support for young people in the EU. Consistent with the substantial heterogeneity of impacts across programmes and, in particular, the tendency reported by Kluve et al. (2016a) for entrepreneurship programmes in HICs to have less positive or even negative impacts, the Eurofound review reported that two of the studies found no impact, three found mixed impacts and four found (modest) positive impacts. Typically, where the studies found mixed effects, this meant in practice positive employment effects and negative income effects. They also noted that the two studies which dealt adequately with issues of sample selection – controlling for both observable and unobservable differences across treatment and control groups – found that the measures had (virtually) no impact. From this small sample, it is impossible to judge whether the finding is attributable to the relatively high quality of the two specific impact evaluations or whether it had something to do with the context – both evaluations concerned French programmes – or whether the French programmes were indeed less effective than other programmes. It is worth noting, however, that the finding that higher-quality evaluations tend to produce less positive measured

---

[22]   Indeed, a little care is advisable in interpreting the results. It is not surprising that the results of the two studies are quite similar, given that they use an overlapping sample. However, the Kluve et al. (2016a, 2016b) meta-analysis is much more extensive in its search for studies, and, at the same time, more selective in its inclusion criteria. Perhaps more significantly, the primary form of estimation differs across the studies. Kluve et al. (2016a) adopted an approach using the standardized mean difference (SMD), but also presented results using a probit model. Eichhorst and Rinne (2015), in line with previous meta-analyses of ALMPs such as Card et al. (2010, 2015), presented results of analysis using only ordered (and dichotomous) probit models. The difference between the two approaches is that using the SMD imposes greater precision on the estimated impact. In the estimates employing the probit model, and in line with results reported by Eichhorst and Rinne (2015), much of the difference in impact across programme types disappears (Kluve et al., 2016a, table 16, p. 105).

[23]   In particular, see the studies by Card et al. (2010, 2015) cited in Chapter 4, as well as Kluve et al., 2016a, considered in some detail here.

Box 5.2. Examples of impact evaluation findings

A number of impact evaluation case studies of self-employment programmes demonstrate the differential effects of interventions. Blattman et al. (2011, 2014) examined the effectiveness of a government programme in Uganda designed to help poor and unemployed young people to become self-employed artisans and craftspeople. The programme invited young people from northern Uganda to submit grant proposals for vocational training and business start-ups. Funding was randomly assigned among eligible participants, allocating an unsupervised sum equivalent to US$382 per individual member of a treatment group. The study found that intervention increased business assets by 57 per cent, work hours by 17 per cent and earnings by 38 per cent. The benefits of the intervention were found for both male and female participants.

Banerjee et al. (2015) conducted a six-country study (covering Ethiopia, Ghana, Honduras, India, Pakistan and Peru) of interventions to enhance self-employment via support, training and coaching. They found significant cost-effective impacts on consumption (influenced by increased income from self-employment) and on the psychosocial health of participating households. Positive effects of the interventions were found to last up to 12 months after completion of the programme.

---

outcomes is echoed in the findings of Grimm and Paffhausen (2015). Moreover, the findings of little or no impact in the European context are also consistent with the results reported by Kluve et al. (2016a), who adopted relatively high standards for the inclusion of studies with regard to the evaluation methodology and who, as noted above, found negative average impacts of entrepreneurship programmes in HICs.

The overall impression from the various recent reviews is that:

- programmes promoting self-employment and entrepreneurship among young people can indeed have significant positive effects on post-programme employment and income;

- there is much heterogeneity in the impact of programmes (the effects of different programme elements are discussed in more detail below);

- the substantial heterogeneity in effectiveness of entrepreneurship and youth employment interventions appears to be influenced by intervention typology as well as by the country context (local labour market and macroeconomic conditions and structures) in which interventions are implemented;

- entrepreneurship and start-up support seem to be most effective in LMICs.

There are two important corollaries to the last finding which, as noted, is common to several reviews: whereas in HICs, the programmes evaluated tend to be large-scale, even national interventions, in LMICs the programmes (and consequently also their evaluations) tend to be of a small scale; this potentially limits the external validity of the findings, in the absence of evidence of spillover effects.[24]

A number of studies – and some individual impact evaluations – have found that positive impacts do not necessarily come from the creation of new businesses, which is typically, the formal aim of such programmes.

Kluve et al. (2016a) highlight this gap in the evidence base. Furthermore, given the limited intervention and evaluation time frame, very few studies are able to report on the cost-effectiveness of interventions or examine the causal mechanisms behind the changes that do occur (Kluve et al., 2016a; Grimm and Paffhausen, 2015, p. 79). This is important information when policy-makers are increasingly asking: what works, why, for whom and how much will it cost?

5.3.1. Different types of intervention

On the basis of the available evidence, self-employment interventions for young people may be divided into three types of interventions and entrepreneurial assistance, following the categorization proposed by Green (2013): (1) enterprise education; (2) soft support (consulting, skills development, advice); (3) hard support (microcredit, grants).

Training for entrepreneurship

The objectives of enterprise education programmes are to enhance awareness of the benefits of entrepreneurship among young people. This may take the form of the delivery of skills such as business-plan writing and management. A number of evaluations of enterprise education interventions have demonstrated an increase in willingness to engage in entrepreneurial activities as a result of targeted educational interventions (Athayde, 2009; Souitaris et al., 2007).

Green's review of the existing evidence base from Europe (Green, 2013, pp. 13–14) notes that it is difficult to assess how effective programmes are in translating personal motivations for self-employment into actual and sustainable labour market activities. The author notes that the effect of enterprise education is only likely to become apparent when individuals become self-employed, which for most people occurs when they are over 30 years old. Alternatively, one could argue that skills such as project planning are generic, and also of benefit to salaried employees.

Cho and Honorati (2013, p. 31) argue that vocational and business training generates more positive outcomes for participants than those gained through

---

[24] Or, more generally, "general equilibrium" effects. That is, such microeconometric evaluations are typically concerned with providing a reply to the question: Did the intervention influence (preferably improve) the post-programme experiences of participants compared to (similar) non-participants? It does not answer the question: What was the impact of the programme on post-programme outcomes of (eligible) young people as a whole? Still less: What would the effects of a scaled-up similar project be on the labour market for young people in the wider context? The apparently contradictory evidence on the pilot and full-scale wage subsidy programmes in South Africa discussed in Chapter 4 above provides a useful illustration of this. In any event, there is clearly still much to learn.

inteventions providing assistance through financial training. Business training appears to be a relatively cost-effective way of promoting performance and income growth. However, McKenzie and Woodruff (2014) have found mixed evidence on the sustained impacts of training. For example, they noted that gaining enhanced business knowledge and skills through training did not always lead to increased incomes for participants.

Premand et al. (2011) provided important evidence with respect to the potential of entrepreneurship training to enhance the skills of young people and assist them in embarking on self-employment. They implemented an experimental intervention evaluation to enhance business training to university students in Tunisia. The programme offered training in designing a business plan in addition to academic work. The research indicated that the entrepreneurship training successfully increased rates of self-employment, although the effects of this development were found to be small in absolute terms.

Soft support

Soft support interventions aim to provide young people with assistance and advice via individuals' social networks or via mentors. Again, from the available evidence, it is difficult to assess the impact of soft support measures on self-employment rates. This is mainly because soft support interventions are rarely rigorously evaluated (Eurofound, 2015a).

Hard support

A third type of intervention is the provision of "hard support", which consists of microfinance loans or grants, both before and after start-up. These measures aim to assist the self-employed to overcome such barriers as difficulties accessing financial capital to help with start-up costs (Eurofound, 2015a).

In terms of financing, Cho and Honorati (2014) found few variations in the effectiveness of cash, in-kind grants and microcredit. The review indicates that accessing the support of the private sector in programme delivery may improve effectiveness, although it is not clear by what methods this could be achieved.

According to Eurofound, impact evaluations of hard support measures have been difficult, owing to variations in funding levels and access to these funds across Member States. For example, in France, minimal funds may be provided for a young person's living expenses, while in Belgium preferential loans (up to €4,500) are accessible (European Employment Observatory Review, 2010; Green, 2013, p. 15) Assessing the impacts of these various measures is difficult, as different programmes use a variety of procedures to screen potential participants. For instance, particular groups of young people such as "the unemployed, ex-offenders, or the disabled may be targeted for specific support" (Green, 2013, p. 16).

A frequently cited example of microfinance being used to support self-employment is that of the Prince's Trust in the United Kingdom. The Trust assists young, unemployed people including ex-offenders and the disabled. It has been repeatedly evaluated using quasi-experimental techniques. For example,

Meager et al. (2003) found that microfinance support increased the earnings of the self-employed and that soft support (mentoring) was negatively associated with earnings from self-employment. Overall, the authors suggested that neither soft nor hard support provision had much impact on the earnings potential or employability of programme participants. However, as with ALMPs and welfare-to-work policy in general, tracking individuals after the expiry of training interventions is highly problematic, owing to both the costs of long-term research evaluations and the logistics of following individuals after the conclusion of programmes. The evaluations that do exist of post-programme work outcomes of UK government policies, such as the New Deal, have found that participants tend to be churned back into unemployment after three to four months, particularly in local labour markets where few jobs are available (Martin et al., 2003).

5.3.2. Policy implications

Existing studies show that policies and interventions that aim to promote a culture of entrepreneurship and entrepreneurial values are of critical importance for supporting the entry of young people into sustainable self-employment (Green, 2013). However, a number of authors note that self-employment and entrepreneurship for young people should not be seen as a policy solution to economic inactivity and unemployment (Eurofound, 2015a).

Overall, Cho and Honorati (2014) propose that programmes and interventions should provide (a) a combination of skills, capital and counselling; and (2) support based on the target group's main constraints. Despite the heterogeneous effects of self-employment interventions reported by Cho and Honorati (among others), as noted above, the existing studies tend to find that labour market and business outcomes are significantly better for young participants than for older people.

In its review of policies and programmes to tackle youth unemployment, Eurofound (2015a) proposed a trio of general "policy triggers" that may be used to enhance the efficacy of self-employment and entrepreneurship interventions for young people in Europe:

1. *Providing entrepreneurial education and skills:* This provision should be delivered in formal and informal environments. It helps people acquire the technical and soft skills, as well as the attitudes and knowledge, necessary to set up and run a business; for example, creating a business plan, critical thinking, problem-solving, self-awareness and creativity (ILO, 2014a). Evidence shows that entrepreneurial education is better acquired at an early age, and when embedded in the formal education system. Employers and schools should be involved in these programmes (Eurofound, 2015a, p. 44).

2. *Supporting awareness-raising campaigns:* This can help increase the "social legitimacy of entrepreneurship" within communities. Young people should be introduced to self-employment and entrepreneurship via youth business fairs, competitions and young businessperson awards (Eurofound, 2015a).

3.   *Improving the image of entrepreneurship and using social networks/learning via vicarious experience:* Successful role models can be used to encourage young people to consider entrepreneurship and self-employment as viable career paths (Eurofound, 2015a).

5.4. Conclusions and policy recommendations

Self-employment: A poor substitute for "regular" (dependent) employment?

Self-employment is not always a favourable employment status for young people in terms of the economic and social impacts it generates. The analysis of the SWTS survey suggests that encouraging self-employment is not necessarily a particularly effective policy mechanism by which to promote upward social mobility or reduce poverty. In many contexts self-employment can be seen as the only feasible way young people in economically depressed areas can generate an income in the absence of formal opportunities, such as may be sought in the already overloaded public sectors of many LMICs. In such circumstances, entry into self-employment can be seen as a coping mechanism both by the individual and his or her family.

Self-employment among young people is often embedded in a family where parents or other family members are self-employed. Encouraging individuals into self-employment without a support network to provide expertise and complementary business support is therefore a risky venture.

Patterns of self-employment for young people in developing countries are rather different from patterns observable in developed countries. For instance, in developing countries the self-employed are often underemployed, rather than working long hours as is typical of self-employed workers in the EU. There are also large differences in the prevalence of self-employment between global regions, even for less developed countries, and probably strong regional differences (for instance, rural vs urban) within these countries. For this reason alone, it is only to be expected that programmes to encourage self-employment will have very different effects in different contexts, in respect of both the number of new self-employment jobs and the quality of those jobs.

On the other hand, the evidence from survey respondents who were currently self-employed does not support the suggestion that self-employment is necessarily a negative status. Job satisfaction scores and sense of job security are not greatly different between the self-employed and employees. Although the weekly working time of self-employed individuals is often well below that of full-time employees, only a minority state that they want to work longer hours. It may be that the rest of their week is taken up with other economic, domestic and/or leisure activities rather than being wasted time, as can be characteristic of unemployment. The tenure data from the work histories suggest that self-employment is, if anything, a more stable status than being an employee. There is evidence for both push and pull factors in entry into self-employment; for women the balance seems to be more push than pull, compared with men, but many respondents provided positive reasons for wanting to be self-employed. It is easy to dismiss these positive aspects of self-employment as either adaptive preferences or ignorance of the longer-term benefits of being an employee, but it would be premature to dismiss all self-employment as inferior to regular employment.

This comparison of the relative *quality* of employment for employees and the self-employed might, in many cases, be further complicated by the same individual being simultaneously an employee and self-employed. This may be because those in the formal labour market (such as teachers and civil servants) in LMICs take second or even third jobs in the informal labour market (as, for example, self-employed newsagents or taxi drivers), complementing the longer-term prospects of employment with additional income from self-employment (Ezrow and Frantz, 2012, pp. 112–113).

From a life-cycle perspective, self-employment compares less favourably with regular employment. Rather than breaking into employment in the formal sector, many career trajectories seem to be stuck in a cycle between self-employment and unpaid family work, which is itself seen as a far more negative state by those currently in that position. While there is a clear upward trajectory in income for employees and employers, those who stay self-employed are likely to remain on low incomes. Although the work histories did not record being an employer as a separate category, it is important to emphasize that the data suggest that only a small proportion of self-employed ever progress to the point of growing a business through employing others. Even the small proportion of employers in the SWTS data set is probably an overestimate, as many of those individuals who claim to be employers probably achieved that status by joining the family business rather than growing their own business. If employing others is the key characteristic of entrepreneurship, the vast majority of self-employed individuals are not entrepreneurs, and much of the rhetoric linking self-employment and entrepreneurship is therefore misleading.

It is difficult to separate out successful and unsuccessful self-employment in the SWTS data, but, according to the meta-analysis review by Gindling and Newhouse (2014), the successful self-employed (defined by household affluence and having employees) in developing countries tend to be older, with a high level of education; they are more likely to work in retail and services, and much less likely to work in agriculture. Men and women who are self-employed are equally likely to be successful, while the self-employed who identify themselves as head of household are less likely to be successful than are spouses and other family members. Rather than asking whether self-employment is better or worse than being an employee, a useful theme for further work might emphasize the greater heterogeneity of self-employment: when it is good it is very good, and when it is bad, it is awful.

Given these misgivings about the quality of self-employment, and the consequent possibility that programmes to increase self-employment might produce more low-quality jobs, perhaps *a focus on the quality rather than the quantity of self-employment* would make more of a contribution to development goals. Programmes with this in mind might upskill individuals who are already self-employed, minimize fiscal disincentives to business growth, and provide sound business advice to improve resilience and future prospects. At a macro level, countries could review their welfare systems to ensure that self-employed individuals have the same levels of social and economic protection and access to health care and pensions as employees.

A solution for young people?

There is now good evidence (as also discussed in Chapter 4), that labour market measures such as ALMPs can be beneficial in helping to promote the employment of young people and their well-being (Card et al., 2015; Coutts, 2009; Kluve et al., 2016a, 2016b). However, evidence from schemes to promote self-employment is less extensive. The findings – in particular for LMICs – are on average positive; among ALMPs for young people, self-employment programmes have the largest average (albeit highly variable) impact on individual employment and earnings (Kluve et al., 2016a).

Yet, since these findings are based on a rather limited number of microeconomic "partial equilibrium" evaluations of small programmes using small samples, it is not yet clear, on the basis of the evidence and data reviewed, that the schemes that have been tried actually created new self-employed jobs; nor is it clear whether these jobs are of sufficient merit to be worth creating. Also, the focus on the short term and the largely economic outcomes (such as rates of job entry) of many studies means that lagged effects of interventions on psychological health, social capital and networks are often not measured. In terms of creating sustainable employment transitions into decent work, these are important influences and outcomes.

Evidence is being accumulated on what works, where and why, and it is reasonable to suppose that, in the future, schemes will be identified that work well to create "good" or decent self-employed jobs in terms of income and sustainability; but to date, evidence remains limited. It is likely that such interventions will work only for specific types of individuals, depending upon, for instance, their existing levels of education, their skills, and the extent to which self-employment is common and well understood in their families. As yet, however, our understanding is partial, and without more and better information, labour market programmes promoting self-employment still run the risk of failing to create jobs, and/or if they do succeed, of creating low-paid jobs with limited sustainability.

Specific recommendations on programmes to promote self-employment: What works, why and for whom?

The evidence collected and analysed through recent meta-analyses is rather encouraging with regard to the impact of self-employment and entrepreneurship programmes, at least in LMICs. In these contexts, they have been found to be, on average, more successful than other forms of intervention, as well as being – along with other forms of ALMP for young people – more successful than analogous interventions in HICs. This suggests that *self-employment and entrepreneurship programmes have a useful role to play as one component of national youth employment strategies.*

Caution is, however, advisable in moving from these findings to the more general proposition that encouraging self-employment and entrepreneurship should be the mainstay of countries' youth employment policy. Moreover, the impact of such programmes is highly heterogeneous, and better understanding is needed of which programme elements work in which contexts and for whom.

Self-employment and entrepreneurship interventions which have been studied in LMICs are, for the most part, small-scale interventions often sponsored and run by non-governmental and/or international organizations. It cannot simply be presumed that such programmes will produce analogous results when scaled up to the national level.

The methodologies employed in evaluating such programmes typically take no explicit account of positive or negative spillovers and more general effects arising from the programmes. They are, by their nature, "partial equilibrium" approaches to evaluation, and typically say little or nothing about substitution or displacement, or about possible positive linkages. Yet even where programmes do produce sustainable and prosperous self-employment for participants, this may lead to unintended negative consequences for others. Self-employed individuals, particularly in MICs, cite market competition as a common problem. Encouraging more businesses into the same limited niches may further depress the incomes of existing self-employed people, or even force them out of business and back to being unpaid family workers. Therefore, *care needs to be taken to encourage self-employment start-ups in market segments where there is unmet demand and potential for growth.*

Throughout the literature on youth self-employment and entrepreneurship, it is noted that promoting these concepts as effective labour market policies should be viewed in the medium to long term. Authors tend to agree that *interventions to create "quick entrepreneurs" and increase rates of self-employment are unlikely to have positive long-term impacts* (Eurofound, 2015a, p. 100; Cho and Honorati, 2014).

Any business requires time to develop, and changing young people's attitudes towards self-employment and entrepreneurship will require prolonged timescales (Eurofound, 2015a, p. 100). Within the context of "active" welfare, reduced fiscal space for welfare and social protection interventions, it appears unlikely that the development and policy backing for funding lengthy self-employment interventions to support business development and facilitate behaviour change is a realistic option. Even if such schemes produced successful outcomes, the cost would probably be prohibitive.

The available evidence also shows that policies targeted at promoting self-employment among young people are most beneficial when they *bring together different actors and policy sectors*, such as the labour market, social protection, education, health-care services (especially mental health), youth business organizations, financial institutions, individual companies and chambers of commerce. As Eurofound (2015a) noted, *government initiatives to support youth entrepreneurship should consider three policy pillars: (1) fostering an entrepreneurial mindset, attitudes and culture; (2) providing information, advice, coaching and mentoring; and (3) removing perceived practical barriers and easing access to credit.*

111

Interventions should provide "a balanced, comprehensive range of support modalities, such as training/skills development, mentoring and counselling, access to networking, dedicated funding or easier access to finance" (Eurofound, 2015a, p. 100).

Participation of diverse stakeholders allows the multiple needs of young people to be addressed. Well-being and psychological health issues may be acting as barriers to entering the labour market, education services are required to rectify basic skills gaps, and access to finance may be needed to support a start-up and purchase initial goods and materials (Eurofound, 2015a). Because the problems experienced by the unemployed and disadvantaged in general are often multidimensional, they invariably require a multi-sector policy response and interventions that reflect these multiple needs. However, it is difficult to see how this sort of comprehensive support could be provided on restricted government budgets.

The existing evidence in relation to the efficacy of self-employment interventions is, as noted above, generally positive (Banerjee et al., 2015; Angel-Urdinola et al., 2013). Notwithstanding this, knowledge remains less than complete. For example, Grimm and Paffhausen (2015), in their review of entrepreneurship interventions, found – in common with Eurofound (2016) – that where evaluations took better account of selection bias, as with those using RCTs, estimated impacts tended to be less positive than for those using other, less rigorous evaluation methods. They go on to suggest that:

> in many of the studies which are based on a weaker identification strategy, selection bias is still an issue. However, it can also not be ignored that many RCTs have low statistical power due to small sample sizes and that they are applied particularly to small programs, very poor areas and very specific target groups. Hence, RCTs seem to paint an overly pessimistic picture with respect to the potential of such policies and interventions to create jobs. (Grimm and Paffhausen, 2015, p. 79)

The gathering and analysis of evidence on the effectiveness of youth employment policies in LMICs is a rapidly developing research area. Clearly, we still need to know more.

6. Contractual arrangements for young workers[1]

6.1. Introduction

One important difference between younger and older workers is the relative lack of work experience of the former. Increasingly, atypical work arrangements – or non-standard forms of employment – introduced with the intention of increasing labour market flexibility have been applied with a view to giving young people the experience they lack, often by encouraging the combination of learning and work. However, this route raises concerns regarding the precariousness of young people's foothold in the labour market. It is not clear to what extent, and under what circumstances, the use of atypical work arrangements and work-based schemes actually helps young people to obtain stable, legally protected jobs as opposed to pointing them towards a vicious circle of unpaid/underpaid and unprotected work.

This chapter seeks to shed light on the issues by examining the legal regulation of employment for young people. The chapter reviews different forms of contractual arrangements which either are aimed specifically at young people or affect young people disproportionately. Trends in the regulation of youth employment are also adressed. The possible influence of these arrangements on the labour rights of young people and more generally on the school-to-work transition is then discussed.

Although a range of "atypical" work arrangements are used to engage young workers (e.g. semi-dependent work, part-time work, employee sharing, job sharing, ICT-based mobile work, voucher-based work, portfolio work, crowd employment, collaborative employment),[2] here the focus is specifically on temporary contractual forms of employment. The next section (6.2) examines contractual arrangements with no training component. Although these are not usually designed specifically for the young, such a focus is justified because of the over-representation of young people in temporary forms of employment (ILO, 2016c, ch. 3; Eurofound, 2015b, p. 20; Quintini and Martin, 2014). Temporary employment refers specifically to working

---

[1] This chapter is largely based on Burchell et al., 2015.
[2] The ILO (2016c) and Eurofound (2015b) both provide quite detailed discussions of the different types of non-standard employment. De Stefano (2016) assesses their implications for workers' rights and the adequacy of existing regulatory arrangements to deal in particular with them.

relationships that deviate from the standard employment relationship in terms of its duration in that they are, at least formally, finite rather than open-ended. Hence fixed-term contracts, temporary agency work and temporary employment contracts, all of which affect a significant number of young people, are reviewed here.

In the following two sections, contractual arrangements for youth involving some kind of training are examined. A distinction is made between apprenticeships on the one hand (section 6.3) and traineeships and/or internships on the other (section 6.4). In its "ideal" form, apprenticeship involves a dualistic form of learning, combining theory and practice, typically through a combination of classroom learning with workplace training. We include here also work-based schemes that do not correspond to this model of apprenticeship, but which are regarded as apprenticeships in specific national contexts. A similar distinction can be made between an ideal model of traineeships/internships and work-based schemes that bear one of those names. In principle, a traineeship/internship involves a work-based learning scheme that facilitates the labour market entry of the trainee/intern; but in some cases these terms are used to cover a variety of situations involving low wages and unprotected labour. Here we consider both forms. In practice, the absence of widely accepted definitions of the terms "apprenticeship", "traineeship" and "internship" means that the lines between these forms of work arrangements, as well as between these types of arrangements and temporary work and/or informal jobs, are often not clear-cut.[3]

The aim here is to give a general overview of these arrangements and to identify the potentially positive and negative outcomes and trends associated with them. One of the key justifications for all of these forms which deviate from the standard employment relation without training is that they will facilitate the school-to-work transition and hence enhance the long-run employment prospects of young people. This is the theme that unifies and justifies the somewhat unusual approach to the subject matter adopted here. The chapter consequently concludes by considering the extent to which different contractual forms can and do facilitate the entry of young people into work, and offers recommendations on whether and how youth work arrangements should be regulated in order to better support the school-to-work transition.

6.2. Contractual arrangements without a training component: Temporary employment relationships

6.2.1. What is temporary employment?

Temporary employment relationships are working relationships that deviate from the standard employment relationship by virtue of their explicitly limited duration. The term over which these contracts extend varies: some terminate on a designated

---

[3] Treating traineeships and internships as synonymous is in line with current European Commission practice. National approaches vary widely, however, as is discussed further in sections 6.3 and 6.4 below.

date, others on the completion of a particular task, and yet others on the occurrence of a specific event (McCann, 2008, p. 102).

Temporary employment includes fixed-term, project- and task-based contracts, as well as seasonal and casual work (ILO, 2015f). Here, we consider all these with the exception of the final category; although casual work is an important source of informal wage employment, above all in low-income developing countries (ILO, 2015a), the end point of the relationship is often not specified at the outset and the legal status of a casual worker is often not clear (McCann, 2008, p. 103). On the other hand, temporary agency work is often not included in discussions of temporary employment, but is included here as a subcategory. Apprenticeship contracts, too, are sometimes defined as fixed-term (temporary) employment contracts, but as they include a training component, they are discussed separately in the following section.

As already observed, young people are over-represented in temporary employment around the world (Quintini and Martin, 2014; Eurofound, 2015b, p. 20). These arrangements may take several forms.

Participation in apprenticeships or training, which are structured as temporary work contracts

In countries with a long apprenticeship tradition (Austria, Denmark, Germany) a major source of temporary work among young people aged 15–24 is vocational education and training (Eurofound, 2013). In countries operating a dual apprenticeship system the prevalence of temporary employment has long been high; in Germany and Switzerland, for example, in 2014 around half of all young workers had a temporary contract (53.4 per cent in Germany and 52.6 per cent in Switzerland), while in Austria and Denmark the proportion is closer to a third.[4] This situation has existed since well before the new millennium and is not associated with the upward trend in temporary employment forms referred to in Chapter 1 above. Indeed, in Denmark the prevalence of temporary employment has fallen in recent years from around 30 per cent in 2000 to just above 20 per cent in 2014. In Austria, Denmark and Germany around 80 per cent of young temporary workers are engaged in an apprenticeship or similar training.[5] In France, Luxembourg and Italy a significant proportion of young people in temporary employment are also on training contracts. In France, 25 per cent of young people in temporary employment are on temporary assisted training contracts, supported by the State; in Luxembourg, large numbers of young people on temporary contracts are involved in publicly subsidized schemes, introduced to help the young to find jobs through workplace training. In Italy, over 40 per cent of young people in temporary jobs are on training contracts (Eurofound, 2013).

---

[4] http://ec.europa.eu/eurostat/web/lfs/data/database.
[5] Eurofound, 2013, annex table 6, p. 39. The report does not include information on Switzerland.

Voluntary temporary employment

Another reason for young people's engagement in fixed-term work is a desire for flexible work arrangements in order to accommodate family, educational or other obligations (ILO, 2015f). For example, in Finland, Ireland, Norway, Slovenia and Sweden, many temporary employees are in fact still students.[6]

Involuntary temporary employment

A substantial portion of young people are in involuntary temporary employment because they have not been able to find permanent positions. In 11 EU Member States (Belgium, the Czech Republic, Cyprus, Greece, Hungary, Latvia, Poland, Portugal, Romania, Slovakia and Spain), involuntary temporary employment constitutes a significant portion of youth employment. For example, in Belgium in 2012, 42 per cent of young workers were involuntarily employed on fixed-term contracts, many of those with durations of less than four months (Eurofound, 2013). On the other hand, in some countries the proportion of youth in temporary employment is very low. Three main reasons emerge for this: (a) extensive employment in the informal economy; (b) weak EPL; and (c) the extensive use of probationary periods. As will be discussed further in Chapter 7 below, in many LMICs a large proportion of young people are involved in informal forms of work, making formal temporary contracts largely irrelevant; under these circumstances, typically, either one is employed with a permanent formal contract, or one has no formal contract at all. Quintini and Martin (2014, p. 20) also point out that: "In the United States, the *employment at will* norm, by which either employer or employee can terminate a work relationship at any time, makes the distinction between permanent and temporary workers meaningless." In some European States (Bulgaria, Estonia, Lithuania, Malta) the small numbers of young people on temporary contracts are counterbalanced by the large proportions of youth who are undergoing the probationary period of their employment contracts (Eurofound, 2013, p. 13). During this probationary period an employer can easily end the contract and therefore this period acts as a "temporary" contract.

6.2.2. International guidance on the regulation of temporary employment

There are several ILO instruments that regulate different forms of temporary employment.[7] The Termination of Employment Convention, 1982 (No. 158), and the corresponding Recommendation, No. 166, regulate and provide guidance on the use of fixed-term and casual employment contracts. Although a member

---

[6]   In Finland, this work takes the form of summer jobs; in Ireland, seasonal work in agriculture, construction, and hotels and restaurants; in Norway, work combined with studies; in Slovenia, student jobs; in Sweden, temporary student jobs or seasonal jobs. See Eurofound, 2013; also http://www.eurofound.europa.eu/observatories/emcc/comparative-information/young-people-and-temporary-employment-in-europe.

[7]   There are no ILO (or EU) Recommendations or Conventions concerning temporary employment specifically for young people.

State may exclude fixed-term and casual workers from all or some of the provisions of Convention No. 158, the Convention also insists on the provision of adequate safeguards against recourse to contracts of employment for a specified period of time the aim of which is to avoid the protection resulting from this Convention.

Recommendation No. 166, which supplements Convention No. 158, suggests measures that may be taken to ensure adequate safeguards against the use of temporary contracts whose purpose is to avoid the protection resulting from Convention No. 158. It suggests that a provision may be made to:

(a) limit recourse to contracts for a specified period of time to cases in which, owing either to the nature of the work to be effected or to the circumstances under which it is to be effected or to the interests of the worker, the employment relationship cannot be of indeterminate duration; and/or

(b) deem contracts for a specified period of time, other than in the cases referred to in (a), to be contracts of employment of indeterminate duration; and/or

(c) deem contracts for a specified period of time, when renewed on one or more occasions, other than in the cases mentioned in (a), to be contracts of employment of indeterminate duration.

The Private Employment Agencies Convention, 1997 (No. 181), requires ratifying States to take measures to ensure that workers recruited by private employment agencies are not denied the right to freedom of association or the right to collective bargaining, and that agencies treat workers without discrimination. Ratifying States must also ensure adequate protection of agency workers and, where relevant, determine and allocate the respective responsibilities of private employment agencies in relation to: collective bargaining; minimum wages; working time and other working conditions; statutory social security benefits; access to training; protection of health and safety; compensation in case of occupational accident or disease; compensation in case of insolvency and protection of workers' claims; and maternity and parental protection and benefits.

In addition to such specific regulation of temporary contractual forms, it is of course also true that the eight fundamental ILO Conventions[8] apply also to temporary workers and apprentices.

At the EU level, two directives on temporary work have been issued.[9] Directive 1999/70/EC on fixed-term work prohibits discrimination against fixed-term

---

[8] These are: the Freedom of Association and Protection of the Right to Organise Convention, 1948 (No. 87); the Right to Organise and Collective Bargaining Convention, 1949 (No. 98); the Forced Labour Convention, 1930 (No. 29); the Equal Remuneration Convention, 1951 (No. 100); the Abolition of Forced Labour Convention, 1957 (No. 105); the Discrimination (Employment and Occupation) Convention, 1958 (No. 111); the Minimum [working] Age Convention, 1973 (No. 138); and the Worst Forms of Child Labour Convention, 1999 (No. 182).

[9] These Directives do allow for exceptions to be made for apprentices and those in vocational training as discussed further below.

workers in respect of their employment conditions compared to employees who work under employment contracts of indefinite duration. The Directive also requires Member States to take measures to prevent the abuse of successive fixed-term employment contracts. These measures include the introduction of objective reasons justifying the renewal of such contracts or relationships, a specified maximum total duration for successive fixed-term employment contracts and/or a maximum number of renewals (Council of the European Union, 1999). Directive 2008/104/EC on temporary agency work defines a general framework applicable to the working conditions of temporary workers in the EU. This Directive aims to guarantee a minimum level of effective protection to temporary workers and to contribute to the development of the temporary work sector as a flexible option for employers and workers. In pursuit of these aims it lays down the principle of equal treatment of temporary agency workers compared to their client enterprise's own workers, and contains provisions that limit Member States' prohibitions or restrictions on the use of temporary agency work.[10]

Thus, international instruments allow (and in the EU even promote) temporary work, but establish rules to avoid the abuse of temporary contracts. Typically, temporary workers should not suffer from poorer working conditions than permanent workers.

6.2.3. National trends in regulating temporary employment of young people

The regulation of temporary employment among OECD countries is weakest in the United States and in Canada. In the EU, although the use of temporary employment contracts is promoted, there are usually restrictions regarding the maximum duration of temporary employment and/or the number of times a contract can be renewed. The details of such regulation and the degree of restriction imposed, however, vary markedly across Member States. The regulation is strictest in Luxembourg and France and least restrictive in the United Kingdom; in the Russian Federation, the regulation of temporary work is less restrictive than the OECD average. In LMICs, temporary employment is typically more restrictively regulated than in HICs.[11]

The reconciliation of flexibility and security takes various forms and has various consequences. Countries that have sought to enhance the adaptability of the labour market mainly by easing regulations on temporary contracts while leaving in place strict regulations on permanent contracts have often seen an increase in labour market dualism, with typically no significant reduction in youth unemployment. Consequently, in these countries young people are considerably over-represented in temporary work and, as a result, are more vulnerable to economic downturns. This is the case in Spain and Italy, but also in France and Germany (Eurofound, 2015b).

---

[10]   Directive 2008/104/EC of the European Parliament and of the Council of 19 Nov. 2008 on Temporary Agency Work, OJ L 327, 5 Dec. 2008, pp. 9–14, arts 2, 4, 5.

[11]   OECD, Employment Protection Legislation Database, Strictness of Employment Protection –Temporary Contracts, http://stats.oecd.org/Index.aspx?DataSetCode=EPL_T.

Figure 6.1. Ratio of youth (15–24) to adult (25–49) unemployment rates in the EU28, 2007 and 2015

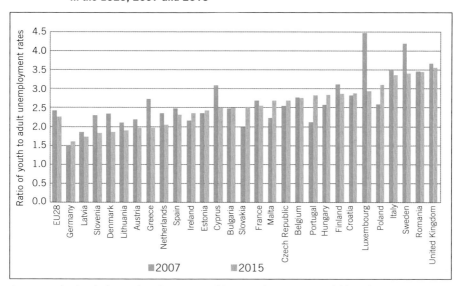

Source: Author's calculations, based on Eurostat labour market statistics available at: http://ec.europa.eu/eurostat/web/lfs/statistics-illustrated.

On the other hand, it has been argued that, in some emerging economies, strict regulations on permanent contracts accompanied by strict rules on the use of fixed-term contracts are likely to result in high and persistent youth unemployment or in a high incidence of informal work among young people. Hence it has been argued that an expansion of temporary work is likely to help to reduce unemployment, the hope being that temporary jobs will lead to permanent ones. Evidence on whether this actually happens in practice is at best mixed (Eurofound, 2013, p. 27; ILO, 2015f).

A look at the current evidence on the ratio of youth to adult unemployment rates does not reveal any obvious pattern (figure 6.1); the ratio is fairly stable over time (with some country-specific exceptions). Germany clearly has the most successful system in terms of integrating young people into the labour market – it stands out as the one country in Europe (indeed, the world[12]) able to maintain a ratio close to one-to-one for a sustained period, although the ratio has increased slightly in recent years, hovering around – or a little above – 1.5 since 2005. We may observe that all the countries operating a dual apprenticeship system are placed at the lower end of the scale (on the left of the figure). This is, however, probably the only clear conclusion one can draw from this simple figure. For example, the countries of Central and Eastern Europe which underwent major structural transformations with the transition to the market economy in the 1990s tend – but not without exception – to be

---

[12]   See e.g. O'Higgins, 2001, 2003.

grouped towards the high end of the scale; it is also true that Italy, with its segmented labour market (and along with Luxembourg), has one of the highest ratios of youth to adult unemployment rates – but so does the United Kingdom, with its highly flexible labour markets (and low rates of temporary employment).

As noted in Chapter 3 above, the empirical evidence about the impact of EPL on youth employment and unemployment rates (but not labour market flows) is also equivocal, with no clear finding one way or the other. Given the unclear and even conflicting findings and claims on the influence of employment regulation, different countries have taken different approaches to regulating temporary work. In some countries regulation was reduced before the global financial crisis. For example, in Germany the regulation of temporary work was thoroughly amended in 2002 as a consequence of the Hartz reforms. Among other things, these abolished some of the restrictions on fixed-term contracts as well as on the maximum duration of temporary agency work. At the same time, a new rule was introduced requiring temporary work agencies to guarantee that temporary agency workers would receive the same pay and treatment as regular workers. Collective agreements, however, may diverge from this principle. Concerning fixed-term contracts, the reform simplified rules and widened the range of cases which may potentially be exempted from the generally rather restrictive regulations (Jacobi and Kluve, 2006, p. 13).

In the Russian Federation, the rules governing fixed-term contracts were amended in 2002 and in 2006, extending their use to a wider range of workers and situations (ILO, 2014c, p. 65). Some countries – notably Greece, Lithuania, the Netherlands, Poland, Romania and Spain – relaxed the regulations during the recent financial and economic crisis in the hope of stimulating job creation (Eurofound, 2013, p. 1). For example, in Greece since 2011 the unrestricted renewal of fixed-term employment contracts is permitted if the renewal is justified by an objective reason. The total duration of successive fixed-term contracts must not exceed three years, rather than the two years stipulated in the previous provision (Eurofound, 2013).

In most EU countries, restrictions on temporary work remained in place during the crisis; in Italy and Slovakia they were even tightened, changing incentives so as to encourage more employers to hire workers on standard contracts. In Slovakia since 1 January 2013 employers are required to pay contributions to compulsory insurance funds not only for open-ended contracts but also for fixed-term agreements (Eurofound, 2013). In Italy since 18 July 2012, as the result of the Monti–Fornero reform, permanent employment has been given preference over temporary employment. Fixed-term work was discouraged by the requirement that additional contributions on temporary contracts be paid to finance the expanded system of unemployment benefits (Clauwaert and Schömann, 2013, p. 3).[13]

---

[13] The Monti–Fornero reform of 2012 also reduced the effective protection afforded by regular employment contracts. On the other hand, in some respects the process for entering into temporary contractual arrangements has also been simplified in Italy following the Monti–Fornero reform, particularly since 2014 (De Stefano, 2014).

In addition to the general promotion and regulation of temporary work, some countries have introduced and regulated fixed-term contracts specifically for young workers or new entrants to the labour market (e.g. first job contracts). Often these overlap with wage subsidy programmes (considered in Chapter 4 above). First job contracts are intended to ease the hiring of young people, thus helping them to get a foothold in the labour market, primarily by lowering hiring costs or by directly subsidizing wages (ILO, 2012b).[14]

In **Spain**, the work experience contract *(contrato en prácticas)* was introduced on 24 March 1995 to aid the school-to-work transition. It was aimed at workers who had obtained a vocational training degree or a tertiary education degree during the previous four years, or six years in case of disabled workers. The length of the contract had to be between six months and two years, and social security contributions were reduced for employers using the scheme. In 2010 the contract was modified to allow young workers with professional qualifications to be hired under this contract, and the maximum period between the completion of education and the conclusion of the contract was extended from four years to five years (Eurofound, 2013, Spain country report).

In **Slovenia**, "student" work is a significant form of temporary employment among young people. Student work is administratively very flexible; employers do not have to go through the normal lengthy procedures required for other workers in order to hire or fire "student" workers. To qualify, students need only proof of student status. Neither students nor their employers are required to contribute to the public pension fund or to pay for social and health services, which makes student workers much cheaper than regular employees. The main burden for employers is a special 25 per cent concession fee, which is distributed to student employment agencies, the Student Organization, and public funds for scholarships and the improvement of educational facilities (Eurofound, 2013). Students receive a wage of at least €4.50 gross per hour (since 1 February 2015).[15] The legal status of student workers as employees in Slovenia is not clear. The courts of the first and second instance have found that the status of an employee and that of a student are mutually exclusive. The Supreme Court of Slovenia, however, has expressed a different opinion, asserting that the existence of an employment relationship should be determined according to its characteristics, and that the two statuses – being a student and being an employee – are not necessarily mutually exclusive (Tičar, 2013). In practice, student work is still treated as a special kind of contract work; although they are paid a wage, student workers are not fully protected by other labour law provisions.

In **Bulgaria**, the Promotion of Employment Act 2001 provides for subsidized temporary employment for young people up to 29 years old for between six months and one year (Eurofound, 2013, Bulgaria country report).

---

[14]   See also the discussion in Chapter 4 above.
[15]   "New student work provisions step into force", *Slovenia Times*, 1 February 2015, http://www.sloveniatimes.com/new-student-work-provisions-step-into-force.

Box 6.1. Approaches to temporary employment of young people in Latin America

In **Brazil** the first job contract is targeted at young people (aged 16–24 years) who have no previous work experience and come from poor families. Employers who hire them for at least one year are compensated to the value of 96 per cent of the minimum wage. The number of young people hired under these contracts is limited in order to avoid the replacement of regular workers.

In **Panama** young people between 18 and 25 years of age can be hired under youth contracts for three to 12 months. These workers receive at least the minimum wage and have a right to annual leave. The employers are entitled to deduct the minimum wage and social contributions paid according to these contracts from their taxable income. The permitted number of youth contracts depends on the size of the enterprise.

In **Mexico** the formalization of young people's work is promoted by tax deductions. Employers who hire young people without previous social security registration can make additional deductions from their taxable income, subject to a maximum of 40 per cent of taxes due.

In **Paraguay** the first job contract is targeted at young people aged between 15 and 28 years, lasts for three to 12 months and entails the payment of at least the minimum wage. Employers have no obligation to pay pension payments, social security payments, family allowance, notice period or holiday payments. They can deduct the amounts of these contributions from their taxable income even if they have not paid them. There is also a first formal job contract, targeted at young people between 18 and 29 years of age who have not paid social contributions for one year. Under this contract, employers receive the subsidy for a maximum of 12 months if the contract lasts longer than eight months. Young people hired under this contract receive at least the minimum wage, have medical insurance coverage and are entitled to maternity leave payment.

Source: Palmi Reig, 2012.

In **Finland**, the "Sanssi card" system is used to support the employment of young people. This is a voucher form of wage subsidy,[16] available to employers who recruit workers aged under 30. The maximum subsidy is €700 per month (for a full-time job) and the employer can receive the support for up to ten months. The subsidy covers both employment relationships and apprenticeships. Young people employed with the help of the "Sanssi card" are covered by general labour law regulations and collective agreements (Eurofound, 2013, Finland country report).

In **France**, the single integration contract in the market sector (*contrat unique d'insertion–contrat initiative emploi*: CUI-CIE) is designed to encourage the recruit-

---

[16] For more on this and other forms of wage subsidy, see Chapter 4 above.

ment of jobseekers with difficulties in accessing the labour market. The instrument was initially targeted at the long-term unemployed, but was later extended to other groups that have trouble finding employment. The employer signs a contract with a local authority (for instance, the PES, *pôle emploi*) and is then eligible to receive subsidies to cover part of the labour costs and, if applicable, training expenses and other benefits for individuals employed under the scheme. The size of the subsidy is determined by regional authorities and cannot exceed 47 per cent of the gross hourly minimum wage. Contracts may be permanent or temporary (from six months to two years). The single integration contract in the non-market sector (*contrat unique d'insertion–contrat d'accompagnement dans l'emploi*: CUI-CAE) is the equivalent of the CUI-CIE in the public sector. The major difference is that wage subsidies are significantly higher – up to 95 per cent of the minimum wage – and that they are eligible for a range of specific exemptions. In the second quarter of 2012, 57.5 per cent of all CUI-CIEs were permanent contracts whereas over 98 per cent of all CUI-CAEs were temporary contracts (Eurofound, 2013, France country report).

In **Latin America**, the main aim of "first employment" contracts is not so much to help young people to enter the labour market as to encourage movement from the informal economy to formal employment (see box 6.1).

6.2.4. Temporary employment and the working rights of young people

Even though the overall regulation of temporary work aims to guarantee working conditions for temporary workers equal to those applying to permanent workers, in practice the short-term nature of their employment means that they often do not qualify for a range of benefits, such as sickness, maternity and unemployment provision. Workers in temporary employment contracts also earn significantly less than permanent staff on average. Pavlopoulos (2009) has verified the existence of a "temporary contract wage penalty" in the United Kingdom and Germany; he shows not only that there is a wage differential between the two categories at the beginning of young people's careers, but also that the penalty persists well into their working lives. In Germany, young people entering the labour market on temporary contracts face a longer-term wage penalty which only disappears after 12.5 years for men and 6.5 years for women; in the United Kingdom, for young men this wage penalty persists throughout their working lives, while young women face no such penalty in either the short or the longer term.

Access to training and education is also important for the career development of young workers, and a number of analyses have found that those in temporary employment are much less likely to be provided with training than those in permanent employment (EC, 2010a). For fairly obvious reasons there is less incentive for employers to invest in training their temporary employees. Given that fixed-term contracts are targeted at specific groups of workers, such as young people, who are already among the most vulnerable as regards labour market entry, progress and retention, the effects of temporary forms of employment risk worsening divisions and inequalities in the labour market (Clauwaert and Schömann, 2013).

An alternative approach starts from the proposition that young people's entry into the labour market can be facilitated either at the expense of their labour rights and/or at the expense of the State, or some combination of both. The example of the *contrato en prácticas* in Spain illustrates the former case: here the school-to-work transition is effected at the expense of the young person, by paying her/him a wage that is below the average for the same job. In Greece, too, even though there is no special fixed-term contract for young people, the law provides for a reduction of the minimum wage paid to workers under 25 years of age to 84 per cent of the adult minimum wage and a reduction of the minimum wage paid to minors of 15–18 years of age to 70 per cent of the minimum wage (Eurofound, 2013, Greece country report). In Slovenia, engaging in student work can exclude a young person from the protection of labour laws other than concerning their right to a wage. In Latin America, the deductions from social security payments allowed to employers who employ young people inevitably influence the young employees' social security. However, if the alternative is informal jobs, perhaps first job contracts can be regarded as a preferable option for young people on the road to decent work.

The weakening of the labour rights of young people has also led to the abrogation of laws. In Paraguay, legislation enacted in 2002 with the aim of promoting youth employment was rejected because it also provided for exclusions from social security contributions, from pension and family allowances, and from leave entitlements, among other provisions. In France, similarly, the 2006 law on the "contract for first employment" of indefinite duration was abrogated only one month after its adoption because it provided for a "consolidation period" of two years during which the employee could be dismissed without any justification (ILO, 2012b, pp. 60–61). In 2011 Greece introduced a new "youth contract" that provided for considerable support measures to encourage the hiring of people up to the age of 25 on wages 20 per cent lower than the previous rate for first jobs, stipulating a two-year probationary period, no social contributions for employers and no entitlement to unemployment benefits at the end of the contract. A complaint was submitted to the European Committee on Social Rights (ECSR) by Greek trade unions, claiming that this new type of contract was in breach of numerous articles of the European Social Charter. On 23 May 2012 the ECSR held that, indeed, this "youth contract violates the rights to vocational training, to social security and to fair remuneration" (Lang et al., 2013, p. 20).

However, efforts to support young people's school-to-work transitions do not have to be accompanied by the reduction of their labour rights. For example, the Finnish "Sanssi card" system, as well as the CUI-CIE and CUI-CAE in France, use state support to include youth in the labour market while guaranteeing them labour rights equal to those of other workers. Also, measures that support young people's transition to permanent employment do not reduce their labour rights.

Another approach which has been proposed in order to combat segmentation and polarization between young people trapped in unstable work and others in relatively stable employment contracts is to abolish or reduce the differences between the legal protection of permanent and fixed-term workers by means of "the single contract". For example, in the "Agenda for new skills and jobs" the European Commission supports this idea (EC, 2010b).[17] However, there are also serious concerns connected with its introduction. In particular, if such reform moves towards too much flexibility in regular contracts, it could lead to the erosion of normal contractual rights. Further relaxation of EPL for regular employment contracts means that incentives for investment in employability and sustainable employment will be reduced for other/wider (age) categories of workers (Tros, 2012, p. 34). Therefore the introduction of a unique employment contract would not necessarily lead to improvement in young people's working conditions, so much as put them in a more nearly equal situation to permanent workers as the protection of other workers was reduced.

6.2.5. Temporary employment of young people and the school-to-work transition

Although the stated intention underlying the use of temporary contractual forms is to relax contractual obligations on employers so as to encourage the hiring of (young) workers, the evidence on the effectiveness of this strategy is mixed. On the one hand, a high degree of labour market flexibility through, say, fixed-term contracts provides an incentive for employers to hire young people whom they might otherwise be reluctant to hire, due to informational uncertainties and other factors, as discussed above. The loss of labour rights would, in this view, be balanced by better chances of immediate employment and also by improved employability in the longer term. However, since temporary employment also discourages training provision, as noted above, it is perhaps not surprising that temporary work can easily become a low-pay trap, as young people are persuaded to accept unstable low-paid and low-skilled jobs in which they risk becoming stuck for many years or even for the rest of their working lives.

The evaluation of the "stepping stone" vs the "dead end" effect is essentially an empirical issue; however, existing evidence does not strongly support either proposition. Studies on the influence of temporary employment on young people's entry into the labour market in different countries have produced variable results. Tros (2012), for example, reports that in France, the Netherlands and the United Kingdom temporary employment contracts have helped young people to enter the labour market, that in Estonia, Spain and Sweden this effect has been only temporary, and that in Hungary and Italy these measures have had negative effects on labour market entry. Similarly, the ILO (2015f, p. 21) reports that the stepping-stone effect is confirmed in Denmark, Italy, the Netherlands and the United States, but not in Japan and Spain; moreover, temporary agency workers in Germany, Sweden and the United States are subject to prolonged periods in this form of relationship characterized also

---

[17] Note, however, that De Stefano (2014) argues both that such a view of dualistic labour markets is over-simplistic and that the response in Mediterranean countries in practice has been more about the reduction of employment protection as a whole rather than a narrowing of the gap, implying also the strengthening of protections for those on temporary contracts; De Stefano argues in particular that the latter element is more apparent than real in recent reforms.

by higher risk of unemployment or economic inactivity. In general, cross-country comparative research suggests that the effect of entering the labour market through a temporary contract on the probability of getting a permanent job is rather weak.

Evidence on the impact of temporary employment contracts on young people's labour market entry is, then, inconclusive. It is not at all clear that temporary employment contracts reduce young people's unemployment. At the same time, engaging in temporary work does inevitably lead to the reduction of a worker's employment rights. Temporary workers receive lower wages than permanent workers and often do not qualify for a range of benefits because of the short-term nature of their work, even in the presence of legislation that guarantees the equal treatment of temporary and permanent workers. The use of temporary contracts for young people that involve the reduction of their labour rights risks deepening labour market segmentation between (adult) insiders and (young) outsiders.

Recent ILO work analysing firms' usage of temporary contracts in a range of LMICs sheds further light on the topic more generally. Aleksynska and Berg (2016) found that, among a sample of over 43,000 private firms in 118 developing countries, different types of firm use temporary contracts in quite different ways. A significant number of firms – around 60 per cent – make no use of temporary contracts at all; a little under one-third use temporary contracts "moderately"; and the remaining firms (a little under 10 per cent of the total) use temporary labour intensively. In addition to major differences between "using" and "non-using" firms, clear behavioural distinctions also emerge between intensive and moderate users: in particular, intensive users closely conform to the internal/external dual labour market model of Doeringer and Piore (1971). In such firms, the possibilities for accessing internal stable employment are severely limited, while among moderate users the behaviour of firms is more consistent with the role of the temporary contract as a probationary entry point to more permanent employment. Although not focused specifically on young people, the analysis suggests a way in which the two forms of use can coexist.

Aleksynska and Berg's analysis also illustrates how the flexibilization of labour markets through the partial use of temporary contracts, leaving in place strict regulation of open-ended contracts, can also contribute to an even deeper dualism in the labour market. First job contracts tailored to young people with no previous training accelerate this trend. If these contracts entail a further reduction of labour rights, young people are less protected not only compared to those in permanent contracts, but also compared to other temporary employees in "standard" temporary contracts. Since the promotion of temporary work among young people implies a reduction of their labour rights,[18] great caution needs to be exercised in suggesting the extension of temporary contractual forms, in particular with a view to the danger of prolonged precariousness of employment.

---

[18] As well as, it has been argued by some, a reduction in collective labour rights in general (De Stefano, 2015).

6.3. Apprenticeships

6.3.1. Definition and general background

Currently there is no uniform international (legal) definition of apprenticeship. Historically, the ILO has revised the definition of apprenticeships used in its Recommendations over time. In the Apprenticeship Recommendation, 1939 (No. 60), apprenticeship was defined as "any system by which an employer undertakes by contract to employ a young person and to train him [or her] or have him [or her] trained systematically for a trade for a period the duration of which has been fixed in advance and in the course of which the apprentice is bound to work in the employer's service" (Para. 1). In 1962 the ILO reformulated its definition in the Vocational Training Recommendation (No. 117), which defined apprenticeship as "systematic long-term training for a recognised occupation taking place substantially within an undertaking or under an independent craftsman" and stipulated that it "should be governed by a written contract of apprenticeship and be subject to established standards" (Steedman, 2012, p. 2). The ILO thus broadened the definition by extending the use of the term "apprenticeship" to the training of all, not just the young, and by allowing apprenticeships to be governed by contracts which are not necessarily employment contracts.

The main characteristics of an apprenticeship according to the ILO, then, were the following:

- it is based in the workplace and supervised by an employer;
- its fundamental aim is learning a trade/acquiring a skill;
- it involves training that is systematic, i.e. follows a predefined plan;
- it is governed by a contract between apprentice and employer;
- it involves training to established standards for a recognized occupation;
- it involves long-term training.

Later Recommendations that have superseded Nos 60 and 117, however, do not define apprenticeship. The up-to-date Human Resources Development Recommendation, 2004 (No. 195), regarding "education, training and lifelong learning", encourages governments to promote the expansion of workplace learning and training, but does not define or specify the different forms of this training.

The existing ILO definition of apprenticeships foresaw workplace-based long-term systematic training, but did not insist on the dual nature of the apprenticeship. The dualist ideal of apprenticeship has, at its heart, "the synthesis of theory and practice, on the one hand, and of the classroom and the workplace, on the other" (Ryan, 2011, p. 2).

Although there is no common legal definition of apprenticeship in the EU, the Member States typically define apprenticeships fairly clearly and consistently. In its policy documents the European Commission has used the following definition:

> apprenticeships are those forms of IVET that formally combine and alternate company based training (periods of practical work experience at a workplace) with school-based education (periods of theoretical/practical

education followed in a school or training centre), and whose successful completion leads to nationally recognised IVET certification degrees. Most often there is a contractual relationship between the employer and the apprentice. (EC, 2013a, p. 3)

The key elements of apprenticeship in the EU are thus the following:

- it is part of a formal education and training programme, typically at upper secondary level;
- it involves systematic, long-term, practical, work-related training at the workplace (either company- or school-based) combined with theoretical education (at an educational institution or training centre);
- an apprenticeship contract, typically a fixed-term employment contract, is concluded either directly between the apprentice and the employer, or via the educational institution;
- apprentices normally obtain the status of an employee or a contracted/employed apprentice and receive remuneration;
- apprentices are awarded accredited initial vocational education and training (IVET) qualifications or certificates;
- apprenticeships are the most tightly regulated and monitored form of combined education and work-based training;
- the social partners are involved (EC, 2013a).

Thus, compared to the ILO, the EU uses a more restrictive definition of apprenticeship; in this view, apprenticeship is not just systematic work-based learning but, more specifically, a mode of learning where class- and work-based learning, theoretical and practical learning, alternate. Here we discuss both dual apprenticeship schemes and those apprenticeships that do not fall within this definition but which are still defined as apprenticeships in specific countries.

In the EU an average of 3.7 per cent of young people (aged 15–29) take part in apprenticeships. Participation is highest in Austria, Denmark and Germany; in France, Italy, Poland and Portugal the proportion is between 1.5 and 5 per cent; and in other EU countries it is below 1.5 per cent (EC, 2013a). In Germany in 2012, 53 per cent of young people (aged 15–24) were fixed-term employees, and 84 per cent of these young people were engaged in training (primarily apprenticeships: Eurofound, 2013, p. 12, table 2). Similarly, in Austria in 2012, 36 per cent of young people were in temporary employment, and 77 per cent of all temporary employment relationships among the 15–24 age group were accounted for by training (Eurofound, 2013, p. 12, table 2). In the United States, the proportion of all apprentices in the overall workforce was very low at 0.3 per cent in 2010 (Smith and Kemmis, 2013, p. 6). In Australia, the corresponding figure for 2016 was 1.5 per cent, over three-quarters of whom were young people aged 15–24.[19]

---

[19] Author's calculations, based on data from the Australian Bureau of Statistics, http://www.abs.gov.au/.

6.3.2. National trends in regulating apprenticeships

In developed countries it has been found that one of the most critical factors in guaranteeing the success of apprenticeship as a mechanism for the school-to-work transition is "the existence of a stable and robust institutional and regulatory framework which sets the overarching context and baseline conditions within which such schemes are implemented" (EC, 2013a, p. 11). More specifically, the European Commission suggests that the framework should:

1. spell out the main training and skills development requirements in order to ensure the learning content and quality of the programme;

2. provide a clear outline of the rights, roles and responsibilities of all relevant parties;

3. specify the status of the apprentice;

4. outline the basic apprentice-related terms and conditions, including (where applicable) entitlement to remuneration and other benefits;

5. determine the (minimum) duration of the placement as well as the distribution of time between school- and work-based training;

6. specify quality assurance mechanisms;

7. define the contractual arrangements between the educational institution, employer and apprentice; and

8. set the minimum qualifications and length of previous professional experience for trainers, both at the educational institutions and within the companies (EC, 2013a, p. 12).

Although the existence of a regulatory framework is crucial for the success of an apprenticeship, no international regulation of apprenticeships exists. At the country level, apprenticeships are typically regulated by labour laws, national apprenticeship-regulated standards (typically, an Apprentice Act) and/or relevant collective bargaining agreements. Rules that govern apprenticeships could also belong to different legal domains (e.g. education law, commercial law, human rights law, etc.) and different areas of policy-making.

Legal measures to promote apprenticeships

In some countries legal measures are taken to promote apprenticeships. Three main mechanisms are used: quotas in the employment of apprentices upon qualification; obligations upon employers to take on a certain number or quota of apprentices; and/or of incentives to employers to take on apprentices.

For example, in Italy employers have a legal obligation to hire a certain share of former apprentices upon completion of training, and a recent reform has increased the applicable ratio (Quintini and Martin, 2014; Eurofound, 2015b). In Colombia, employers with more than 15 workers are obliged to offer one apprenticeship for each 20 employees that are hired (Baker & McKenzie, 2014, pp. 94–95). In Brazil, employers also have a legal obligation to offer apprenticeships, the proportion being based on the size of their workforce. For medium and large enterprises, between 5 and 15 per cent of the workforce must be apprentices. In return, firms receive a payroll subsidy in the form of a lower deposit into the workers' guarantee fund for length of service: 2 per cent instead of the standard 8 per cent. In addition, there are no penalties for unjustified dismissal (OECD, 2014b). Despite this, due to a lack of monitoring of the implementation of the law, it is estimated that in 2008–09 less than 0.3 per cent of young people aged 15–29 were apprentices (Neri, 2012).

In Turkey, companies with over 50 employees are obliged to take on at least one apprentice (Gopaul, 2013, p. 40). Apprentices' social security insurance premiums and the insurance contributions for occupational accident, disease and sickness are paid by the State. Employers are also exempt from revenue stamps, income tax, severance payments and other financial requirements. Employers can declare the wages paid to apprentices as expenditures (Smith and Kemmis, 2013, p. 131). In India and South Africa, too, there are legal obligations on companies to take on apprentices (Gopaul, 2013, pp. 29, 38).

In Canada, the Apprenticeship Training Tax Credit is a refundable tax credit for companies and businesses employing apprentices in certain skilled trades during the first three years of an apprenticeship programme. The employer can claim up to 5,000 Canadian dollars (CAD) each year up to a total of CAD15,000 per apprentice. In France, public subsidies for apprenticeships take the form of exemptions from employer and employee social security contributions. In addition, employers hiring apprentices benefit from a tax credit amounting to €1,600 per apprentice (on a full-year equivalent basis) (Eurofound, 2015b).

In countries with dual apprenticeship systems such as Austria, Denmark and Germany, there are neither quotas nor subsidies for employers who hire apprentices. Employers' benefits from apprenticeships include the screening of potential employees and the chance of developing employer-specific skills. Low apprentice wages (around 30 per cent of the normal wage) also work as an incentive for employers to hire apprentices (Ryan, 2011).

The outcomes of these measures differ in practice. It is argued that the quota approach can be counterproductive inasmuch as it can undermine the willingness of employers to take on apprentices (Eurofound, 2015b). With regard to Brazil, despite the legal obligation (and attached sanctions), many enterprises were found to incline towards relatively low-cost means of taking on labour, e.g. through internships and casual jobs, because apprenticeships were usually perceived as costly, in particular because of their training component (Ryan, 2011). In India and South Africa, too, there appears to be little appreciation or understanding of the benefits of the apprenticeship system, and only a small percentage of qualified apprentices move into employment (Gopaul, 2013, p. 12).[20]

---

[20]   In India, a particular problem is the evident reluctance of employers to take on apprentices. This is due to a large extent to the onerous requirements placed on employers who do take on apprentices, coupled with heavy penalties (including prison terms) for any breach of the regulations (ILO and World Bank/IBRD, 2013).

Contracts governing apprenticeships and the legal status of apprentices

Employer-based training may function under a training contract, an employment contract or both. Although the apprenticeship ideal suggests that the apprenticeship contract should "be clearly distinct from the employment contract, with the apprenticeship contract spelling out formally the training-related rights and duties of the apprentice and the employer, while the employment contract does the same for the service-related rights and duties of the employee and the employer" and that "apprentices should hold a training contract only" (Ryan, 2011, p. 15), in practice different contractual arrangements are used to regulate apprenticeships. The most common practice is to regulate apprenticeships through an employment agreement that encompasses not only working conditions but also training requirements. It is also possible to conclude two different agreements: an employment agreement to clarify working conditions and a training agreement for the training part of the apprenticeship. The third way is to conclude only a training agreement.

The contractual basis of the apprenticeship significantly influences whether the apprentice qualifies as an employee. In particular, it determines whether the apprentice falls under the scope of labour law and is thereby protected. Table 6.1 classifies a variety of countries for which information is available according to whether or not apprentices are covered by national labour law. It is apparent that the typical situation in HICs is for apprenticeship to be regulated by labour law, whereas in the few LMICs covered in the table, exclusion from the provisions of labour law is more usual. If the apprentice cannot be regarded as an employee, her/his rights may be protected through other branches of law (for example, educational or contract law), labour law protection may be extended in part only to apprentices, or the relationship may even be entirely unregulated.

Whether the apprenticeship contract is regarded as an employment contract or as a training contract varies across countries and over time. For example, at the time of writing in both Germany and Switzerland, unless explicitly stated otherwise, an apprentice has the status of an employee. However, before 1969, when the new Vocational Education Act came into force, apprentices in Germany were only trainees (Ryan, 2011, pp. 15–16).

In England, historically, apprenticeship contracts have been distinct from employment contracts, but the difference between the two has been eroded, and since the 1970s legal experts see the apprenticeship contract simply as another form of employment contract, distinguished primarily by its fixed duration and training-related requirements. Apprenticeship agreements were explicitly recognized as employment contracts by the 2009 Apprenticeships Act (Ryan, 2011, pp. 16–17).

In Italy, the Consolidated Act of 14 September 2011, modified by Law No. 92 of 28 June 2012, defines apprenticeship as a "permanent employment contract for youth training and employment". The definition introduces the concurrent dual nature of apprenticeship, but leaves no room for doubt that apprenticeship is an employment relationship (Rustico, 2013, p. 21). Apprentices are also defined as employees in Denmark (ETUC, 2013, p. 43), Estonia (ETUC, 2013, p. 44), Ireland (ETUC, 2013, p. 61), France, Slovakia, the Netherlands (EC, 2012a, p. 70), the United

Table 6.1. Coverage of apprentices by labour law, selected countries

Country	Covered by labour law	Not covered by labour law
Australia	X	
China		X
Cyprus		X
Denmark	X	
Estonia	X	
France	X	
Germany	X	
Indonesia		X
Ireland	X	
Italy	X	
Jordan		X
Netherlands	X	
Slovenia	X	
South Africa		X
Switzerland	X	
Turkey	X	
United Kingdom	X	
United States	X	

Source: Jeannet-Milanovic and Rosen, 2016.

States (US Code of Federal Regulations, Title 29, part 520.300), Australia (Stewart and Owens, 2013, p. 40) and Turkey (Smith and Kemmis, 2013, pp. 130–131).

However, there are States that do not consider apprentices as employees, for example Cyprus (ETUC, 2013, p. 42). In the case of Poland, the contract is signed exclusively between the training centre and the enterprise or such other entities as may arrange vocational placements or in-company training. In Jordan, the ILO technical assistance project "Towards a national apprenticeship system in Jordan" includes among its components the revision of the labour code in order to ensure that apprentices benefit from the protection afforded to every worker working under the code. In China, according to the Labour Law of 1995,[21] students' work (apprenticeship) should not be regarded as employment under a formal labour relationship ("employment relationship"). There is no contractual or labour/ employment relationship between the student and the company, so the student keeps

---

[21] Strictly speaking, it is according to the "opinion" of the Ministry of Labour on the Law in question.

her/his student status and is not regarded as an employee. Nevertheless, an employer may conclude an agreement with an apprentice on a voluntary basis, determining the apprentice's duties and possible remuneration therein; however, this agreement cannot be identified as a classical employment contract (Wang, 2014).

In Indonesia, as in China, apprentices are not considered as employed and therefore are not protected by labour law. In South Africa, even if apprentice and employer conclude an apprenticeship agreement, this does not mean that apprentices are employed. The employee status of apprentices varies across sectors and companies. At the same time, black apprentices are less likely to be formally employed than white apprentices (Smith and Kemmis, 2013, p. 111).

National regulations with a clear concept of apprenticeship

In some countries the concept of apprenticeship is clear and the organization of apprenticeships tightly regulated. This is usually the case with dual schemes, but also applies to some other types of apprenticeship.

In Germany, a transparent legal basis founded on collective agreements between the social partners sets out the legal responsibilities of stakeholders. The national Vocational Training Act and the *Ländesschulgesetze* (Education Acts at the level of the regional states or *Länder*) set out the legal responsibilities of government, employers and other partners, such as chambers of industry and commerce, education institutions and trade unions, with regard to all aspects of apprenticeships. Problems and ideas are discussed between the key stakeholders to enable apprenticeships to evolve over time (O'Higgins, 2001, p. 104).

Dual study programmes combine in-company vocational training with theoretical work. The contents of apprenticeship contracts are highly standardized because the content of training is fixed by law. The duration of the apprenticeship is also fixed by law, and has been open to more variation since the 2005 Law on Vocational Education and Training (BBiG). In addition to a probationary period of one to four months, the duration of the apprenticeship itself can now be 24, 36 or 42 months. Training costs are shared between the enterprises and the State (ibid.).

Apprentices' allowances are highly standardized and based on collective agreements. Although the allowance is the subject of individual negotiation, employers do not usually deviate from the established standard pay rate since apprentices can challenge a lower allowance in court (Le Deist and Winterton, 2011, p. 31). Apprentice allowances are set as fixed monetary sums, not as percentages of the base rates of skilled employees; relative pay rates start somewhat below one-third of the skilled worker's pay rate and rise only slowly thereafter (Ryan, 2011). Apprentices are willing to accept lower wages (in the form of the allowance) as they expect, in return, to acquire skills that will guarantee their employability. In turn, these modest allowances constitute an incentive for enterprises to take part in the scheme (O'Higgins, 2001, p. 104). The legal framework does not impose an upper age limit for apprenticeships.

In Denmark, the apprenticeship system is characterized by the strong involvement of social partners at all levels. The Danish Law on Vocational Education and Training 2015 establishes the framework for, and the overall objectives of, the system. The dual apprenticeship system involves periods of school-based education and training alternating with on-the-job training. Apprenticeships consist of a basic course that lasts nine months or so and a main course lasting two to four years. Wages and other employment conditions are negotiated between the social partners. In addition to the main sectoral collective agreements, supplementary agreements on apprentices are normally agreed, including issues such as: cooperation and how to deal with complaints; working hours; compulsory school attendance; school preparation and training evaluation; wages, including overtime pay; holidays and days off; illness and injury; and work clothing and tools to be provided by the employer. Apprentice wages depend on the stage of the apprenticeship and on the apprentice's age. Adult apprentices (over 25 years old) and apprentices in their later years of apprenticeship earn more. Apprentice wages are typically between 50 per cent and 79 per cent of a regular worker's wage (Jeppesen and Siboni, 2015; Andersen and Kruse, 2016).

In France, the legal regulation and contracting of apprenticeship are also based on collective agreements between the social partners. Important changes have been made with the reform of apprenticeship training initiated in 2002. The aim of the reform is to optimize the division of roles and responsibilities between enterprises, sectoral stakeholders, training providers and regional authorities.

Any individual aged between 16 and 26 years old can be offered an apprenticeship. Those under 16 years of age can also be accepted if they have completed the lower level of secondary education. Disabled individuals over the age of 26 may also be allowed to take up an apprenticeship. A special form of work contract between the apprentice and the employer is concluded. The duration of this contract is usually equivalent to the required period for obtaining the qualification through apprenticeship, which can vary between one and three years depending on the occupation and the type of the qualification to be obtained. The apprenticeship contract can be terminated by the employer or the apprentice within a two-month trial period. Once this trial period has passed, the contract can be terminated by the employer only for one of the following reasons: grave misconduct, repeated breaches of duty, proved inaptitude of the apprentice or certification obtained in advance of the expected date.

Under this contract the apprentice usually alternates education/training and work on a pattern of one week of training courses within an apprenticeship training centre (CFA) followed by two to three weeks of work-based training within the enterprise. Within the CFA, two-thirds of the curriculum are devoted to general transversal courses and technical vocational courses, while the remaining third is devoted to practical technical and vocational training connected with the speciality of the apprentice.

Apprentices are entitled to a minimum apprenticeship wage calculated as a percentage of the general minimum wage, taking into account the age of the apprentice and the stage of the apprenticeship. The wage of an apprentice forms 25 per cent to 78 per cent of the minimum wage (Smith and Kemmis, 2013, p. 83).

National regulations without a clear concept of apprenticeship

In England and Wales, apprenticeship denotes any publicly funded programme of work-based learning that satisfies the (frequently undemanding) requirements for public subsidy, however limited its educational content. It is important to distinguish apprenticeship contracts as governed by common law from the apprenticeship programme organized and funded by government, and regulated by the 2009 Apprenticeships Act. Ryan suggests that "in such a situation, the use of the term 'apprenticeship' is often confusing, cosmetic and objectionable" (2011, p. 6). It has also been found that:

> Apprenticeship is not a "course" or a "qualification" but merely a label. Some apprenticeships are highly prized, very selective, and lead to well-paid careers with professional pathways and qualification hierarchies. For example, the Advanced Apprenticeship in the engineering sector has entrance qualifications at least as demanding as A levels, in the shape of General Certificate of Secondary Education (GCSE) grade C or above in English, Maths and Science, as well as extensive interviews, and cognitive and practical aptitude tests. At the other end of the spectrum are apprenticeships that demand little if anything in the way of entry requirements, offer no opportunity for off-the-job education and training, and limit the apprentice to a restrictive diet of on-the-job experience. These apprenticeships might last for less than a year and provide no real foundation for progression beyond [ISCED] level 2. (Le Deist and Winterton, 2011, p. 39)

The identification of an apprenticeship agreement as a contract of employment and not as a contract of apprenticeship recognized in common law means that in these apprenticeships, work-based learning is predominant and the vocational and technical education part marginal. In the literature this has been found to be an indicator of the weakening of the apprenticeship ideal (Ryan, 2011, p. 20). Also, in England and Wales the distinction between school- and work-based training may not be sufficiently marked to qualify the system as a dual one. While general or technical training content does exist for some qualifications, the general training can be provided at the workplace; in addition, compared to Germany more weight is given to firm- or occupation-specific skills. The Government has no obligation to involve social partners in legal consultations concerning the regulation of apprenticeship (Biavaschi et al., 2012, p. 50).

In comparison to apprenticeships under common law, the Apprenticeships Act has also reduced the legal protection of apprentices under apprenticeship agreements with regard to conditions for dismissal. As apprenticeship agreements have the same status as contracts of service, apprentices engaged under such agreements can be dismissed in the same way as ordinary employees. However, employers have only a limited right of dismissal in relation to apprentices engaged under traditional common-law contracts of apprenticeship. In the event of a wrongful termination of a contract of apprenticeship, different principles apply to the assessment of damages, which will include the loss of wages, loss of training and loss of status. Damages for the breach of a common-law contract of apprenticeship are therefore potentially much greater than damages for breach of an apprenticeship agreement which is deemed to be a contract of service (Yarrow and Pugh, 2013).

Nevertheless, the Apprenticeships Act has improved the remuneration of apprentices by requiring that from 2011 all apprentices working under apprenticeship agreements should be paid a wage in line with national minimum wage regulations.[22] Individuals must be employed for a minimum of 30 hours, except in situations where the learner cannot do 30 hours, in which case the minimum is 16 hours (Smith and Kemmis, 2013, pp. 74–75).

Traditionally, apprenticeships in England and Wales have been exclusively young people's working arrangements. From around 2005 onwards, however, there have been experiments with offering adult apprenticeships, and apprenticeship is now viewed by the Government as an "all age program" (Smith and Kemmis, 2013, p. 74). A comprehensive apprenticeship reform was initiated in 2013 in acknowledgement of the risk of losing sight of the core features of what makes apprenticeships work and what makes them unique. Indeed, it has been argued that the original concept of apprenticeship and its intended purpose has been bent so far out of shape by labour policies in order to address youth unemployment that it has lost its purpose (Richard, 2012, p. 2). Recent years have seen a significant reform of apprenticeships in England. In 2015, the Government announced a target of 3 million new apprenticeships to be established by 2020, and the 2016 Welfare Reform and Work Act placed an obligation on the Government to report annually on its progress in meeting that target. The 2016 Enterprise Act also established a new independent body – the Institute for Apprenticeships – led by employers, to regulate the quality of apprenticeships. An apprenticeship levy on firms was also established, coming into force in 2017 (Mirza-Davies, 2016).[23]

In Italy, the 1955 apprenticeship contract put an emphasis on training, whereby "an entrepreneur undertakes to teach an apprentice to become a skilled worker (blue-collar) and the apprentice engages to work under the employer's direction".[24] This labour contract entitled apprentices to a lower wage than regular workers (Treu, 2007, p. 50). Owing to changes in the labour market – in particular, changes in the demand for certain skills – training was gradually relegated to a secondary aim and the courts have become stricter in recognizing the existence of this contract, considering the apprentice as a regular worker if the work is too simple to require training (ibid.).

---

[22] Albeit at the reduced "apprentice" rate. The reduced rate is applied to all apprentices aged 16–18, and for the first year of apprenticeships for those aged 19 and over. Until October 2015 this stood at 72 per cent of the national minimum wage (NMW) for 16–17-year-olds, 53 per cent of the NMW for 18–20-year-olds and 42 per cent of the adult NMW for those aged 21 and over. On 1 October 2015, the apprentice rate was raised significantly – well beyond the request of the Low Pay Commission – bringing it up to 85 per cent of the NMW for 16–17-year-olds, 62 per cent of the NMW for 18–20-year-olds and 49 per cent of the adult rate (21 and over).

[23] In 2016 the apprenticeship system underwent further significant reform including an apprenticeship levy on large employers and changes to the process and approach to developing apprenticeship standards.

[24] Art. 2 of Act No. 25/1955.

The legal reforms of 2003, which sought to distinguish apprenticeship from ALMPs, recognized three forms of apprenticeship: "right and duty" *(diritto-dovere)*, organized as part of upper secondary education; "occupational" *(apprendistato professionalizzante)*, geared to particular employers' needs; and "higher" *(alta formazione)*, at post-secondary level. The first and the third of these streams must contain part-time off-the-job vocational education, not just work-based training, and as such fall under the definition of an ideal apprenticeship. The second stream typically involves no requirement for part-time vocational education, so it generally falls outside this definition – and is by far the largest, accounting in 2009 for 72 per cent of all "apprentices". Many "apprentices" in Italy thus do not undertake an ideal apprenticeship (Ryan, 2011, p. 7).

In 27 October 2010 the Government, regions, provinces and social partners signed an agreement to relaunch the apprenticeship contract, the use of such contracts having declined considerably in the preceding years (EC, 2012a, p. 45). However, the degradation of the training component of apprenticeship continued. In 2011 apprenticeship was literally defined as a permanent employment aimed at training young people,[25] and collective agreements were set to regulate the duration of the training (CEDEFOP, 2012).

In 2012 the Monti–Fornero labour reform was introduced in reaction to, inter alia, increasing use of apprenticeships as a means of reducing labour costs to the detriment of training, as it was assumed that "shorter durations are incompatible with the completion of a meaningful training program" (OECD, 2014c, p. 13). In 2013 the apprenticeship contract was further amended in respect of sanctions for the failure of an employer to provide training; whereas such acts would previously have resulted in the apprenticeship contract being automatically converted into a contract of employment, the reform abolished this sanction if it occurred during the first year of apprenticeship (Morosini, 2013). The 2014 reform simplified employers' commitments even further by allowing them to define individual training programmes themselves.[26] Apprentices in Italy earn between 60 and 95 per cent of the salary of a qualified worker and apprenticeships are designed for young people up to 29 years of age.[27]

Although in the Netherlands a fairly clear system of traditional apprenticeships exists, the concept of apprenticeship has been blurred with the introduction of a new style of apprenticeship. There are now two types of apprenticeship in the Netherlands: traditional apprenticeship places, with both a learning contract and an employment contract; and new-style apprenticeship places, with only a learning contract. The wages of apprentices in traditional apprenticeships are set by sectoral agreements, and apprenticeship places of this type are most prevalent in economic

---

[25] Legislative Decree No. 167 of 14 Sep. 2011, referred to as the Consolidated Act on Apprenticeships *(Testo Unico (TU) sull'apprendistato)*.

[26] Italian Act No. 78 of 2014.

[27] "Basic information about mobility of apprentices in Italy", available at: http://www.euroapprenticeship.eu/en/italy.html.

sectors that traditionally used the apprenticeship system as a means to train workers. The respective shares of these different types of contract vary according to the specificities of sectors and their needs in human resources, but nowadays the proportion of new-style apprenticeship places is substantial. In 30 per cent of training firms, apprentices have only a learning contract, and 9 per cent of firms employ apprentices through such cooperation arrangements between firms and training institutions (Le Deist and Winterton, 2011, p. 37).

Apprenticeship contracts detail the status of an apprentice and the rights and obligations of the contracting parties. In traditional apprenticeship contracts the apprentice has the status of an employee; in new-style apprenticeships training takes place off the job, and the tasks and practical assignments of training (to be fulfilled in the enterprise) are established by the school. Contracts also cover the functions of supervisors: each apprentice has a supervisor from the school and a supervisor from the training enterprise (ibid.).

Sectoral collective agreements between trade unions and employers' associations often stipulate different conditions and requirements of apprenticeship contracting. Educational institutions and employers jointly organize apprenticeship programmes, all of which are governed by the 1996 Adult and Vocational Education Act. Apprentices work four days at the firm and attend class one day a week. Apprentices attending class receive full (apprentice) pay for a maximum of eight hours per week. Employers are partly compensated for the productivity loss they incur while employing an apprentice (ibid.).

Countries in Latin America have implemented a range of work-based schemes that have some similarities with apprenticeships in the sense that they combine theoretical education and work-based training, but are not sufficiently systematic to count as ideal apprenticeships. Jóvenes ALMPs began in the early 1990s targeting mainly disadvantaged youth, such as those from low-income families, the poorly educated and the un- or underemployed. Chile created the first programme, which was subsequently imitated in Argentina, Colombia, the Dominican Republic, Paraguay, Peru, Uruguay and the Bolivarian Republic of Venezuela. Governments did not manage or regulate the Jóvenes programmes. Training was offered through a bidding system in which both public and private firms could take part and which was, therefore, demand-driven (Eichhorst et al., 2014, p. 9). Currently apprenticeship-type schemes exist in most Latin American countries, often supplemented by financial incentives for the employers hiring young people under these schemes.

Regulated versus informal apprenticeships

There are also countries where formal apprenticeships are flanked by unregulated informal apprenticeships, and others where only informal apprenticeships prevail. It is estimated that informal apprenticeships involve approximately 50–90 per cent of young people in countries such as the Gambia, Ghana, Madagascar, Malawi, Mali, Senegal, the United Republic of Tanzania and Zambia. In sub-Saharan Africa, informality is not necessarily a result of cumbersome regulations and mistrust in public institutions and taxation, but is driven rather by significant economic pressure on job creation to sustain livelihoods, given the doubling of the population aged between 15 and 24 years in the region from 1985 to 2010 (Eichhorst et al., 2014, p. 17).

Continuous efforts have been made to upgrade and formalize informal training systems.[28] However, this is difficult because the flexible character of traditional apprenticeship can easily be deformed, leading to just another supply-driven training programme. For example, it has been found that the steps taken by the Ghanaian Government to formalize informal apprenticeships (especially through the partial takeover of training costs) neglected the complex system of pecuniary and non-pecuniary payments made between apprentices, their families and the craftspeople, and could force poor apprentices to leave their placements before completion and therefore with insufficient skills. However, the establishment of practical short-term training courses run by public or private institutions to accompany work-based training, as well as specific training of craftspeople to guarantee a minimum apprenticeship quality, have been found to be successful in Ghana, Kenya and the United Republic of Tanzania (Eichhorst et al., 2014, p. 17).

In Turkey, apprenticeships are thoroughly regulated by law. Dual-structured apprenticeships target young people between 14 and 18 years old, but are also open to older people. Apprenticeships are mainly carried out in state-owned vocational training centres and workplaces, and study periods alternate with practical work periods. Apprenticeships are governed by contracts and last two to four years. Apprentices have employee status and earn a wage which is at least 30 per cent of the minimum rate (Smith and Kemmis, 2013, pp. 129–131). In practice, informal apprenticeships also exist, whereby young people work at small workplaces as apprentices but do not have apprenticeship contracts and do not attend apprenticeship training. There are no definitive numbers of informal apprenticeships, but especially in larger cities, where inspection of the apprentices is more difficult, it can be assumed that there are several times as many apprentices working unregistered in the informal sector as registered apprentices. Since 1977, when the first law on apprenticeship training was enacted, there have been efforts to formalize the informal sector, and these efforts are continuing (Smith and Kemmis, 2013, p. 128).

Although (mainly informal) apprenticeships have existed in Egypt for thousands of years, attempts to establish a modern apprenticeship system, initiated in 1956, have not yet proved successful. There is no "national system" of apprenticeships in Egypt, but four different types of apprenticeship schemes have been established. Three of them are offered by governmental bodies and the fourth by an employers' organization. The common characteristics of these schemes are the following: (a) completing basic education is a prerequisite for admission; (b) duration is usually three years; and (c) graduates are granted either a technical secondary school certificate or a diploma at the same level (Smith and Kemmis, 2013, pp. 64–65).

---

[28] The ILO has been active in this area. For a summary of the approach, see ILO, 2011. More in-depth analyses are available at: http://ilo.org/skills/projects/WCMS_158771/lang--en/index.htm [2 Feb. 2017].

6.3.3. Regulation of apprenticeships and the labour rights of young people

In the majority of countries considered here, apprentices have employee status and are typically covered by labour law protection. However, this does not mean that they enjoy precisely the same rights as regular employees. For example, apprentices' wages are typically significantly lower than those of qualified workers, ranging from around 30 per cent to 95 per cent of the latter.

The limited duration of apprentices' employment has conflicting effects on their rights. On the one hand, the short-term nature of apprentices' employment often does not allow them to fully qualify for a range of benefits, such as those related to unemployment, sickness and maternity. In this respect, some countries choose to amend existing legislation while others enact new law in order to extend such protection to apprentices. For example, in Italy unemployment benefits are extended to apprentices as of 2017 (Clauwaert and Schömann, 2013, Italy country report, p. 9).

In the EU, apprentices' rights are more limited than the rights of other fixed-term workers. The Directive on fixed-term work, which aims to avoid unjustified discrimination against fixed-term workers, and to prevent the abuse of successive fixed-term contracts, explicitly allows Member States to exclude initial vocational training relationships and apprenticeship schemes from its scope (Council of the European Union, 1999, clause 2(2)). This means that it is possible for EU countries to leave apprentices without the guarantees provided by the Directive. For example, in the United Kingdom, the Fixed-Term Employees (Prevention of Less Favourable Treatment) Act 2002 excluded those employed under a common-law contract of apprenticeship; and in 2013 it was further clarified that apprentices under apprenticeship agreements regulated by the Apprenticeship Act 2009 were also covered by this exclusion (Yarrow and Pugh, 2013).

On the other hand, in EU countries apprentices typically possess some additional rights compared to regular workers. First, they are often entitled to off-the-job as well as work-based training. The extent to which this applies varies. Off-the-job training rights are strongly protected in countries operating dual schemes, but much weaker in countries such as the United Kingdom or Italy, where apprenticeship typically denotes a more specifically work-based training arrangement. Indeed, the success of the former type of apprenticeship in facilitating young people's entry into the labour market has often been explained by its dual nature. If the apprenticeship does not include an off-the-job learning component, its effectiveness tends to decrease.

Second, the contractual requirements applying to apprenticeships are typically more protective than those of temporary or other training contracts. For example, in Italy apprenticeship contracts are considered permanent contracts. In Australia, a formal contract is compulsory in the case of an "apprenticeship", or training in any prescribed vocation,[29] while it is optional for other types of training arrangement (Stewart and Owens, 2013, p. 96).

---

[29] That is, in occupations designated as "apprenticeable" by state legislation.

The key difference here appears to be whether or not apprentices are defined as employees. Whether or not there is a causal link, there is a clear association between "regular" employee status and the effectiveness of the apprenticeship as a mechanism to smooth the transition from school to work, as demonstrated by the relatively low unemployment rates of young people compared to adults in countries operating such schemes. Apprentices regarded as employees are rather well protected; the differences between the rights of regular workers and of apprentices derive mainly from the nature of the apprenticeship and, as such, are reasonable.

Apprentices who are not defined as employees are in a far more precarious situation. They are sometimes covered by educational or contract law, but there are also cases in which they are completely unprotected. In the latter case it is difficult to distinguish between "unprotected" apprenticeships and other work-based schemes – or, indeed, other types of precarious work.

6.3.4. Apprenticeships and the school-to-work transition

One of the key advantages of apprenticeships compared to purely school-based schemes is precisely the facilitation of rapid school-to-work transitions for students. In Europe the majority of apprentices – usually about 60–70 per cent, in some cases as many as 90 per cent – secure employment immediately upon completion. Furthermore, the proportion of apprentices who secure employment within six months to a year after completing the scheme is even higher, often over 80 per cent (EC, 2013a, p. 8).

Patterns of transition from school to work are smoother in countries with strong apprenticeship systems (e.g. Germany) than in those without strong work-based training integrated into the formal school system (e.g. Italy or Spain). Apprenticeships perform very favourably, both compared to school-based education at the same level of training and across different qualification levels, resulting in more rapid school-to-work transitions (EC, 2012a, p. 93). Apprentices achieve better job matches, higher wages, shorter periods of unemployment before finding a first job and a longer duration of their first job compared to individuals with low educational attainment or school-based vocational education (EC, 2013a, pp. 10–11).

Still, this generally positive picture turns out to be more complex when examined in detail. The positive effect of apprenticeships on wages emerges most strongly when compared to workers with low education and no apprenticeship training, less so when compared to workers having completed full-time vocational education. The advantages of apprenticeships compared to school-based vocational paths tend to be stronger at the beginning of working life and decline or disappear over the longer term. The beneficial effects on transition and pay seem not to hold true for women in all countries, mainly because of occupational and sectoral segregation. Studies in Germany have shown that the size of the training firm appears to affect the labour market perspectives of former apprentices, with better employment and earnings prospects for those who received their apprenticeship training in large firms than for those trained in smaller firms. Also, the positive effects of apprenticeships on labour market conditions are related to the quality of the apprenticeship (EC, 2013a, pp. 10–11).

There is also evidence that informal apprenticeships can contribute to a better school-to-work transition. For example, studies on Malawi and the United Republic of Tanzania showed that most informal apprenticeship graduates were employed either within their former training companies or with another employer. Informal apprenticeships respond more easily and more quickly to changes in current skills demands, and therefore graduates find work more easily than vocational school graduates. Also, as informal training has no formalized entry criteria, it is often the only opportunity for some school-leavers to obtain vocational education. A study conducted in Ghana showed that individuals with low levels of formal schooling benefited significantly from informal training, with earnings increasing by 50 per cent. However, in general, the effects of informal training on earnings seem to be somewhat disappointing (Eichhorst et al., 2014, p. 28).

The effectiveness of the transition from apprenticeship into permanent employment is difficult to assess because of the lack – with some limited exceptions – of appropriate follow-up data. In France, 67 per cent of apprentices found employment in February 2009; of these, only 63 per cent had a permanent contract. In 2008, 65 per cent of young people on "professionalization contracts" had found jobs, 57 per cent of them with permanent contracts (37 per cent of all participants). In Italy, 40 per cent of those in apprenticeships in 2005 had a permanent job five years later, compared to 45 per cent of those who were in an apprenticeship in 2000 (Eurofound, 2013, pp. 27–28). Evidence shows that in Italy, having been an apprentice increases the probability of having a permanent contract in the future: apprentices have a 16 per cent higher probability of a stable job than young fixed-term workers (EC, 2013a, p. 10).

6.3.5. Apprenticeship: Stepping stone or dead end?

Apprenticeships in their ideal form have performed well in supporting young people's school-to-work transition. Strongly regulated apprenticeships in Europe in general appear to work more effectively than work-based schemes which bear the same appellation, but lack an off-the-job education element. However, in Latin America Jóvenes programmes, which are not traditional dual apprenticeship schemes, have also contributed to effective school-to-work transitions. Moreover, in Africa even fully informal apprenticeships have increased the employability of young people. Therefore, the success of apprenticeships seems to depend not only on their conformity to the ideal apprenticeship model, but on the specific context.[30]

Although the apprenticeship model has proved to be successful in aiding young people's entry into the labour market, there are two main concerns connected to its use: social partnership and cost. In ideal apprenticeship models, success appears to

---

[30] The ILO has recently produced a number of documents and guides on "quality apprenticeship" going into some detail as to what these entail. See ILO, 2017, for a summary and sources of further information.

be strongly associated with the deep involvement of social partners. The willingness of employers to take on apprentices cannot be increased simply by setting out a legal obligation to participate in these schemes. The provision of subsidies reduces the costs of apprenticeships and motivates employers to take on apprentices. Even so, the educational content and quality of apprenticeships needs to be guaranteed by legal regulation or collective agreements in order to avoid the use of apprentices as cheap (and even subsidized) labour.

Subsidized apprenticeships have been found very costly to the countries that have operated them. However, these costs can be avoided or reduced through the engagement of social partners and specifically through an appropriate structuring of incentives, for example, allowing employers to screen potential employees and develop employer-specific skills, and specifying a low wage level for apprentices. The first two incentives refer to the need to tailor apprenticeship programmes to the needs of labour market; the third, a low wage rate for apprentices, can be used as an incentive only if this is accompanied with quality training – otherwise such an apprenticeship will end up as simply another form of low-paid, low-quality precarious work for those young people who have no other options open to them.

Work-based schemes that are called apprenticeships, but are insufficiently regulated and/or exempt apprentices from the scope of labour law, cannot guarantee quality learning and are likely to become dead-end jobs. Instead of increasing the employability of young people who participate in them, such schemes will tend to lead them towards precarious work.

6.4. Traineeships, internships and other work-based training programmes

6.4.1. Definition and general background

The concept of a traineeship/internship is still less clear than that of an apprenticeship. No common (legal) definition of a traineeship/internship exists; a reasonable working description is that they are work-based schemes whose purpose is to provide skills and knowledge in the workplace. A distinction is typically made between traineeships, internships, stages or even volunteering on the one hand, and apprenticeships on the other; the former terms may denote the same, similar or different work-based schemes, depending on national legal regulation. A common definition at the international level with regard to apprentices, interns and trainees would be valuable in order to enable distinctions to be made between such categories. However, recent discussions at the International Conference of Labour Statisticians have noted the difficulties in making such distinctions specific, given the variety of national practices (ILO, 2015g, pp. 47–48).

In its policy documents the EU defines traineeship as a limited period of work practice spent at a business, public body or non-profit institution by a student or a young person having recently completed their education, in order to gain some valuable hands-on work experience ahead of taking up regular employment. The

EU uses the term "traineeships" as a synonym for "internships" and/or "stages" (EC, 2012b, p. 7; 2012c, part 1). In the Quality Framework for Traineeships a traineeship is defined as a limited period of work practice, whether paid or not, which includes both learning and training components, undertaken in order to gain practical and professional experience with a view to improving employability and facilitating the transition to regular employment.[31] Although the definition of a traineeship used in EU policy documents does not explicitly include the combination of both learning and work experience components, the Quality Framework insists that some learning possibilities need to be provided in addition to work experience.

Even though the Commission does not include an explicit learning component in the definition of traineeships, it explains that "a traineeship is a work practice including a training component". The Commission also explains that "traineeships allow to document practical work experience as part of the individual CV ... or to gain work practice for the purpose of facilitating the transition from education and training to the labour market. They are predominantly short- to middle-term (a few weeks up to 6 months, in certain cases 1 year)." They can form part of the curriculum of vocational or higher education, can be administered as ALMPs or can be conducted after graduation in the open market. Trainees are often not regarded as employees, but work under traineeship agreements (EC, 2012b, pp. 7–8).

Among Member States the definition of "traineeship" varies. However, in countries where definitions of traineeship exist, they usually involve a strong link between education and work experience. Usually a trainee is a pupil, a student or a person who is working temporarily to acquire on-the-job experience which is relevant to his/her studies. Hence, in most Member States the legal position of a trainee is not equal to the legal position of a regular employee or apprentice (EC, 2012d, p. 132).

In common-law countries the term "internship" is more commonly used. There is no uniform legal definition of either traineeship or internship in the United Kingdom. Work-based schemes outside formal education are referred to as "internships", although an "intern" is not a specific legal status; the legal position of interns depends, rather, on the nature of the work undertaken as part of the internship. The term can be used to describe placements which vary considerably in terms of content, quality and remuneration. Traineeships as part of higher education courses are often referred to as "sandwich placements" or "work placements" (EC, 2012d, p. 132). No legal definition of an internship exists in the United States either. In practice, what defines an internship depends largely on who is doing the defining (Perlin, 2012, pp. 25–26), and the word "intern" is a kind of umbrella covering a range of intermittent and precarious roles that might otherwise be called volunteer, temp, summer job and so on (Perlin, 2012, p. xi).

In Australia, as in some other English-speaking countries, the term "internship" has historically referred to medical graduates gaining supervised (and generally

---

[31] Council Recommendation of 10 March 2014 on a Quality Framework for Traineeships, OJ C 88, 27 Mar. 2014, pp. 1–4, preamble 27.

paid) practical experience before obtaining their licences to practise, but it has now come to refer to a wide range of arrangements for the performance of paid or unpaid work for businesses, non-profit organizations and government agencies (Stewart and Owens, 2013, p. 51). The term "traineeship" in Australia refers to a kind of subgroup of apprenticeships. Traineeships were introduced in Australia in the 1980s and expanded into occupational areas that had not previously supported training, such as retail, tourism and hospitality. Now they form a part of the Australian apprenticeship system and trainees have the same rights as apprentices (Smith and Kemmis, 2013, pp. 43–44).

As with apprenticeships, in the case of traineeships/internships a distinction can be drawn between, on the one hand, an ideal model of traineeship/internship as a work-based learning scheme that combines theoretical and practical learning, and, on the other, work-based schemes that are called traineeships/internships but which cover a variety of forms of cheap and unprotected youth employment.

6.4.2. International guidance on the regulation of traineeships/internships

There are no legal instruments adopted by the ILO to explicitly guide the regulation of internships/traineeships. Nevertheless, the issue of youth employment, including internships, has been high on its agenda. The 2012 resolution and call for action of the International Labour Conference (ILC) on "The youth employment crisis" suggested inter alia that governments improve the links between education, training and the world of work through social dialogue on skills mismatch and standardization of qualifications in response to labour market needs, and enhanced technical vocational education and training, including apprenticeships, other work experience schemes and work-based learning. It further suggested that governments regulate and monitor apprenticeships, internships and other work experience schemes, including through certification, to ensure that they allow for a real learning experience and do not replace regular workers; and that they raise awareness about the labour rights of young workers, interns and apprentices (ILO, 2012c, paras 26(b), 27(d)).

The EU has initiated the regulation of traineeships through the promotion of the mobility of trainees. Recommendation 2001/613/EC on mobility within the Community for students, persons undergoing training, volunteers, teachers and trainers is aimed at fostering, among other things, "the mobility of students and trainees" by recommending that Member States "take measures to remove the legal and administrative obstacles to the mobility of these persons" (European Parliament and Council of the European Union, 2001, p. 30). In the following Recommendation 2006/961/EC on transnational mobility within the Community for education and training purposes (proposing a "European Quality Charter for Mobility"), the EU accepted the need to focus not only on increasing mobility in quantitative terms but, above all, on improving its quality. The EU recommended the adoption and promotion by Member States of the Quality Charter, which envisages the provision of information and guidance, including general and linguistic preparation, to students or trainees embarking on studies or traineeships abroad. The document also recommends the drawing up of a learning plan, the personalization of the training, the provision of logistical support and mentoring, and the recognition and evaluation of the study or placement period abroad (European Parliament and Council of the European Union, 2006, p. 5). Recommendation 2006/961/EC regulates only transnational traineeships, where the traineeship is carried out in a Member State different from that of the trainee's residence, and it does not cover open market traineeships or traineeships carried out in the framework of ALMPs.

In the Quality Framework for Traineeships the EU has taken a further step by regulating not only transnational but also domestic traineeships. The Quality Framework does not cover placements that are part of the curricula of formal education or vocational education and training (EC, 2012c). Rather, this recommendation regulates privately offered (sometimes called open market) and/or ALMP traineeships. This is explained in the explanatory memorandum accompanying the Commission's proposal for a Quality Framework (EC, 2013b), which states that the Quality Framework covers only traineeships agreed between a trainee and a traineeship provider without the involvement of a third party, generally conducted after completion of studies and/or as part of a job search. However, the Quality Framework itself does not exclude from the scope of regulation ALMP traineeships, nor does the definition of a traineeship used in the Quality Framework (EC, 2012c) state that the recommendation is applicable only to open market traineeships.

The Quality Framework is not a logical follow-up to the two previous recommendations, but rather seeks to regulate traineeships that have previously been unregulated at the EU level. A written traineeship agreement is the main element stipulated to guarantee the learning content of the traineeship and improve the working conditions of the trainee. The Quality Framework proposes obligatory conditions to be included in the traineeship agreement; recommends the promotion of best practices as regards learning and training objectives; encourages traineeship providers to designate a supervisor for trainees; recommends that Member States guarantee the rights and working conditions of trainees under applicable EU and national law (including limits to maximum weekly working time, minimum daily and weekly rest periods and minimum holiday entitlements); and requires the clarification of the terms of health insurance and compensation provided to trainees. The Quality Framework also proposes a reasonable duration for traineeships, with a maximum of six months, and calls on Member States to clarify the conditions under which traineeship agreements may be extended and renewed, as well as the conditions for the termination of such agreements (EC, 2012c, paras 10–12).

Thus international efforts – both by the ILO and by the EU – have focused on two issues concerning traineeships/internships: first, encouraging governments to improve the quality, structure and scope of skills provision; and second, emphasizing the need to protect the labour rights of trainees/interns. However, these provisions are advisory rather than regulatory, and therefore the main responsibility in regulating traineeships/internships remains with national governments.

6.4.3. National trends in regulating traineeships/internships

As one might expect in this context, there is no one approach towards the legal regulation of traineeships/internships. Legislative and regulatory diversity exists not only between different countries but also between the different types of traineeships. These work-based schemes can be fully unregulated, regulated through laws which explicitly apply to traineeships, or regulated through laws associated with education, training and/or employment policies. Sometimes traineeships which form part of academic study curricula are regulated by the educational institution itself.

Not only the diverse approaches of governments to the regulation of traineeships/internships, but also the working components of these arrangements, make it difficult to frame and study these relationships. More specifically, the absence of legal regulation governing traineeships/internships does not mean that there are no legal issues connected with these schemes; the question of trainees'/interns' labour law status and their coverage under labour law protection arises.

Labour law status of trainees/interns

The labour law status of trainees/interns is even more unclear than that of apprentices. At the same time it is, in principle, far more important from the viewpoint of the protection of trainees/interns, since traineeships/internships are more often unregulated than apprenticeships in other respects.

In most **EU countries**, a traineeship is explicitly *not* an employment contract. For example, in Greece, traineeships that are part of study curricula are not regarded as employment relationships. In Estonia, Italy and Sweden, traineeships linked to educational programmes do not entail employment contracts but rather an agreement between the sending organization, the company and the trainee (EC, 2012d). In Finland, vocational education traineeships are explicitly exempted from the regulation of labour laws (Rosin and Muda, 2013, p. 292). In France, trainees are not explicitly exempted from labour law protection, but according to court practice, a trainee working in order to fulfil the aims set out in the *convention de stage* (traineeship agreement) does not thereby qualify as an employee (Rosin and Muda, 2013, p. 301). In the United Kingdom, workers who are participants in a scheme designed to provide them with training, work experience or temporary work, or to assist them in seeking or obtaining work, where the scheme is either provided under arrangements made by the Government, or funded by the European Social Fund, are exempted from the National Minimum Wage Regulations (Stewart and Owens, 2013, p. 227).

In **Argentina**, interns are not considered as employees and therefore such contracts are exempt from social security contributions (Baker & McKenzie, 2014, p. 3). In **Brazil**, internships aimed at vocational and tertiary education students are regulated by a separate law and are not considered as conferring employee status (OECD, 2014c, p. 113).

In **China**, only a student who has not yet obtained his or her graduation certificate or diploma can enter into an internship agreement with a company. According to the Labour Law 1995, No. 309, a part-time work–study arrangement is not considered employment. Although the employer does not have to sign a labour contract with the student, employers are strongly recommended to conclude internship agreements with students entering into this relationship (China Briefing, 2014). It has been found that classifying technical and vocational school students as interns who are not covered by labour law, and using them to perform ordinary labour without any educational benefits, results in the abuse of these workers in the labour market. Currently, private employers in China use increasingly unprotected intern labour as a major component of their workforce. It has also been argued by some that the exploitation of vocational or technical school interns without providing them with education is contrary to the ILO Conventions prohibiting forced labour (Brown and DeCant, 2014, pp. 149–195). Internships after graduation in China are not allowed; an employer is obliged to sign an employment contract when taking on a graduate student. If the employer fails to sign a written labour agreement within a month of work commencing, the employee may claim double salary for each month worked without a written contract. As the contract is now deemed a labour contract, the employer will have to comply with social insurance and minimum wage requirements (China Briefing, 2014).

In **Japan**, under the Industrial Training and Technical Internship Programme, foreign nationals can enter the country as "trainees" for one year and become "technical interns" for another two years; they are required to go back to their own country thereafter. In 2010 the programme was revised with a view to strengthening the protection of trainees and technical interns, who thereby acquired protection under labour laws and regulations, such as the Labour Standards Law and the Minimum Wage Law. However, conditions for foreign trainees have not improved: they are still forced to work under the threat of deportation, they are not allowed to change their employer, and they remain vulnerable to abuse by employers.[32]

In the **United States**, the Fair Labor Standards Act 1938 exempts from the category of employees those individuals who volunteer to perform services for a public agency which is a State, a political subdivision of a State, or an interstate governmental agency, provided such individuals receive no compensation and the services performed are not the same type of services as the individual is employed to perform for such a public agency. Also, individuals who volunteer their services solely for humanitarian purposes to private non-profit food banks and who receive groceries from the food banks are not employees. The Wage and Hour Division of the US Department of Labor stipulates that unpaid internships in the public sector and for non-profit charitable organizations, where the intern volunteers without expectation of compensation, are generally permissible (Rosin and Muda, 2013, p. 296).

---

[32] Observation by the ILO Committee of Experts on the Application of Conventions and Recommendations (CEACR), adopted 2012, published 102nd ILC Session (2013), Forced Labour Convention 1930 (No. 29) – Japan (Ratification: 1932). Available at: http://www.ilo.org/dyn/normlex/en/f?p=NORMLEXPUB:13100:0::NO::P13100_COMMENT_ID,P13100_LANG_CODE:3081910,es.

In **Australia**, the Fair Work Act 2009 provides that the terms "employee" or "national system employee" do not include persons who are "on a vocational placement". A vocational placement is a placement that is: (a) undertaken with an employer for which a person is not entitled to be paid any remuneration; (b) a requirement of an education or training course; and (c) authorized under a law or an administrative arrangement of the Commonwealth, a State or a Territory (Stewart and Owens, 2013, p. 75).

In **Canada**, the provinces are responsible for much of the legislation regulating work. In Ontario, for example, secondary school students performing work under a work experience programme authorized by the school board that operates the school, and individuals performing work under a programme approved by a college of applied arts and technology or a university, are not employees. Also in Ontario, individuals receiving training that corresponds to the US six-step test[33] are exempted from the category of employees according to law (Stewart and Owens, 2013, pp. 191–192).

Although the exemption of trainees/interns from the scope of labour laws may seem to clearly exempt these workers from labour law protection, the issue is far more complicated. According to the ILO's Employment Relationship Recommendation, 2006 (No. 198), the determination of the existence of an employment relationship "should be guided primarily by the facts relating to the performance of work and the remuneration of the worker, notwithstanding how the relationship is characterized in any contrary arrangement, contractual or otherwise, that may have been agreed between the parties" (Para. 9). This Recommendation refers to three important principles: first, the existence of an employment relationship should be determined on a case-by-case basis; second, the guiding criteria in the determination of an employment relationship are the performance of work and the payment of remuneration; third, the "label" on the working relationship is not decisive in determining whether it constitutes an employment relationship. Many national labour laws contain provisions on the employment relationship. Despite certain similarities, not all national labour laws provide exhaustive or equal coverage of the subject. Some provisions deal with the regulation of the employment contract as a specific contract; other provisions are intended to facilitate recognition of the existence of an employment relationship. In general terms, the employment relationship creates a legal link between a person who performs work and the person for whose benefit the work is performed in return for remuneration, under certain conditions established by national law and practice. In many countries, the legislation contains a substantive definition of the employment contract that establishes the factors that constitute such a contract and distinguish it from other similar contracts. In other countries, the legislation is less detailed and the task of determining the existence of an employment contract is largely left to case law (ILO, 2005, p. 19). The most commonly used factors for determining whether work is

---

[33] As established in the *Portland Terminal* case; see p. 154 below.

being performed under an employment contract are dependency and subordination, or the performance of work under the direction, authority, supervision or control of the employer, or for the employer's account (ibid., p. 20).

Taking into account the principle that the existence of an employment relationship is determined on a case-by-case basis, the employee status of the trainee/intern should be considered according to the factual circumstances. Therefore, the non-existence of regulation covering traineeships/internships, the regulation of traineeships/internships through a separate body of norms, or even the explicit exemption of these relationships from the scope of labour laws does not mean that trainees/interns do not qualify as employees. The qualification of trainees/interns as employees is more important in countries where no regulation of these relationships exists, because in those cases protection under the labour law is the only kind of protection available to the trainee/intern. If traineeships/internships are regulated through some other body of norms, trainees/interns are not without protection even if they are not regarded as employees. Still, even in those conditions it is not straightforward to deny the employee status of trainees/interns if the conditions of an employment relationship are met.

Regulation of traineeships/internships by a separate body of norms

In the EU, the countries which legally regulate traineeships do so either explicitly or through their national legislation on secondary, including vocational, and tertiary education.

France is usually identified as an example of a country with comprehensive legislation on traineeship, as it regulates all traineeships and requires that they be embedded in educational programmes. All traineeships must be formalized in a tripartite agreement *(convention de stage)* by the sending education/training provider, the host organization and the trainee (EC, 2012d, pp. 42–43). This agreement is not regarded as an employment contract, but includes conditions that guarantee the educational component of a traineeship, as well as reasonable working conditions. The obligatory conditions of a traineeship agreement include agreed working tasks for the development of skills; the date of the beginning and the end of a traineeship; weekly working time; the amount of compensation; other benefits granted to a trainee; the social protection and occupational accident insurance of a trainee; supervision; the issuing of a certificate on the completion of a traineeship; the conditions for suspension and termination of the contract; the conditions of a trainee's right to leave of absence; and the applicable internal regulations of the workplace (Education Code, art. D612-30[34]).

Trainees are entitled to compensation in the case of traineeships lasting more than two months within the same academic year regardless of the number of hours worked (Education code, art. L124-6). The compensation is paid not on the basis of

---

[34] *Code de l'éducation* (France). Available at: https://www.legifrance.gouv.fr/affichCode.do?cidTexte=LEGITEXT000006071191

a labour contract but on the basis of the traineeship agreement. At the same time, the overall duration of a traineeship is limited to six months (Paulin and Thivin, 2010, p. 148). The host organization has to pay the trainee at least 15 per cent of the minimum wage (Education Code, art. L124-6), and receives token compensation for its expenses from the state (Paulin and Thivin, 2010, pp. 170–171).

In **Spain**, the 2006 *Ley Orgánica de la Educación* regulates pre-university and university levels of vocational training and covers compulsory vocational educational training traineeships. There are also two specific employment contracts which link education with work experience (open market traineeships): the training contract *(contrato para la formación)* and the work experience contract *(contrato en prácticas)*. Training contracts are targeted at students whose study curricula require that part of their time at the workplace be devoted to training activities, while work experience contracts are aimed at recent graduates. The upper age limit for both types of contract is 25 years (EC, 2012d, p. 44).

Since 1995, numerous labour reforms have taken place in Spain. Of particular relevance to training was the renaming in 2011 of the 1995 training contract *(contrato para la formación)* as the training and learning contract *(contrato para la formación y el aprendizaje)*. In 2012 it underwent further changes – including extension of the age eligibility criterion, permissible working time and duration of the contract – which brought about a shift towards work and away from the initial aim and purpose of the contract, i.e. training. Furthermore, while the 2011 provision stipulated that training must be provided by a recognized training centre, the 2012 reform allowed for the provision of training within the company as well. The two reforms were in fact contradictory: the 2011 reform reinforced the training content of the contract, while the 2012 reform subordinated the training content to the goals of employment promotion, as exemplified in the extension of the maximum working time permitted under the contract (Eurofound, 2013, Spain country report).

Italy is characterized by a plethora of traineeship-related regulations. All the traineeship models included in the study curricula in both secondary and tertiary education are governed directly by the specific regulations of schools, colleges and universities. Summer traineeships integrated into vocational training courses were also introduced by Law 30/2003. These can last no more than three months, and participants are paid up to €600. Traineeships integrated into the study curricula of those aged 15–18 attending both high schools and vocational training schools were introduced by Law 53/2003 *(Legge Moratti)*. Additionally, vocational and orientation (non-curricular) traineeships are defined and regulated at the national level by separate laws (EC, 2012d, p. 43).

As part of the Monti–Fornero reform adopted in June 2012 in Italy, measures have been introduced to facilitate access to apprenticeships and traineeships. In addition to the requirement that trainees be paid a "decent wage", the Government has been requested by the Parliament to adopt one or more legislative decrees setting down fundamental rules and requirements for traineeships based on the following principles: (a) general revision of traineeship regulations; (b) measures to prevent the abuse of traineeships through the accurate description of the trainee's activities and the traineeship's qualifying elements; (c) provision of some form of remuneration to trainees (Lang et al., 2013, p. 23).

In **Greece,** traineeships that form a part of the study curricula of technical education institutes (TEI) are regulated. These traineeships last six months and are undertaken in the last semester of study. TEI trainees are entitled to compensation and insured against occupational risks. The TEI traineeships are organized according to the requirements and focus of the specific study curriculum and are supervised by the relevant teaching staff. All aspects of traineeships are defined in the "traineeship guide" which is compiled for each profession. Higher education traineeships are not uniformly regulated and are organized according to each university department's own traineeship guide; nevertheless, these trainees are also entitled to compensation and insurance coverage against occupational risks and work accidents (EC, 2012d, pp. 313–314).

In **Estonia** and **Finland**, only vocational education traineeships and traineeships carried out as part of ALMPs are regulated. In these cases, traineeships require the establishment of a traineeship agreement. The obligatory conditions of the traineeship agreement in vocational education are mainly aimed at guaranteeing the educational component of the traineeship. In Estonia, the traineeship agreement in vocational education should include conditions on the organization of the traineeship and the rights and obligations of the parties. The aim of the traineeship, the tasks conferred on the trainee, the studies carried out before the traineeship and the expected outcomes of the traineeship are fixed in a traineeship programme that forms part of the traineeship agreement (Vocational Education Institutions Act, sec. 30(3));[35] Aaviksoo and Holm, 2013, sec. 4(1)). Finnish laws envisage similar obligatory conditions of the traineeship agreement; in addition, the hours and duration of the traineeship, and the supervision and evaluation of the trainee should be agreed (Initial Vocational Education Act, ch. 3, sec. 16;[36] Decree on Vocational Education, ch. 4, sec. 9 and ch. 5, sec. 6).[37]

The obligatory conditions of a traineeship agreement concluded as part of an ALMP in Estonia do not guarantee the learning quality of the traineeship, but rather are concerned with the regulation of working conditions. Estonian regulation is very brief and sets out only that the number of persons participating in the traineeship, the content and the duration of the traineeship must be agreed in the administrative contract concluded between the PES and the employer (Labour Market Services and Benefits Act, 2005, sec. 15(2)).[38]

---

[35] *Kutseõppeasutuse seadus* (Estonia), 12 June 2013. Available at http://www.riigiteataja. ee/en/eli/505022014002/consolide

[36] *Laki ammatillisesta koulutuksest*, 1998 (Finland). Available at: http://www.finlex.fi/ fi/laki/ajantasa/1998/19980630?search%5Btype%5D=pika&search%5Bpika%5D=Laki%20 ammatillisesta%20koulutuksesta

[37] *Asetus ammatillisesta koulutuksesta*, 1998 (Finland). Available at: http://www.finlex.fi/ fi/laki/ajantasa/1998/19980811

[38] *Tööturuteenuste ja – toetuste seadus*, 2005 (Estonia). Available at: https://www. riigiteataja.ee/en/eli/ee/Riigikogu/act/528042014001/consolide

Finnish regulation is more detailed and states that the traineeship contract concluded between the PES, the employer and the trainee should establish the aim of the traineeship, the duration and the place of work, weekly and daily working time, the working tasks, and the supervision and evaluation of the trainee (Labour Market and Enterprises Services Act, ch. 4, sec. 5).[39] In the case of traineeships forming part of higher education, no regulation of the traineeship agreement is prescribed in either Estonia or Finland. It is up to the parties to the traineeship (educational institution, trainee and employer) to decide whether and under what conditions to conclude a traineeship agreement. No regulation of market-based traineeships exists in these States.

In **Brazil**, internships are aimed at vocational and tertiary education students and governed by law. The maximum number of hours interns may work is generally 20 per week for students at non-tertiary level and 30 for those at tertiary level (OECD, 2014c, p. 113). Students older than 14 years can be hired as interns and work under a tripartite internship agreement. The intern must be supervised and evaluated and is covered by occupational accident insurance. The maximum duration of internship is two years and the maximum number of interns in an enterprise is ten. The payment of a stipend to the student is optional if the internship is a compulsory part of an educational curriculum and mandatory in the case of voluntary internships (Gama and Migliora, 2009).

In **Argentina**, the regulation of internships prescribes the conclusion of an internship agreement between the employer and educational institution to establish an internship programme. Internships have a training purpose and are available only to students. The internship has a minimum term of two months and a maximum term of 12 months, which may be extended once for six additional months. The work schedule may not exceed 20 hours per week and no social contributions are paid for interns (Baker & McKenzie, 2014, p. 3).

In **China**, according to the law, only students who have not yet obtained their graduation certificate or diploma can enter into an internship agreement with a company. The conclusion of an internship agreement is not compulsory, but is strongly recommended. The host organization is not obliged to pay social welfare contributions or a severance payment at the termination of the agreement, and minimum wage standards are not applicable to interns (China Briefing, 2014).

Ad hoc regulation of internships through the establishment of employment status

In common-law countries internships are for the most part not separately regulated, so that the only way for an intern to obtain some protection of her/his labour rights is by obtaining employee status. This is determined on an ad hoc basis, and court practice provides some guidance on which relationships named as internships can

---

[39] *Laki julkisesta työvoima – ja yrityspalvelusta*, 2012 (Finland). Available at: http://www.finlex.fi/fi/laki/ajantasa/2012/20120916

be implemented without labour law protection and which constitute employment relationships.

In the **United States**, the Supreme Court's decision in the *Portland Terminal* case (1947) is one of the most important decisions from which the rules governing unpaid interns are derived. A trainee or intern is not an employee if the internship satisfies the six requirements laid down in the *Portland Terminal* judgment:

1. training, even if it includes the operation of the employers' facilities, is similar to that which would be given in a vocational school;

2. training is for the benefit of the trainee;

3. trainees do not displace regular employees, but work under close observation;

4. the employer that provides the training derives no immediate advantage from the activities of the trainees, and on occasion the employer's operations may actually be impeded;

5. trainees are not necessarily entitled to a job upon completion of the training period;

6. the employer and the trainee agree that the latter is not entitled to a wage covering the time spent in training. (Bacon, 2011, pp. 67–96)

If the internship does not satisfy these requirements, the intern is covered by the protection of the Fair Labor Standards Act. When the courts have applied the test to interns, the interpretations have varied. The US courts of appeal are divided as to whether an employer must satisfy all six requirements to avoid having a labour relationship with an intern, or may fail on one or more points if the totality of the circumstances establishes that the intern is not an employee (Bacon, 2011, p. 74). The six-step test has received much criticism in the US academic literature (Braun, 2011; Bennet, 2011). It has been found that many internships cannot satisfy the standard of unpaid internship and are therefore in violation of the law.

There has long been concern as to the legal position of interns under other US statutes. For example, protection from discrimination is provided only for employees. In the notorious case of *O'Connor v. Davis* (1997) a young woman, as part of her college degree in social work, undertook an internship at a hospital for the mentally disabled. She was subjected to a range of inappropriate sexual remarks from one of the psychiatrists. In determining her appeal in relation to discrimination, the Court of Appeals held that remuneration was an essential condition in this case. Because of the absence of any payment, Ms O'Connor was regarded as a volunteer by the court (Stewart and Owens, 2013, p. 238).

In the **United Kingdom** it has been suggested that internship arrangements are not enforceable (employment) contracts because of the absence of the intention to create legal relations, or the non-satisfaction of the requirement of mutuality, or because interns have no obligation to work and are volunteers. Even so, there are two cases where the employment tribunal has ruled that the interns were entitled to statutory rights to wages and holiday pay under the National Minimum Wage Act (Stewart and Owens, 2013, p. 228).

In the 2008 case *Vetta v. London Dreams Motion Pictures*, Ms Vetta had worked as an art director's assistant with the respondent company for several weeks following her application and subsequent interview for the position. The advertisement promised a position that provided an opportunity to show artistic work and make lots of contacts. In addition, it stated that the only remuneration was for expenses. Ms Vetta was paid her first set of expenses, but no other payments were made. The court ruled that she was a worker within the meaning of the term in both the National Minimum Wage Act and the Working Time Regulations. Ms Vetta was not a volunteer, and, given the nature of the work, she was not in a training programme (ibid., pp. 228–229).

In 2011, in *Hudson v. TPG Web Publishing Ltd*, a young intern worked on the Village website for TPG for six weeks. She worked from 10.00 a.m. to 6.00 p.m. every day for several weeks, had responsibility for collecting and scheduling articles, and was put in charge of a team of writers and the recruitment of other interns. There was no written contract of employment, although she had had some discussions about pay. This, along with the nature of the work undertaken, indicated the existence of an employment relationship. Accounts of the case suggest that the judge indicated that, even if a worker was taken on as an intern and agreed to work without payment, they would nonetheless be treated as a worker for the purposes of the minimum wage legislation if they were doing a real job and not being trained (ibid., pp. 229–230).

In **Australia**, work experience can be regarded as constituting employment under contract and falling within the scope of the Fair Work Act and other labour statutes, if the parties intended to create legal relations and if the requirements of mutual consideration and obligation are satisfied. If so, it must then be determined whether the contract concerned is one of employment or a contract for services. In practice, it is highly unlikely that a person seeking to gain work experience on an unpaid basis could be regarded as an independent contractor. The key issue is whether a contract exists at all, or at least some form of bilateral commitment under which the person "works" in return for something (Stewart and Owens, 2013, p. 137).

Court practice on periods of work experience in Australia varies. In some cases, work experience schemes have been found not to involve employment. For example, in *Pacesetter Homes Pty Ltd v. Australian Builders Labourers Federated Union of Workers* (1994) a builder had agreed with a youth organization to give unemployed school leavers a chance to gain work experience. One worker stayed for six months and, having started out mostly observing, was performing productive work by the end of this period. He was paid throughout the period below the standard rate for the job. The court held that there was no contract of employment. It suggested that the fact that the worker was never under any obligation to turn up for work demonstrated the absence of the necessary mutuality of obligation, and that neither party had intended to create legal relations (ibid., p. 140).

There are also cases where work experience schemes have been found to constitute an employment relationship. In *Cossich v. G Rossetto & Co Pty Ltd* (2001) the applicant aimed to attain an associate diploma in wine marketing, in which one subject required her to perform 240 hours of work experience within the wine industry. The applicant worked at a wine cellar for 39 days. This in addition to hours worked earlier at a winery would have satisfied the requirement of her course. However, she continued to work for a further eight months. The respondent's manager paid the applicant 50 Australian dollars per day. The respondent said this money was paid to assist the applicant with travelling expenses, but there was no attempt to estimate those expenses. The applicant received minimal instruction and tuition. The court found that there was an employment relationship in question, basing this conclusion mainly on the lengthy period of the work experience (ibid., pp. 141–142).

In Ontario, **Canada**, the leading case discussing the six conditions of an unpaid internship was *Girex Bancorp Inc* v. *Hsieh & Sip* (2004). Girex was an e-commerce company which had previously hired several employees to develop a software program; these individuals had since departed. Its director decided to make "training opportunities" available to Ms Hsieh and Mr Sip, both of whom were in the final stage of their studies, with the intention of later offering them employment. When the anticipated funding failed to materialize, they were both offered work, but only as independent contractors. They instituted claims for wages during the training period. The Ontario Labour Relations Board held that the claimants had not been promised they would be taken on as employees after training, nor that they would be paid for the training. Nonetheless, Girex was not able to prove four of the six conditions necessary to show that the claimants were persons in training. For example, in the question of the similarity of training to that in a vocational school, the board found that lack of formal instruction, supervision or evaluation meant that the training could not be characterized as "similar to that which is given in vocational school" (Stewart and Owens, 2013, p. 196).

6.4.4. Regulation of traineeships/internships and the labour rights of young people

Because of the heterogeneity of the regulation of traineeships/internships across countries and different types of traineeships/internships, it is difficult to draw any universal conclusions on the labour rights of young people engaged in these schemes. The regulation of traineeships/internships is often unstructured; legislation tends to regulate only some incidental aspects of traineeships/internships, and in some contexts these schemes are completely unregulated.

The reason for this diversity in regulation seems to be the lack of clarity about the concept of a traineeship/internship. In some countries these schemes are regarded as learning; here the emphasis is on the participant obtaining skills and knowledge in the workplace, and therefore the learning part of the traineeship/internship is regulated. In contrast to the treatment of apprenticeships, it is often forgotten that reasonable working conditions for a trainee/intern should also be guaranteed. This is the case, for example, in Estonia and Finland, and under EU regulation. At the same time some States, for example Italy and Spain, see traineeships/internships primarily as a means of obtaining work experience, and hence regulation focuses mainly on working conditions. Both of these approaches seem to guide trainees/interns towards a precarious work track. On the one hand, if only the educational part of the work-based scheme is regulated, trainees/interns may suffer from poor working conditions. On the other, guaranteeing trainees/interns some rights concerning their working conditions (but not the full protection of labour law) without requiring the existence of a learning component turns them into a source of cheap labour. However, some States, for example France, succeed in regulating both components of these schemes, ensuring not only the educational quality of the traineeship/internship, but also reasonable working conditions for trainees/interns.

Another important characteristic of the regulation of traineeships/internships is the exemption of trainees/interns from the scope of labour laws. In contrast to apprentices, trainees/interns are typically explicitly or implicitly regarded as non-employees. This means that their labour rights are not automatically protected; a special regulation of traineeships/internships is needed to protect their labour rights, or else certain labour law protection has to be explicitly broadened to cover these workers. However, specific regulation of traineeships/internships appears to be rare. Also, in common-law countries the working conditions of trainees/interns who cannot be regarded as employees are unregulated.

The exemption of trainees/interns from labour law protection leads on to the even more difficult question of the actual status of these workers under labour law. As trainees/interns usually perform work in subordination to the employer, they fulfil one of the most important characteristics of an employment relationship. Another important condition of the employment relationship is the payment of remuneration. In some cases trainees/interns are also paid. Therefore the conditions of an employment relationship are met. If traineeships/internships are unpaid, the training provided by the employer can constitute a valuable consideration and therefore again the conditions of an employment relationship are fulfilled. The explicit exemption of traineeships/internships from the scope of labour law even though these relationships satisfy the conditions of an employment relationship is therefore questionable.

6.4.5. Traineeships/internships and the school-to-work transition

There is a very limited number of impact evaluation studies in the field of traineeships/internships. Given this, along with the heterogeneity of traineeship/internship schemes, it is difficult to assess their impact on young people's school-to-work transition. The recent guide issued by the Commission (EC, 2013a) suggests that the most effective traineeships in facilitating school-to-work transitions are those undertaken during education and, in some instances, those linked to well-structured ALMPs. The proportion of trainees participating in traineeships connected with academic or vocational study curricula who secured employment ranged between 35 per cent and 87 per cent. The schemes associated with technical and other vocational education showed the highest employment entry rates. Of the ALMP-linked traineeship programmes, the proportion of trainees who secured employment immediately upon completion ranged from 13 per cent to 90 per cent. However, consideration of the positive employment outcomes in the case of ALMP traineeships should take into account the fact that subsidized employment with an employer typically continues after the completion of the scheme on condition that the trainee is retained for a specific period of time.

The EC review of apprenticeship and traineeship schemes brings out the key elements of successful apprenticeship and traineeship arrangements:

- a robust institutional and regulatory framework;
- active social partner involvement;
- strong employer involvement;
- close partnerships between employers and educational institutions;
- funding, including employer subsidies and other incentives;
- close alignment with labour market needs;
- robust quality assurance;
- high-quality guidance, support and mentoring of apprentices/trainees;
- appropriate matching of apprentice/trainee to host organization;
- combination of theoretical, school-based training with practical, work-related experience;
- existence of an apprenticeship/traineeship agreement;
- certification of acquired knowledge, skills and competences;
- flexible approaches that are tailored to the needs of vulnerable young people (EC, 2013a).

Interestingly, the key success factors of apprenticeships and traineeships are the same, which suggests that in order to guarantee the effectiveness of traineeships/internships, they should be organized on a basis similar to that of dual apprenticeship schemes.

On the basis of data from the EU-wide REFLEX survey of graduates, the OECD has estimated that "study-related work experience increases a graduate's likelihood of finding a job immediately upon graduation by 44%, lessens the probability of overqualification by 15%, and reduces the occurrence of skills mismatch by 26%" (EC, 2013a, p. 11).

6.4.6. Traineeships/internships: Stepping stones or dead ends?

There is no clear concept of traineeship/internship, which means that a range of work arrangements can fall into these categories. As traineeships/internships can, on the one hand, be highly structured schemes where learning is combined with work practice and, on the other hand, constitute a form of unpaid and unprotected labour, they can be either stepping stones or dead-end jobs.

Because of the novelty and the heterogeneity of these schemes, it is difficult to find reliable data on the effectiveness of traineeships/internships in the school-to-work transition of young people. However, according to the evidence which does exist, it can be concluded that traineeships/internships do help in the school-to-work transition if they are similar to dual apprenticeship schemes.

The likelihood of traineeships/internships turning into dead-end jobs is reinforced by the explicit or implicit exemption of trainees/interns from the scope of labour laws. Even though in practice trainees/interns perform work similar to employees, they are often not entitled even to minimal labour law protection. In this way these schemes seem to provide a legal channel for firms to employ unprotected workers. It is difficult to see the justification for the unequal treatment of apprentices on one side and trainees/interns on the other. If the main aim of both of these forms is to promote skills and knowledge development in the workplace, and apprentices as well as trainees/interns perform work, then including apprentices under the scope of labour laws and exempting trainees/interns cannot be objectively justified.

6.5. Conclusions and policy recommendations

There is a clear trend in many countries towards the introduction of more flexible working arrangements. This chapter has been concerned in particular with various (broadly) working forms which have been introduced with the aim of facilitating young people's entry into employment and which have in common a (usually) limited duration. In pursuit of a more comprehensive view of the full variety of these arrangements, and because in many countries they involve a large proportion – even the majority – of young labour market entrants, the chapter has considered not just temporary employment contracts per se, but also apprenticeships and other forms of work-based training and/or work experience programmes. The question underlying the evidence presented here is: Do (and, if so, under what conditions) such "arrangements" promote the integration of young people into long-term stable employment?

In order to approach an answer to this question, the chapter has gone into some detail in describing the variety of forms which may be found under the three headings of temporary employment contracts, apprenticeships, and traineeships/internships. Given the heterogeneity of the modalities and definitions, it is hard to draw universal conclusions about the effectiveness of different work arrangements; still, it is possible to identify some characteristics in the regulation of youth work and their influence on young people's labour rights and school-to-work transition. Table 6.2 sets out a broad summary of the implications of the different contractual forms discussed above, with the caveat that it does provide a rather simple overview of the considerably more complex picture emerging from the above discussion.

Terminology

The distinctions between temporary contracts, apprenticeships, and traineeships/internships, and even informal jobs, are both blurred and overlapping. There is no common definition of what constitutes an apprenticeship, let alone what is meant by "traineeship" or "internship", which means that a range of work arrangements can fall into these categories. Moreover, apprenticeships and other forms of work-based training also commonly fall under the definition of temporary employment contracts, if indeed

Table 6.2. Principal contractual forms and their influence on the school-to-work transition

Contractual form		Implications	
		Reduction of labour rights	Effects on school-to-work transition
Temporary employment contracts	Temporary employment contracts	Minor	Mixed
	First job contracts	Minor	Limited
	Subsidized work	None/Minor	Limited
	Permanent job recruitment incentives	None	Slightly positive
Apprenticeships	Dual schemes	Moderate	Substantial
	Non-dual schemes	Substantial	Limited
	Informal apprenticeships	Substantial	Moderate
Traineeships/Internships	Education-based	Substantial	Mixed/positive
	ALMPs	Significant	Moderately positive
	Open market	Substantial	No evidence

the relationship between trainee and firm is defined in law as one of employment. The analysis has shown that *there is a clear need to reduce the ambiguity of terminology in this area, and clearer international guidelines on the usage of such terms would be helpful.*

Temporary employment contracts

Temporary employees are covered by labour law protection, and therefore, as a rule, are guaranteed some basic labour rights. Still, *engaging in temporary work inevitably leads to the reduction of protections afforded to workers.* The mere fact that employment is available or guaranteed only for a limited period of time reduces the quality of the job as compared to permanent employment.

Temporary workers typically receive lower wages and often do not qualify for a range of benefits because of the short-term nature of their work, despite legislation that prescribes the equal treatment of temporary and permanent workers. In some countries, promoting the employment of young people at the expense of their labour rights has been seen as acceptable. *Special temporary contracts for young people which involve a further reduction of their labour rights risk creating or deepening segmentation between adult insiders and young outsiders in the labour market.*

As the promotion of temporary work among young people is often connected with the reduction of their labour rights, it is important that great care is taken not to promote young people's precariousness in the labour market; an alternative focus, such as measures designed to help young people to engage in open-ended contracts, can be effective in reducing youth unemployment as well as promoting the stable employment of young people.

The content of work-based learning

The effectiveness of apprenticeships and traineeships/internships in helping young people's school-to-work transition depends largely on their actual content. Ideal apprenticeship schemes which combine theory and practice, on the one hand, and classroom learning with workplace training, on the other, have been found to be effective. These apprenticeships are also characterized by systematic legal regulation and certification of skills acquired. Also, apprenticeships that combine learning and on-the-job training, but do not constitute the ideal model, have been successful in some countries. Surprisingly, even informal apprenticeships can help in the school-to-work transition, but as it is difficult to determine their actual content, it is difficult to identify the reasons for their success. However, apprenticeships that are called apprenticeships, but do not include a training component, have been found unsuccessful in helping young people's school-to-work transition.

Social partnership

In ideal apprenticeship models, the strong involvement of social partners seems to be a major factor underlying the success of apprenticeships. Moreover, it is not easy to achieve this social partnership involvement by regulation alone; as we have seen here, the willingness of employers to take on apprentices cannot be ensured by simply establishing a legal obligation to participate in these schemes. The provision of subsidies has proved a more effective means to motivate employers to take on apprentices. However, in these cases the quality of apprenticeships needs to be guaranteed in order to avoid the use of apprentices as cheap (subsidized) labour. Subsidized apprenticeships have been found to be very costly.

An alternative and more cost-effective way to engage social partners is through other forms of incentive, e.g. allowing employers to screen potential employees and develop firm-specific skills, as well as establishing a (relatively) low apprentice wage level. The first two incentives imply the need to tailor apprenticeship programmes to the needs of the labour market. A low wage rate for apprentices can be used as an incentive only if this is accompanied with quality training; otherwise apprentices will seek other forms of (quite possibly precarious) work.

Traineeships/internships

The key success factors for traineeships/internships have been found to be similar to those for apprenticeships: that is, in order for a traineeship/internship to be effective in facilitating the school-to-work transition, it should include both work-based and training components. However, as traineeships/internships are rather new forms of young people's work, there are as yet few studies of their impact and effectiveness, and there may well be even more diversity in these schemes than in the case of apprenticeships.

Labour rights

Although neither apprenticeships nor traineeships/internships enjoy an underlying clear and unequivocal conceptual basis, and both arrangements share the same success factors, *the labour rights of apprentices and of trainees/interns differ markedly.* Apprentices are typically covered by labour laws as a special category of employees, whereas trainees/interns almost always fall outside the scope of employment law. Apprentices typically benefit from limited rights compared to regular employees, but the differences can usually be explained by the nature of the apprenticeship as a form of work-based learning.

There is, however, little basis for the exemption of trainees/interns from the scope of labour law. Like apprentices, trainees/interns also perform work in subordination to the employer, even though they (often) do not receive remuneration. The work experience itself, with its presumptive training function, is their main form of remuneration. Therefore, in most countries they could reasonably qualify as employees according to labour law. The explicit or implicit exemption of trainees/interns from the scope of labour law turns them into a group of workers who do not enjoy even the protection of their basic labour rights (for example, health and safety, equal treatment, protection from discrimination, etc.).

Some countries have tried to regulate traineeships/internships outside labour law, but in most cases these work arrangements are treated as learning experiences and therefore only learning quality is guaranteed. Although regulating the learning component of these schemes helps to avoid the use of trainees/interns to perform purely menial tasks, it does not guarantee them reasonable working conditions.

The effect is much the same in common-law countries, which differentiate between trainees/interns and employees on a case-by-case basis, mainly by evaluating the learning component of the arrangement, and do not regulate the working conditions of trainees/interns not regarded as employees. A second group of countries treat traineeships/internships as work experience placements, and guarantee trainees/interns some rights concerning their working conditions (albeit not the full protection of labour law) without requiring the existence of a learning component. In this case one of the success factors of a traineeship/internship is absent, and instead of helping young people to find a permanent job, such schemes run the risk of becoming simply a source of cheap labour.

Stepping stone vs dead end

Compared to both temporary work and apprenticeships, traineeships/internships seem to be the arrangements that are most at risk of pushing young people into persistent precariousness rather than supporting their entry into decent work. In order to avoid this outcome, it would be helpful if countries included trainees/interns within the scope of labour law in a fashion similar to apprentices, or regulated both aspects of traineeships/internships – the learning and the working component – separately and thoroughly.

7. The quality of work: Informal employment in low- and middle-income countries

7.1. Introduction

Informal employment refers to "all employment arrangements that do not provide individuals with legal or social protection through their work, thereby leaving them more exposed to economic risk ...". This definition includes both workers employed in the informal sector and workers in informal employment outside the informal sector (ILO, 2013b). Recent estimates by the ILO show that in a majority of developing countries over half of the workforce are involved in informal employment relationships (ILO, 2013c). As observed in Chapter 1, for young people in these countries informal forms of employment are the predominant experience of work: in developing and emerging economies three out of four young workers experience informal employment as they enter the labour market.

> By the nature of their situation,
>
> informal workers and entrepreneurs are characterized by a high degree of vulnerability. They are not recognized under the law and therefore receive little or no legal or social protection and are unable to enforce contracts or have security of property rights. They are rarely able to organize for effective representation and have little or no voice to make their work recognized and protected. They are excluded from, or have limited access to public infrastructure and benefits. They have to rely as best as they can on informal, often exploitative institutional arrangements, whether for information, markets, credit, training or social security. (ILO, 2002, p. 3)

This chapter describes and analyses the prevalence, determinants and costs of informality, and, considering its findings, discusses potential policy remedies to reduce young people's involvement in informal employment. To this end, the chapter draws on the ILO SWTS covering 34 LMICs, a collection of rich micro-level data sets that offer valuable insights into the dynamics of the formal and informal employment relationships of youth aged 15–29 in LMICs. As noted in Chapter 1, although informal employment is also present, and in some cases fairly extensive, in HICs, it is not the dominant labour market experience of young people as it is in

LMICs.[1] In HICs that role is played more and more by short-term but, in principle, regulated temporary contracts of one kind or another. Thus, the analysis here may be also seen as complementary to that in Chapter 6 on non-standard contractual arrangements.

The remainder of the chapter is structured as follows. Section 7.2 examines the nature of informal employment among young women and men and how this varies across regions. This is followed by an examination of the key determinants of informality in section 7.3, before section 7.4 analyses the economic and social costs of informal employment that are borne by individuals as well as by societies at large.

In June 2015, the 104th Session of the International Labour Conference (ILC) adopted the Transition from the Informal to the Formal Economy Recommendation, 2015 (No. 204), along with an accompanying resolution urging governments to adopt measures to give full effect to the Recommendation. This was followed in November 2015 by an action plan for the implementation of the Recommendation. In the light of this and the preceding discussion, section 7.5 concludes the chapter by examining possible policy remedies to reduce young people's involvement in informal employment.

7.2. Characteristics and prevalence of informal employment

In 2002, the 90th Session of the ILC adopted a landmark resolution regarding decent work and the informal economy. The document broadened the notion of informality, moving beyond the concept of the "informal sector" to the idea of "informal employment" encompassing all "employment that lacks legal or social protection, whether in informal enterprises, formal enterprises or households" (ILO, 2013d). The specific concept of informal employment used in the SWTS – and here – follows the guidelines recommended by the 17th International Conference of Labour Statisticians in 2003, which recognize that formal and informal employment correspond to differing types of status in employment. As noted in the introduction to this chapter, informality is captured by two broad categories: (1) (self-)employment in firms operating exclusively in the informal economy, and (2) informal (self-) employment in firms operating in the formal economy.

Taking both categories together, informal employment is clearly the dominant form of employment for young people throughout developing and

---

[1]   See e.g. Schneider, 2005 – recently updated by Hassan and Schneider, 2016 – for estimates of the size of the informal economy in a large range of countries of differing levels of economic development. Overall, the informal economy in HICs is less than half the size that it represents in LMICs. Given that size here is measured in terms of informal economy output as a percentage of GDP, and that the informal economy is associated with low-productivity economic activity, the divergence in informal *employment* between developing and developed economies is likely to be significantly wider.

Figure 7.1. Prevalence of informal employment in LMICs among young workers (age 15–29)

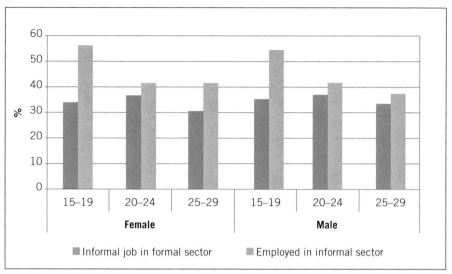

Note: The figure reports the two basic categories of informal employment (and their sum) as a percentage of total (age-specific) youth employment. For details on the SWTS, the countries included and how aggregation was undertaken across the survey to arrive at regional and "global" estimates, see Appendix. The figure excludes data from Samoa, since the breakdown of informal employment into its two major types is not available in this survey.

Source: Author's calculations based on SWTS data.

emerging economies.[2] Figure 7.1 displays the prevalence of informal employment among young workers (age 15–29) in the LMICs covered by the SWTS. In total, about three-quarters (76.8 per cent) of young workers are informally employed. Moreover, employment in the informal economy is slightly more common than informal employment in the formal economy among young people, accounting for 56 per cent of informal employment. Figure 7.1 also shows that informal employment becomes less prevalent with age, primarily as a result of falling rates of employment in the informal economy, while the rate of informal employment in formal firms remains roughly constant across age groups. Overall, the prevalence of informality among young men (76.9 per cent) and young women (76.5 per cent) is very similar. Compared to women, men are slightly more likely to take up informal work in the formal economy.

---

[2]   An important point to bear in mind throughout the discussion is the intrinsic heterogeneity of informal employment. Informality is not defined by the possession of one or more common characteristics, as is the case with, say unemployment, temporary employment or indeed employment as a whole, but rather by the absence of formality. Any form of employment which does not fulfil certain characteristics is by definition informal. Thus, informality is inherently heterogeneous, covering a wide variety of employment forms.

Figure 7.2. Prevalence of informal employment in LMICs among young workers (age 15–29): Regional estimates

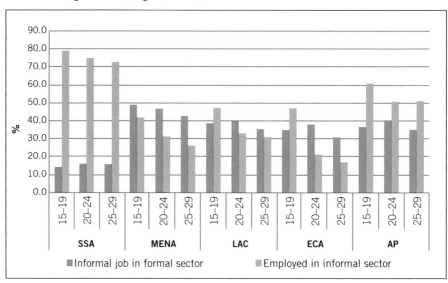

Note: The figure reports the two basic categories of informal employment (and their sum) as a percentage of total (age-specific) youth employment. For details on the SWTS, the countries included and how aggregation was undertaken across the survey to arrive at regional and "global" estimates, see Appendix. The figure excludes data from Samoa, since the breakdown of informal employment into its two major types is not available in this survey.

Source: Author's calculations based on SWTS data.

As noted in the literature (e.g. Shehu and Nilsson, 2014), these "global" aggregates hide much (national and) regional variation.[3] Figure 7.2 plots the prevalence of informal employment by region for the countries included in the SWTS. In sub-Saharan Africa (SSA) and Asia and the Pacific (AP), nine out of ten young workers (90.7 per cent and 90.5 per cent respectively) are informally employed. In Eastern Europe and Central Asia (EECA), informal employment involves "only" around one out of every two young workers (54.3 per cent). In between, the percentages for the Middle East and North Africa (MENA) at 75.4 per cent and Latin America and the Caribbean (LAC) at 72.9 per cent are close to the "global" aggregate. Perhaps even more striking are the variations in the relative weights of the two forms of informality; in the relatively developed regions of EECA, LAC and

---

[3] The figures reported here almost always refer to global or regional aggregates; however, there is also of course significant heterogeneity across countries. The appendix on the SWTS below reports the major statistics on informality and other important indicators used in the book, with details at national level.

Figure 7.3. Prevalence of informal employment by employment status in LMICs among young workers (age 15–29)

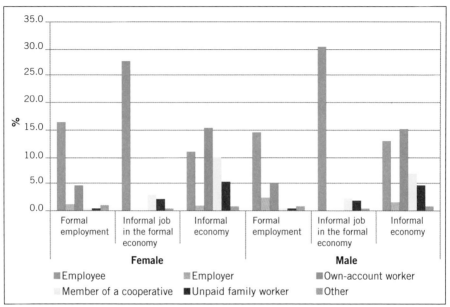

Note: The figure reports the employment status as a percentage of total (formal and informal) employment. For details on the SWTS, the countries included and how aggregation was undertaken across the survey to arrive at regional and "global" estimates, see Appendix. The figure excludes data from Samoa, since the breakdown of informal employment into its two major types is not available in this survey.
Source: Author's calculations based on SWTS data.

MENA, informality predominantly means informal employment in the formal economy. Moreover, the tendency of informal employment to fall with age is much more pronounced in these regions. This, again, is mainly accounted for by the sharp reduction in the prevalence of informal economy employment that occurs with age.

In contrast, informality in SSA is almost entirely (over 80 per cent) accounted for by employment in the informal economy. The AP region lies somewhere between the two extremes, but still with a clear predominance of informal economy employment over informal employment in the formal economy. The tendency for informality to fall with age is also less pronounced in these two regions, particularly in SSA, where the prevalence decreases only modestly from 92.8 per cent among teenagers to 88.6 per cent among 25–29-year-olds. Here too this trend is attributable to the age profile of employment in the informal economy which, in this case, decreases more slowly.

As already observed, informal and formal employment correspond to differing types of status in employment. Following the guidelines recommended by the 17th International Conference of Labour Statisticians, figure 7.3 gives an overview of these different forms for female and male workers.[4] It reveals striking heterogeneities between employment status and informal and formal employment. While working as an employee is the most common form of employment in the formal economy, it accounts for only about a quarter of workers in the informal economy for men and less than a third for women. The overwhelming majority of wage employment – through either a formal employment relationship or informal work – is with firms in the formal economy. Moreover, the figure shows that young people working in cooperatives are almost exclusively informally employed. Once again, gender differences across employment categories appear small.

7.3. What determines informal employment?

Given the prevalence of informal employment among young people in LMICs, it is all the more important to explore who exactly is affected by it and why. That is, what factors, characteristics and attributes of individuals are pushing (or pulling) young people into taking up jobs in the informal sector or informal jobs in the formal sector? This section examines the determinants of informal employment and their relative importance.

We have already seen that the prevalence of informal employment falls with age. At least superficially, this seems to provide some support for the notion that exit from informality is relatively common; or, to put it differently, even if informal employment typically has serious negative effects on socio-economic outcomes (see section 7.4 below), it may be largely a temporary phenomenon for most young people.

A more careful look, however, suggests that this conclusion is not justified. In the first place, as has been pointed out by, among others, Shehu and Nilsson (2014), the SWTS data set confirms that as well as falling with age, the prevalence of informality tends to be concentrated among the least educated in the labour force, and the prevalence of informality (and its form) fall sharply with educational attainment (figure 7.4). Moreover, and importantly, young people with higher levels of education on average enter the labour market later than those with lower levels; thus, informality falling with age *and education* is consistent with the idea that a high proportion of young people entering the labour market relatively early with few educational qualifications gravitate towards the informal sector (and remain there), while those entering later and with higher levels of education are much less likely to enter informality.

---

[4]   Specifically, the calculation includes the following subcategories of workers: (a) paid employees in "informal jobs", i.e. jobs without a social security entitlement, paid annual leave or paid sick leave; (b) paid employees in an unregistered enterprise with fewer than five employees; (c) own-account workers in an unregistered enterprise with fewer than five employees; (d) employers in an unregistered enterprise with fewer than five employees; and (e) contributing family workers. Subcategories (b)–(d) are used in the calculation of "employment in the informal sector", subcategory (a) applies to "informal jobs in the formal sector", and subcategory (e) can fall in either grouping dependent on the registration status of the enterprise that engages the contributing family worker (Elder and Koné, 2014).

Figure 7.4. Prevalence of informal employment by educational attainment (age 15–29)

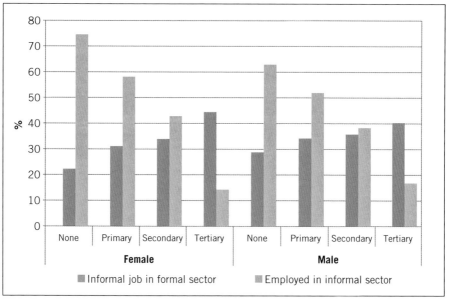

Note: The figure reports the two basic categories of informal employment (and their sum) as a percentage of total youth employment by educational attainment level. For details on the SWTS, the countries included and how aggregation was undertaken across the survey to arrive at regional and "global" estimates, see Appendix. The figure excludes data from Samoa, since the breakdown of informal employment into its two major types is not available in this survey. The figure also includes dotted lines tracking the linear tendency for each series to facilitate the discussion in the text and to clarify the argument concerning the relationship between age and prevalence of informality.

Source: Author's calculations based on SWTS data.

Thus, the inverse relation between age and informality may – in part – be explained by the late entry into the labour force of those (with higher educational qualifications) who are less likely to be engaged in the informal economy, rather than by the tendency of young people to move from informality to formality as they get older. Figure 7.5 plots informal employment rates by (single years of) age, controlling for educational level, and suggests that this scenario is indeed plausible. More precisely, the analysis suggests two significant refinements to the relationship between age, educational attainment and informal employment. First, *conditional on age* the likelihood of being informally employed falls sharply with educational attainment, as also suggested by figure 7.4.

Second, *the higher the level of education, the more informality falls with age.* For those with less than primary education, the rate of informality falls hardly at all with age; for those with just primary education, it falls slightly; while among those who achieve secondary, or even more so tertiary education, the gradient becomes significantly steeper. The implication is that, for those with low levels of education, informality is an almost permanent state, while those entering informal employment once

Figure 7.5. Prevalence of informal employment by single-year age group and educational attainment (age 15–29)

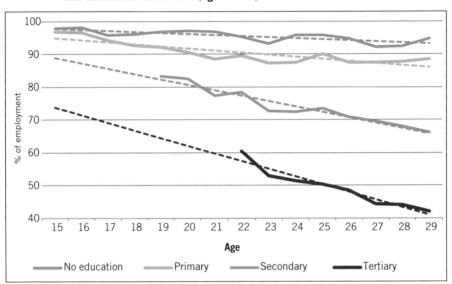

Note: The figure reports informal employment as a percentage of total youth employment by age, distinguishing between different levels of educational attainment. For details on the SWTS and the countries included and how aggregation was undertaken across the survey to arrive at regional and "global" estimates, see the appendix. In this case, given the high degree of disaggregation across age and educational level, we report a three-year unweighted moving average giving the figure that corresponds to the upper limit, so that, for example, the number reported for age 17 is the average for the three years 15, 16 and 17.

Source: Author's calculations based on SWTS data.

they have achieved secondary or tertiary educational qualifications are much more likely to be able to make the transition to formal employment. This is because (a) individuals with at least secondary education show a considerably lower probability of being informally employed when graduating, and (b) chances of finding formal employment improve continuously after graduation.

Thus, the difficulties faced by those who wish to make the transition from informality to formality are greatest at the lower end of the educational scale. This is not particularly surprising, but it does emphasize the need to pay special attention to those most at risk of remaining permanently in informal employment – namely, informally employed young people with low levels of educational attainment.

Besides education, other factors may also be important in explaining why some individuals find themselves persistently in informal employment throughout their youth and, indeed, their entire working lives. In the case of Latin America it has been argued that *initial* poor labour market integration becomes a hard-to-overcome obstacle, and that this is in particular true for less educated youth (ILO, 2015h). Thus: "The first job and its work conditions largely determine the employment and personal paths of young people. A formal, quality first job with good working conditions improves working conditions in subsequent jobs by at least 50%. This advantage intensifies with age" (Dema et al., 2015, p. 39).

To shed more light on the determinants of informality among the young, the chapter now turns to a more general microeconometric model for the SWTS countries. As the above discussion has shown, it is important to examine whether and to what extent an informal first job (relative to a formal first employment) determines future labour market outcomes. Unfortunately, while the SWTS contains retrospective panel information on the employment and educational histories of respondents, it does not contain complete information on the formality or informality of jobs held prior to the current one. It does, however, contain information on past vulnerable employment and, in some countries, whether a job as employee was based on a contract. While vulnerable employment is a concept which is of interest in its own right, it was introduced by the ILO primarily as an easily obtainable proxy indicator for informality.[5] Moreover, whether a job was based on a contract has often been used to distinguish between formal and informal employment.

Cavero and Ruiz (2016) have used information on vulnerable employment for the first job for the case of Peru to understand better the determinants of currently holding a high-quality (i.e. formal) job now (as opposed to an informal one).[6] Although this does not directly confront the issue of persistence in informality, it is strongly indicative. The study found that having a formal first job was an important determinant of whether young people currently held a formal job in Peru. Specifically, the authors found that having had a first job which was formal raised the probability of currently being in formal employment by between 12 and 16 percentage points[7] – a substantial impact.

Turning to results for all SWTS countries, table 7.1 shows the results of an analysis of the determinants of (1) the probability of employment for labour market participants and (2) the probability of being in a formal job for all those in employment.

Taking each model in turn, the key results from estimating the probability of being in employment (column 1) suggest that the likelihood of finding employment increases with education. Perhaps more importantly, obtaining a first job which was vulnerable (as opposed to non-vulnerable, i.e. as an employee or as an employer with employees) increases by around 3 percentage points the probability that an individual will have a job at the time of the survey; however, it also reduces by around 6 percentage points the probability that that job will be formal. Inter alia, this suggests that there is persistence in informal employment, as was found for Peru by Cavero and Ruiz (2016); having had a first job which was vulnerable is likely to lead to informality in the future. Thus, we observe that individuals whose first job was vulnerable are more likely to be in (any form of) employment (as opposed to being NEET) at the time

---

[5]   Vulnerable employment comprises own-account workers plus unpaid family workers – the two largest categories of employment in the informal economy.

[6]   Specifically, a high-quality job *now* is equated with current formal employment. A high-quality *first job* is defined as a first job was which either with a contract or as an own-account worker or unpaid family worker; the latter two categories correspond to vulnerable employment.

[7]   According to whether selection into employment is controlled for or not.

Table 7.1. Determinants of employment, informality and wages

Explanatory variables	Dependent variable	
	(1) Employment/ NEET	(2) Formal/ informal
Secondary education	0.002	0.094***
	(0.005)	(0.006)
Tertiary education	0.066***	0.294***
	(0.006)	(0.011)
Rural	0.025***	−0.051***
	(0.004)	(0.004)
Female	−0.122***	−0.001
	(0.004)	(0.004)
Married	−0.041***	0.007
	(0.004)	(0.005)
Age group 20–24	0.007	0.051***
	(0.006)	(0.009)
Age group 25–29	0.030***	0.070***
	(0.006)	(0.008)
First job was vulnerable	0.031***	−0.064***
	(0.004)	(0.005)
Ln(experience employed)		0.009***
		(0.002)
Country fixed effects	YES	YES
Observations	49,949	37,278
Pseudo R-squared	0.108	0.233

Note: The table reports the marginal effects of two models: (a) a probit model of the probability of being in employment (as opposed to being NEET); (b) a probit model of the probability of being in formal employment (as opposed to being in informal employment). The R-squared is McFadden's pseudo R-squared. For details on the survey and how aggregation was undertaken across survey to arrive at regional and "global" estimates, see Appendix. Standard errors in parentheses. Statistical significance indicated as follows: $^* = p < .10$; $^{**} = p < .05$; $^{***} = p < .01$.

Source: Author's calculations based on SWTS data.

of the survey, but that that job was *much* more likely to be informal. A reasonable interpretation of the positive "effect" of a first vulnerable job on later employment probability is that many young people may not be able to afford the luxury of waiting for a "non-vulnerable" employment opportunity, but rather must accept what they can find more immediately. Unfortunately, accepting such a job entails the risk of condemning the incumbent to long-term informality.

As one would expect, the probability of being in formal employment (column 2) also increases with educational attainment – significantly more so than entry into employment per se – and falls for those living in rural areas. Being female does not, overall, affect informality, as was reflected also in the descriptive statistics reported above.

7.4. Is informal employment a problem and, if so, why?

We have seen that informal employment is a widespread phenomenon among young people today and the "normal" state of employment for most young workers in a majority of developing countries. Moreover, the degree of youth labour market (in)formalization depends largely on the regional and country contexts; also, the chance of finding formal employment varies greatly with an individual's characteristics. Before turning to potential policy options, it is important to ask what informal employment implies. To put the question differently, is informal employment really such a serious problem? What – if any – are the economic and social costs for individuals in informal employment and for societies whose labour markets are characterized by a high level of informality?

At the macroeconomic level, informality is strongly linked to a country's level of development (La Porta and Schleifer, 2008, 2014; McCaig and Pavcnik, 2015). The SWTS confirms that this finding also holds for youth labour markets. Figure 7.6 plots the percentage of informally employed youth in the entire youth workforce against GDP per capita (PPP). Further regression analysis shows that a 10 per cent increase in GDP per capita (PPP) on average is associated with roughly a 1.3 percentage point decrease in youth labour market informality. This might lead one to suppose that the main solution to informality lies in promoting economic growth.

Countries covered, by region, are: Benin, Congo, Liberia, Madagascar, Malawi, Sierra Leone, United Republic of Tanzania, Togo, Uganda, Zambia; Egypt, Jordan, Lebanon, Occupied Palestinian Territory, Tunisia; Brazil, Colombia, Dominican Republic, El Salvador, Jamaica, Peru; Armenia, Kyrgyzstan, the former Yugoslav Republic of Macedonia, Republic of Moldova, Montenegro, Russian Federation, Serbia, Ukraine; Bangladesh, Cambodia, Nepal, Samoa and Viet Nam.

However, informality has become increasingly usual in many developing countries; for example, in Latin America and South-East Asia the share of informal employment has increased between 1980 and 2010 despite strong economic growth (OECD, 2009).[8] Focusing on the 19 countries where two surveys were administered in the SWTS confirms these concerns. Figure 7.7 plots the (percentage-point) change in informality against the percentage change of GDP per capita (PPP) and reveals that there is no statistical relationship between the change in GDP and the change in informality over time.[9] Thus, while we clearly

---

[8] In more recent years this trend has been reversed in Latin America owing to the concerted efforts of governments in the region to formalize employment and economic activity. Indeed, Latin America provides a number of examples of approaches to formalization, also regarding young workers specifically, which will be returned to below.

[9] Note that the difference between figure 7.6 and figure 7.7 is not driven by a sample selection effect; running the regression presented in figure 7.6 for the restricted sample of 19 countries for which two rounds of the sample survey were conducted (and which was used for the regression reported in figure 7.7) produces almost exactly the same estimates – a coefficient of −0.124 with t-ratio of −3.34 ($p = 0.004$) and an R-squared of 0.396.

Figure 7.6. Youth labour market (in)formalization and economic development

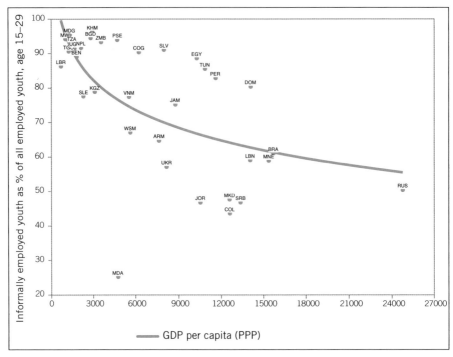

Note: Regressing the prevalence of informality on log GDP (per capita, PPP) produces a coefficient of -0.129, a t-ratio of -4.39 ($p < 0.001$) and an R-squared of 0.376. Countries covered, by region, are: Benin, Liberia, Madagascar, Malawi, Togo, Uganda, Zambia; Egypt, Jordan, Occupied Palestinian Territory; El Salvador, Jamaica; Armenia, the former Yugoslav Republic of Macedonia, Republic of Moldova, Russian Federation, Ukraine; Cambodia, Viet Nam.

Source: Author's calculations based on SWTS data.

observe a correlation between informality and the level of economic development *across* countries, this association seems to be much less clear-cut *within* any given country. This also provides macroeconomic-level confirmation for the point made above based on the microeconometric estimates: informality clearly depends on more than just a country's level of per capita income.

A sustainable employment and economic growth strategy can be an important element in confronting informality; however, waiting for growth to reduce informal employment is evidently not an advisable strategy. Indeed, at least in the short and medium term, economic development can also create and contribute to new forms of informal employment (Kucera and Roncolato, 2008). For example, strong rural–urban migration may leave local urban labour markets with an excess of labour supply, pushing young migrants into informal employment, while at the same time weakening traditional social protection mechanisms through families and communities.

Figure 7.7. Youth labour market (in)formalization and economic development: Changes over time

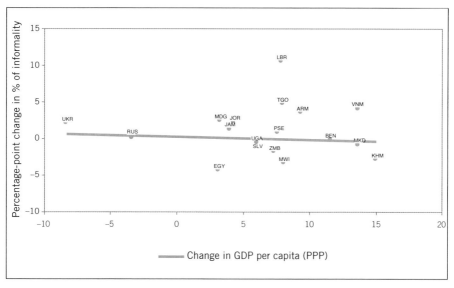

Note: As may be observed from the figure, there is practically no relationship between the percentage-point change in informality and economic growth. Regressing one on the other does produce a slightly negative slope; however, the (adjusted) *R*-squared is less than 0.001 and the coefficient on economic growth has a *t*-ratio of 0.05 (*p* = 0.964), indicating a complete absence of statistical significance. For countries covered, see note to figure 7.6 above.
Source: Author's calculations based on SWTS data.

Moreover, informality itself also impedes development. In many countries, the informal sector is populated by small, unproductive firms which are largely disconnected from the formal economy and exhibit little growth potential. These labour-intensive firms are mostly run by poorly educated micro-entrepreneurs and have little potential for integration into the formal sector (Elbadawi and Loayza, 2008; Gatti et al., 2011; La Porta and Schleifer, 2008, 2014). Furthermore, for a given level of public spending, a higher share of informal employment implies an increasing tax burden on the formal sector, which might hold back new and productive (formal) firms that – in contrast to their counterparts in the informal economy – may have the potential for driving growth. Furthermore, while informal workers and firms use and congest public infrastructure, they do not contribute to the tax revenues needed to maintain and renew it (Gatti et al., 2011). Thus, it is not surprising that informality puts a brake on growth.

However, informal employment is not only related to the level of economic development and a country's growth capabilities. The same factors cited above which link informality and growth are also largely responsible for the clear association that also exists between the size of the informal economy and income inequality (Perry et al., 2007; Loayza et al., 2009).

Table 7.2. Gini coefficient of earnings inequality, formal and informal economy workers

	Formal workers	Informal workers
Global	0.25	0.36
SSA	0.37	0.58
MENA	0.23	0.33
LAC	0.26	0.32
EECA	0.26	0.30
AP	0.21	0.27

Source: Author's calculations based on SWTS data.

Analysis of the SWTS data confirms this general finding also for young people. Table 7.2 displays Gini coefficients – a standard measure of inequality – based on wage data for young people in both formal and informal employment globally and by world region. For LMICs as a whole, but also for each of the regions (and indeed, although this is not reported here, for all but one of the countries in the SWTS database[10]), inequality is higher in the informal than in the formal economy. Again, this does not come as a huge surprise, yet it is an important confirmation; inter alia, it is also consistent with the narrowing of the gap between formal and informal wages as GDP per capita increases, discussed further below. Moreover, the gap in income equality between formal and informal workers, at 21 percentage points, is largest in SSA. It is also very substantial in MENA (10 percentage points) and rather less so in AP, LAC and above all EECA (4 percentage points).

Informal employment also imposes direct costs on the participants, and it is the purpose of the remainder of this section to look at the consequences of informality from the (micro-)perspective of the young people who are engaged in it. An important point already made, to which we will return below, is the extremely heterogeneous nature of informality; similarly, the costs of informality – for individuals and countries – also vary widely according to its form and location.

By definition, informally employed workers lack access to social security and work-related rights (Elbadawi and Loayza, 2008). Thus, for example, because of the lack of employment protection they are more vulnerable to increases in turn-over and to higher separation rates (Shapiro, 2013). Seeking to extend such rights – for example, the provision of social protection to workers who remain in the informal economy – can, however, have unintended negative consequences. Evidence from Argentina suggests that offering child allowances only to unregistered workers results in a large disincentive of these workers to formalize (Garganta and

---

[10] The exception is Armenia, where the Gini coefficient is 0.274 for informal workers and 0.276 for formal workers. A higher Gini coefficient indicates greater inequality.

Gasparini, 2015). More generally, informal employment means lower-quality employment. Shehu and Nilsson (2014) also find that both underemployment and skills mismatch are more prevalent among young workers in the informal economy than among their counterparts in formal employment.

Furthermore, data from the LMICs included in the survey confirm that informal jobs are clearly less desirable from young people's perspectives. Job satisfaction is lower among informal workers, and a much larger proportion of those in informal employment would like to change their jobs, compared to those in formal employment: across all young people, around half of those who were informally employed wished to change their jobs (54 per cent of those employed in the informal sector and 49 per cent of those informally employed in formal firms), while under one-third (31 per cent) of those in formal employment wished to do so.

Informal employment typically also implies a substantial wage penalty. This has been documented in several countries. Shehu and Nilsson (2014) analysed survey data from the first round of the SWTS in 20 developing countries and found informality to be associated with lower pay for both young wage earners and the young self-employed. This is in line with the findings of Daza Báez and Gamboa (2013), who, employing a non-parametric decomposition method suggested by Ñopo (2008), found substantial earning differences between formal and informal workers in Colombia.[11]

Perhaps of equal importance is the fact that the penalty varies substantially across different characteristics of individuals and jobs; not all informal employment is equally bad for incomes. Shehu and Nilsson (2014) found that while the exact earnings gap depends on the specific country context, in general it tends to decrease with earnings, to the extent that at high levels of income informal workers sometimes earn more than formal workers. This is confirmed also by Nordman et al. (2016), who examined informal earnings penalties in Madagascar, distinguishing between informal wage earners and the self-employed. While the study found a huge wage gap at the bottom of the earning distribution, this narrowed sharply towards the upper levels of the distribution, eventually being reversed. Moreover, the gap was particularly large for wage workers and much less so – or even reversed – for informal self-employed workers.

Table 7.3 presents results from a "Ñopo" decomposition analysis (analogous to the analysis of Daza Báez and Gamboa (2013) using the SWTS.[12] The analysis allows an examination of the informal/formal (or informality) wage gap, controlling for differences in background factors – namely, level of education, gender, rural/urban location, age and country, as well as year of survey – which are clearly associated with both wages and participation in informal employment itself. Above all, the approach is non-parametric and overcomes the need to make

---

[11] Controlling for individual characteristics including education, and using household-level data for the period 2008–12.

[12] In order to allow comparison across countries here and below, a simple normalization – to the male formal wage – was applied.

Table 7.3. Decomposition of the informal/formal wage gap, young people (age 15–29)

Variables	All	SSA	MENA	LAC	ECA	AP
Total gap (as % of average male formal wages)	30.6	70.1	28.9	40.2	–1.4	30.1
Unexplained gap (as % of average male formal wages)	20.7	36.8	21.6	31.5	–2.4	22.1
Unexplained gap (as % of total gap)	67.5	52.5	74.8	78.2	100	73.5

Note: The unexplained gap is always statistically significant at $p < 0.01$. For the reasons noted above and in the Appendix, these estimates do not include data from Samoa.
Source: Author's calculations based on SWTS data.

additional assumptions for situations – such as with informality – in which there is a lack of common support; that is, where the two groups under examination differ markedly in the aforesaid characteristics.[13]

The results of the decomposition are revealing. As a whole, the wage gap is significant, comprising over 30 per cent of male average wages. Taking background factors into account, around two-thirds of this difference remains, leaving the global unexplained informality wage gap at 20.7 per cent. Again, this hides enormous regional differences: the gap is largest in SSA, where informality is most prevalent and the wage gap corresponds to 70.1 per cent of formal workers' wages. At the other extreme, in EECA, where informality accounts for "only" around half of employed young people, the informal/formal wage gap is even slightly negative. However, leaving aside EECA, in AP, where the rate of informality is similar to SSA, the wage gap is rather modest, equivalent to only 30 per cent of the male formal worker's average wage, although three-quarters of this cannot be explained by education or location. Thus, although broadly consistent with the notion that the wage gap narrows with the prevalence of informality, there are clearly other factors at work.

Across all regions, however, the proportion of the wage gap which cannot be explained by education and location through a "Ñopo" decomposition remains relatively stable at between around two-thirds and three-quarters of the gap.

These findings are confirmed through an alternative parametric analysis where the natural logarithm of the wage is regressed on several explanatory variables as well as a dummy for informal employment. Column (1) of table 7.4 reports estimates of a global unconditional formal/informal wage gap of around 26 per cent – roughly

---

[13] For more details on the methodology, the interested reader is directed to the Ñopo (2008) paper referred to in the text. O'Higgins (2015) also applies this methodology for decomposing the Roma/non-Roma wage gap in south-eastern Europe. As well as providing a simple, but more exhaustive, explanation of the methodology, the latter paper also offers an example of this approach being used to deal explicitly with a situation in which level of education – a key determinant of earnings – is taken into account.

Table 7.4. Regression analysis of the informal/formal wage gap, LMICs, young people (age 15–29)

Explanatory variables	Dependent variable: log wages		
	(1)	(2)	(3)
Informal job	−0.257***	−0.184***	−0.237***
	(0.009)	(0.008)	(0.017)
Secondary education		0.163***	0.084***
		(0.011)	(0.016)
Tertiary education		0.349***	0.188***
		(0.014)	(0.020)
Secondary*informal			0.065**
			(0.020)
Tertiary*informal			0.139***
			(0.029)
Secondary*informal* female			0.135***
			(0.045)
Tertiary*informal*female			0.164***
			(0.053)
Rural		−0.056***	−0.057***
		(0.009)	(0.009)
Female		−0.243***	−0.163***
		(0.009)	(0.035)
Female*informal			−0.191***
			(0.040)
Female*secondary			−0.038
			(0.038)
Female*tertiary			0.041
			(0.040)
Married		0.027***	0.026***
		(0.010)	(0.010)
Age group 20–24		0.120***	0.114***
		(0.014)	(0.015)
Age group 25–29		0.207***	0.204***
		(0.015)	(0.015)
Ln(employment experience)		0.025***	0.025***
		(0.003)	(0.003)
First job was vulnerable		−0.002	−0.002
		(0.015)	(0.015)
Country fixed effects	YES	YES	YES
Observations	22,629	22,629	22,629
Adj. R-squared	0.213	0.276	0.280

Note: The table reports the results of estimating OLS regressions of the determinants of the (natural logarithm of) hourly wages estimated for 33 LMICs in the SWTS (excluding Samoa as before). For details on the survey and how aggregation was undertaken across the survey to arrive at regional and "global" estimates, see Appendix. Standard errors in parentheses. Statistical significance indicated as follows: * = p <.10; ** = p < .05; *** = p < .01.

Source: Author's calculations based on SWTS data.

in line with the 31 per cent reported in table 7.3.[14] Adding individual background characteristics in column (2) narrows the gap to around 18 per cent.[15]

We may also observe that, in contrast to its detrimental effect on the chances of finding a formal job, having had a first vulnerable job does not bring with it a further wage disadvantage – beyond that attaching to the informal nature of the job itself. Thus, while a vulnerable first job significantly increases the chances of informal (rather than formal) employment (see table 7.1 above), it does not imply an additional wage penalty. In other words, the result in column (2) suggests that the wage gap between two individuals with the same background characteristics, one in formal employment and one in informal employment, is proportionate at around 18 per cent and does not seem to be particularly sensitive with regard to previous informal employment spells (approximated by vulnerability).

Moreover, returns to education appear to be quite strong even among the relatively young people in the sample: having a secondary education raises earnings by around 16 per cent on average – compared to primary or less than primary education – while obtaining a tertiary degree increases wages by around 35 per cent, a further 19 percentage points compared to secondary education. This relatively pronounced increase is plausibly due to the relatively short time tertiary graduates in the sample will have had to realize their greater earnings potential compared to those with only secondary and primary attainment. The regression also reflects the wage penalties associated with living in a rural area (6 per cent) and the wage gap between males and females (around 24 per cent overall).

Finally, the specification in column (3) of table 7.4 includes interaction effects of informality with gender and with education, as well as higher-order interaction terms with informality, education and gender. The results illustrate that the wage gap falls with education and is larger for young women. To understand better the specific implications for wages of these estimates, figure 7.8 plots the average wages by education, gender and employment status (formal/informal) implied by this model. The figure fixes the average formal wage for men with primary or less education at 100.

At least two important findings emerge. First, the informality wage gap narrows as educational attainment rises – an effect that is more pronounced for women than for men. This suggests that the disadvantages faced by more educated informal workers are less severe. This might be because formal and informal jobs become more similar in nature when requiring higher levels of education. Importantly, for young women with primary or less education the informality wage penalty is considerably more severe (around 35 per cent) than for their male colleagues with the same educational background (21 per cent).

---

[14]   While the specification in column (1) does not include any individual background characteristics (such as gender, age, level of education), it includes a full set of country dummies.

[15]   As the dependent variable in our models is log wages, we can interpret coefficients close to zero roughly as percentage-point changes. For all coefficients that (in absolute value) exceed 0.1 we calculate exact effects: percentage change = $100 \cdot (\exp(\text{coefficient})) - 1$.

Figure 7.8. Estimated formal and informal wages by education and gender

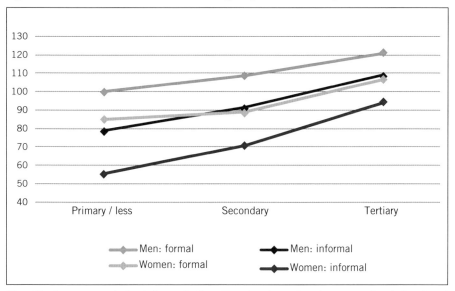

Note: The figure reports the level of wages by formality, education and gender compared to the benchmark (= 100) of formally employed primary-educated men.

Source: Author's calculations based on estimates reported in table 7.4, column (3).

While the wage gap narrows for both genders with rising educational attainment, this catching-up process is stronger for young women. Informally employed women with tertiary education earn on average 12 per cent less than those who are in formal employment, compared to a 10 per cent wage penalty for men with a university degree. This finding would certainly bear further investigation, for example to look at how this varies across countries and regions. This would go beyond the scope of the present analysis; however, the point serves to emphasize the importance of the protections provided by formal employment to young workers.

Second, gender wage differentials also decline as educational attainment rises, but only for young people in informal employment. For formally employed young women and men, the gender pay gap does not vary systematically by level of educational attainment: it is 15 per cent for those with primary or less education, 20 per cent for those with secondary education and 14 per cent for those with tertiary education. By contrast, for informally employed workers, the wage difference between women and men decreases markedly from 24 per cent for young women with primary or less education to 15 per cent for those with a university degree. Evidently, it is easier to discriminate against young women when they are informally employed and hence have no recourse to formal legal protection. At the same time, it is encouraging to see that gender differences in terms of pay – while remaining substantial – are almost halved as educational attainment increases.

181

To summarize, this analysis adds three important findings on informality:

1. More highly educated young people in informal employment not only find it easier than the less educated to exit informality, as shown in figure 7.5, but are also subject to a much smaller wage penalty while they are informally employed, further emphasizing the heterogeneity of informal forms of employment.

2. Although young women have, on average, around the same chances as young men of finding themselves in informal employment, those who do face a much more severe gender-based wage penalty than do formally employed young women. Thus, the greater cost of informality to young women manifests itself in terms of a more substantial informal wage penalty rather than a greater incidence of informality per se.

3. Both the informality and gender-based wage penalties experienced by young women fall with education level – in other words, the labour market disadvantage arising with informality is greatest for young women with low levels of education.[16]

Taken together, results from the "Ñopo" decomposition and the regression analysis come to very similar conclusions, which strengthens the confidence in these findings. Inter alia, it is rather implausible to suggest that such a large, unexplained gap is consistent with young people "choosing" informality over formality.

7.5. Conclusions and policy recommendations

Approaches to formalization

Williams and Lansky (2013) describe an "international consensus" on promoting formalization that includes "shifting formal workers into formal jobs, ... registering and taxing formalized enterprises, providing informal workers and operators with benefits such as access to legal and social protection as well as support services (e.g. skills or business training), and enabling them to be represented in relevant rule-setting, policy-making and collective bargaining processes" (p. 368).

To categorize formalization policies, the framework developed by Williams and Lansky (2013), distinguishing between a "hard" and a "soft" approach, proves helpful. The "hard" approach, which can also be described as "sticks and carrots", aims at (implicit) cost–benefit calculations of economic agents that underpin choices

---

[16] One might be tempted to add that this implies that the largest return to education accrues to young informally employed women; however, it should also be remembered that both participation in informality and wage rates are endogenously determined. A more sophisticated simultaneous, or at least recursive, model taking into account these interactions – and in particular movements between informal and formal employment – would be needed to establish causality before a statement of this sort could justifiably be made. Moreover, this is not really the point here; rather, the issue is which groups suffer most from informality.

and dynamics leading to (in)formal employment relationships. Through deterrence measures (costs) and economic and social incentives (benefits), employers and employees are encouraged to formalize jobs in the informal economy and to create new formal jobs.

By contrast, the "soft" approach relies on the idea of fostering a culture of commitment, including raising awareness about the advantages of holding a formal job and running a formal enterprise. In addition, economic and social development – for example, through policies that promote quality employment, entrepreneurship support and enhanced levels of social protection – contributes to formalization processes.

Most policies for promoting formalization processes are not mutually exclusive but can coexist, be combined with each other or be implemented sequentially. "Country experiences globally confirm that there is no universal policy framework but rather a very diverse array of possible responses that can be combined into integrated policy frameworks and adapted to each specific country context" (Williams and Lansky, 2013, p. 371). This is precisely the idea emerging from the examination of informality contained here, with the emphasis on its diversity across countries and regions.

The resolution concerning decent work and the informal economy, adopted in 2002 by the ILC, provided an overarching framework for the ILO's work regarding the informal economy. It proposed a comprehensive tripartite platform for action, and acknowledged the diversity of informal work and the many possible ways of shrinking the relative size of the informal economy in a process of gradual formalization involving multiple policy areas. The resolution supported an integrated general approach to the informal economy organized around three principles: (i) a systematic approach by all ILO programmes to deepen their understanding and work with respect to the challenges of informal employment; (ii) an integrated and coherent perspective to analyse and support the transition to formality across the four decent work objectives (employment, social dialogue, social protection, labour rights); and (iii) responsiveness to the diversity of local demands.

In 2013 the ILO published an integrated and comprehensive policy resource guide on the informal economy and decent work (ILO, 2013d), and in 2015 the adoption by the ILC of Recommendation No. 204 on the transition from the informal to the formal economy provided additional impetus to efforts to combat informality. The strategy proposed is based on three areas of intervention: (i) facilitating the *transition* of workers and economic units from the informal to the formal economy; (ii) promoting the *creation of enterprises and decent jobs* in the formal economy; and (iii) *preventing the informalization of formal jobs*. It strongly advocates measures to reduce informal employment rates among youth, for example by promoting the implementation of an integrated employment policy framework that includes a focus on activation measures to facilitate the school-to-work transition, such as youth guarantees, and by pressing for the formalization of micro and small economic enterprises through entrepreneurship training, skills development and, importantly, improved access to social security coverage.

The analysis undertaken in this chapter underlines the need for immediate measures in all these policy areas, but it also draws attention to the importance of implementing formalization policies specifically targeting young people. The remainder of this section recapitulates the central findings of the foregoing analysis, derives relevant policy implications, and sketches some policy proposals for two important approaches to formalization – innovative training-based programmes and increased social protection coverage.

The central conclusions and related policy implications are as follows:

For young workers in developing countries today, informal employment is the norm rather than the exception. Informality not only implies a lack of social protection and a deficit of basic work-related rights but, as the analysis presented above has documented, is associated with lower job satisfaction and – more tangibly – a substantial wage penalty. This all points to the conclusion that for a majority of young people *informal employment is not a choice but at best an inferior outcome with few – if any – alternatives.* The analysis of this chapter also underlines *the importance of policies that effectively combat informality and promote formalization.*

The analysis above has also firmly established the inadvisability of a "promote growth and wait" approach to the formalization of employment. Apart from the immense social and economic costs that come with high shares of informal employment right now, *it remains unclear how long a "growth-only" formalization strategy would take to have any effect, given the substantial number of countries that did not see a notable decline in informal employment rates despite solid GDP growth. Moreover, informality also impedes economic growth, putting some countries at risk of getting stuck in a low-growth, high-informality spiral.* Furthermore, growth that triggers substantial rural–urban migration that outpaces formal sector development might itself be responsible for rising or persistent levels of informal employment (Williams and Lansky, 2013; Kucera and Roncolato, 2008). In brief, *promoting growth alone is insufficient to combat high levels of informality.*

There is a clear need for tailored, country- and context-specific policy solutions which typically involve a range of complementary actions adopted simultaneously or in a sequence as circumstances demand. *Approaches towards encouraging formality should be carefully adapted to different national realities.* For example, a country with a high share of informally employed workers in the formal economy might want to consider reforming hiring incentives for formal firms. In other contexts, focusing on the supply side and promoting training and formal education might be more appropriate. Generally, policies should aim to simultaneously reduce informal employment and improve the quality of formal employment (Kucera and Roncolato, 2008).

Furthermore, the analysis in this chapter suggests that, while informality per se is a cause for concern, it is of most concern for those with low levels of education, in particular for women. In addition to being more common among less-educated young people, it is particularly hard for this group to move out of informal relationships as they grow older. In addition, having had a first "vulnerable" job significantly increases the probability of further informal employment. Taken together, these observations favour *championing approaches which focus on young people at the bottom end of the educational spectrum, including solutions that specifically target young women. Priority should be given to interventions that aim at preventing entry into informality,* rather than relying exclusively on measures which promote the formalization of employment of those operating in the informal economy.

The foregoing analysis also supports the notion that policies to reduce informality levels should pay special attention to the promotion of rural development to reduce rural poverty and, in so doing, also slow down rural–urban migration (Kucera and Roncolato, 2008). This is particularly relevant for youth inasmuch as it is primarily the young who take the decision to migrate and hence drive rural–urban migration patterns.

Formalization through training

A number of innovative approaches have been suggested that specifically address youth needs and demands when it comes to formalizing informal employment relationships. For example:

First job first: This is specifically linked to the idea that improving access to a *formal first job* is key to reducing informality, in line with the findings outlined above. For example, "first job" programmes, policies and laws have recently become popular in Latin American countries and elsewhere, aiming to influence work trajectories by improving young people's first experiences in the labour market (Dema et al., 2015; ILO, 2015h). These programmes promote learning processes through quality apprenticeships, traineeships and internships, as well as hiring subsidies and special youth employment arrangements. These mechanisms seek to compensate young people for the disadvantages they face in terms of work experience and limited productivity when they enter the labour market. To avoid replacing long-term workers by "subsidized youth", some of these programmes restrict eligibility by imposing conditions on employers concerning the hiring of regular staff (ILO, 2015h). Specific examples of this type of programme include the Entrenamientos para el trabajo (Job Training) programme in Argentina, Bécate in Mexico, Yo estudio y trabajo (I study and work) in Uruguay and "Quality of informal apprenticeships" in Zimbabwe.

Training for transition: "Formalization strategies have been addressing informality from a productivity perspective", including the provision of coaching and mentoring programmes for (micro)enterprises that choose to formalize (ILO, 2015h, p. 19). The focus here is primarily on promoting formalization processes for micro-entrepreneurs and self-employed workers. Programmes already in place include Microempreendedor individual (since 2008) and Simples Nacional (since 2000) in Brazil, "Enterprise formalization" in Nepal, "Recognizing informal apprenticeships" in the United Republic of Tanzania and "Empowerment of the rural economy" in Zimbabwe.

Linking formalization to increased social protection coverage

To strengthen social protection floors as well as encourage formalization, some countries have chosen to simplify registration processes and lower social security contributions for micro-entrepreneurs and self-employed workers (ILO, 2015h). For example, Costanzi et al. (2013) focus on a policy in Brazil that offers micro-entrepreneurs and self-employed workers below a certain income level simplified administrative procedures (including online registration), benefits (e.g. loans) and much reduced social security contributions. The authors estimate that through this programme, millions of micro-entrepreneurs and self-employed are now covered by social security, with one-third of beneficiaries being below the age of 30.

Although some interventions have been evaluated, there remains a need to gather more information and evidence on the effectiveness of different policy approaches in different contexts.

8. Towards more effective youth employment policies and programmes

This book has considered the effects of different economic contexts, institutions, policies and programmes on the quality and quantity of employment available to young people. While the discussion and analysis has not sought to be comprehensive, it has treated – sometimes in an unusual way – aspects of all the major policy areas affecting the integration of young people into the world of work. In this regard, it takes as its reference point the five pillars of the ILO's call for action on the youth employment crisis, discussed in the introduction. The various reviews and analyses which the book encompasses have produced numerous specific policy recommendations; it will be useful at this point briefly to draw together some of the main findings and their implications for youth employment policy as a whole, and to consider some of the actual and potential interactions between policy areas. This final chapter also offers an opportunity to suggest some directions for future research, to point out what we still need to know – or to know better.

8.1. Main findings

8.1.1. Fiscal and sectoral policies

Chapter 2 emphasized the potential for macroeconomic and sectoral policies to address problems faced by young people entering the labour market. In particular:

The analyses reported in the chapter presented clear evidence of a beneficial role – under certain conditions – for expansionary fiscal policy. Discretionary fiscal policy is a useful policy tool to promote youth employment during lows in the economic cycle, that is, during recessions. To be effective, however, it also requires that government finances be in relatively good shape. Inter alia, this implies that, once recession sets in, a fiscal expansion should be implemented immediately, before the recession itself leads to a significant worsening of the budget balance.

Fiscal policy was shown to be even more effective – albeit marginally – as a tool to counteract youth unemployment than it is in ameliorating prime-age adult joblessness.

However, discretionary fiscal policy is not a cure-all. It is a remedial measure to be adopted during periods of recession; although it can promote youth employment during periods of expansion as well, the effects are relatively modest – and, if the government's finances are not in order, can even be deleterious for youth employment.

Regarding sectoral policies to promote youth employment, while *there is much evidence to support the idea that sectoral strategies can effectively support the expansion of youth employment*, there is no single "sectoral" path to decent work for young people.

Rather, there are many possible sector-specific strategies for promoting youth employment, with correspondingly specific costs and benefits. For example, a focus on lower-productivity sectors, and above all on the development of the agricultural sector, can be an effective sector-specific strategy for promoting youth employment, particularly in MICs; however, a focus on low-productivity sectors brings with it the risk of encouraging low-wage, low-quality employment growth.

8.1.2. Minimum wages and other labour market institutions

Chapter 3 looked at the youth employment effects of minimum wage legislation using a meta-analytic approach. Through the analysis of a large number of both recent and less recent estimates of the effects of changes in minimum wages on youth employment, the chapter drew the following main conclusions:

First, it reaffirmed previous findings that the youth employment effects of minimum wages are, in the vast majority of cases, zero or slightly negative, and that they tend to become larger (more negative) as the minimum wage approaches the average wage.

The chapter also added to previous work in identifying EPL and, to some extent, collective bargaining arrangements as important complementary institutions which affect the impact of the minimum wage on youth employment. In particular, the results of the analysis reported in the chapter show that *minimum wages and EPL are mutually supportive institutions*, and that the negative impact on youth employment of the introduction or raising of minimum wages will be less in the presence of strong EPL. EPL and minimum wage legislation can therefore be used as complementary labour market measures to improve the quality of work for young people.

More generally, the development of minimum wage legislation needs to take account of the existence and functioning of other labour market institutions in the country.

8.1.3. Wage subsidies and other active labour market policies

Chapter 4 went on to look at ALMPs and, in particular, to examine in detail the factors influencing the effectiveness of wage subsidy programmes, broadly defined. Wage subsidies can have a significant impact on the employment and employability of young people; however, numerous factors must be borne in mind in the design and implementation of such programmes if they are to be effective. The following important issues were identified:

It is crucial to include appropriate *targeting and conditionalities* in the programme design; these can improve the efficiency of programmes by, inter alia, *reducing deadweight and substitution costs.*

In order to promote the longer-term employment prospects of young people beyond the duration of the programme itself, such interventions need to involve an increase in participants' longer-term employability. This is usually achieved through the informal acquisition of job-related skills in effective on-the-job learning or via an explicit training component incorporated into the programme design. To this end, programmes need to be of sufficient duration to allow participants to develop job-related competences and to "prove themselves" in the specific work environment.

As elsewhere in this book, here too the importance of taking into account possible interactions between wage subsidy programmes, the economic context and other labour market institutions was emphasized. For example, subsidized employment interventions may be particularly useful when the overall demand for young workers is low, as for example during times of recession. Complementarities and interactions with other labour market institutions are also important, and wage subsidy programmes should take into account their presence and likely impact. To mention just two such possible interactions: first, the presence, regulation, conditionality and generosity of passive labour market policies may well affect the willingness of young people to participate in wage subsidy programmes, particularly if those programmes are aimed at encouraging low-wage employment; and second, the regulation of wage subsidies should avoid possible conflict with minimum wage legislation.

8.1.4. Self-employment and entrepreneurship

Chapter 5 considered self-employment among young people and the effectiveness of entrepreneurship programmes.

The descriptive analysis, based on data from the ILO's SWTS, focused on LMICs and found that, while recourse to self-employment is often a coping mechanism for individuals and families lacking alternative opportunities, it is by no means a universally negative option. Indeed, the picture emerging from an analysis of the evidence is more nuanced, with a great deal of heterogeneity among the self-employed in terms of job quality and satisfaction. Self-employment can be an extremely positive experience, particularly for the more highly educated and those with family experience in it.

Similarly, the evaluation evidence on the effectiveness of programmes to promote entrepreneurship among young people is mixed; the recent meta-analysis (Kluve et al., 2016a) discussed in the chapter suggests that *on average* entrepreneurship programmes produce the most favourable labour market outcomes for young people of all types of ALMP, but that such programmes also demonstrate the *greatest variability in outcomes.*

Given the substantial heterogeneity both in the observable quality of self-employment and in the labour market outcomes attributable to entrepreneurship programmes, an important message emerging from both parts of the chapter is the need for *a focus on the promotion of quality self-employment and entrepreneurship.*

This in turn requires that we expand our knowledge base on the effectiveness of specific programmes.[1] It is clear that entrepreneurship programmes cannot on their own solve the challenge of promoting decent work for young people; nevertheless, they can constitute a useful complement to other, more general, ALMPs.

8.1.5. Contractual arrangements

Recent years have seen a proliferation of different "non-standard" contractual forms used with the express intention of facilitating young people's entry into work. Chapter 6 examined, in particular, different forms of time-limited contracts, both with and without explicit training components. A number of issues promoting or impeding the effectiveness of such arrangements as a bridge to stable employment for young people were discussed. Clearly there is a major issue of definition and terminology: indeed, one of the main problems is the large variety of con-tractual (and non-contractual) arrangements going under a variety of names. In particular, as things stand, arrangements called traineeships or internships are particularly vulnerable to misuse. Two lines of action stand out as requiring fairly urgent attention:

Identification of the key elements of what constitutes quality traineeships/in-ternships. Chapter 6 made progress in this direction; however, more work is needed to collate and evaluate the evidence.

Implementation of appropriate regulatory frameworks in this under-regulated area. In particular, there is little basis for the exclusion of trainees/interns from the scope of labour law.

8.1.6. Informal employment

If temporary contractual forms are rapidly becoming the typical vehicle for entry into employment for young people in HICs, informal employment forms dom-inate the experiences of their peers in LMICs. Chapter 7 discussed and analysed the determinants and consequences of informal employment among young people. It also went on to discuss possible approaches to formalization of employment. Some of the major findings were as follows:

For young workers in developing countries today, informal employment is the norm rather than the exception. Informality implies a lack of social protection and a deficit of basic work-related rights, as well as being associated with lower job satisfaction and a substantial wage penalty.

There is a great deal of heterogeneity among informality. The "worst" forms, where the wage penalty is largest and the possibilities for escaping to formal employ-ment are lowest, are found among the least-educated young people.

---

[1] This is an area in which the ILO's Youth Employment Programme has been particularly active in recent years. In addition to the meta-analysis of Kluve et al. (2016a), see also the recent Taqueem initiative: http://www.ilo.org/global/topics/youth-employment/projects/evaluation/lang--en/index.htm.

Although there is a clear inverse association across countries between the level of economic development and the prevalence of informality, the chapter demonstrated the inadvisability of a formalization strategy based *purely* on encouraging economic growth. Such a strategy would be slow, with an uncertain outcome, not least because informality itself impedes growth; also, development itself brings with it new forms of informality.

The high costs of informality for young people, and the difficulties they face in getting out of informal work once they have set out upon that path, make it clear that policy approaches in this area should not be limited to the formalization of existing informal work, but should follow a two-pronged strategy involving also the facilitation of access to a first formal job for young people to pre-empt the vicious cycle that traps so many in informality. Moreover, given the huge amount of variation in types and forms of informality, here more than anywhere policy approaches need to be tailored to specific forms and contexts.

8.2. Complementarities and interactions

Throughout the book, analyses and reviews have repeatedly emphasized the importance of complementarity between context, institutions, policies and programmes influencing the entry of young people into quality employment. Clearly, a strategy to promote decent work among young people requires action at different levels. The book has suggested at many points, either implicitly or explicitly, how such policies and programmes may interact. Some of these findings are brought together here.

8.2.1. Macroeconomic and microeconomic policies

Both discretionary fiscal policy and wage subsidies are likely to be most effective when the demand for youth labour is weak. Expansionary fiscal policy has the greatest remedial effect during recessions, when implemented promptly, and wage subsidies fulfil an income support function as well as being *relatively* effective (compared to training) in promoting the longer-term employment prospects of young people during such periods.

These findings support the introduction of youth employment guarantee subsidies, which have the function of automatic stabilizers. Thus, for example, a right of access to subsidized employment or training within four months of leaving work or education would "automatically" increase government expenditure during times of low labour demand, and reduce it during periods of expansion. Indeed, this is close to what has been aimed at – albeit for different reasons – in the EU with the establishment of the Youth Guarantee, such that young people in neither employment nor education should have the opportunity of participating in some form of subsidized employment-related activity (including further educational participation). The advantage of such automatic stabilizers, as opposed to discretionary policies, is that they expand immediately (indeed, automatically, as the name implies) when economies fall into recession and do not require any further, inevitably time-consuming, deliberation and decision-making by government.

The discussion of the potential of sectoral development policies along with the analysis of informality suggests that approaches to sectoral development, aimed at promoting productivity and employment growth, might effectively combine with policy components encouraging the formalization of economic activities.

8.2.2. Labour market institutions and labour market policies

Chapter 3 focused on the youth employment effects of minimum wages, reaffirming existing findings, as noted above, that although minimum wages can sometimes discourage the employment of young people, they often do not, and where such disemployment effects do exist, they are generally small. The chapter also produced a number of findings on complementarities among institutions. Specifically, stronger EPL tends to reduce any disemployment effects associated with the introduction or raising of minimum wages.

Similarly, the disemployment effects of minimum wages are less pronounced where trade union coverage is extensive and well coordinated but also decentralized, allowing for variations in minimum wages to respond to local conditions.

These findings tend to support the notion that LMICs should seek to develop concurrently a comprehensive set of appropriate protective labour market institutions, rather than introducing, say, ad hoc minimum wage legislation.

It appears clear that minimum wages can play a useful role in raising low youth wages. However, the rapidly growing participation of young people in non-standard forms of employment, as discussed in Chapter 6 on contractual arrangements, implies that the application of minimum wage legislation and other labour market institutions needs to take into consideration their effects on the increasingly unprotected young workers in non-standard forms of employment.

This is perhaps most important among the nominally "self-employed" workers in the "gig" economy – a subject which has not been specifically treated here, but which certainly deserves further consideration. The analysis of self-employment in Chapter 5 brought out strongly the importance of distinguishing good (and very good) forms of self-employment from bad (and very bad) forms.

Although the investigation here has not explored this directly, the evidence presented above on wage subsidies suggests that subsidized employment forms might plausibly also be used as a mechanism to reduce or counteract any disemployment effects of minimum wages.

We need to know more about the effects of minimum wages on youth employment in LMICs, particularly in respect of their interaction with informality. Despite the apparent plausibility of the argument, it is by no means established that raising minimum wages encourages informality, since there often appears to be a "lighthouse effect", with minimum wages in the formal sector raising (rather than reducing, as one might expect) wages in the informal economy.

8.2.3. ALMPs, wage subsidies and informality

Although not considered explicitly in either Chapter 4 on wage subsidies or Chapter 7 on informality, an obvious way in which wage subsidies might provide added value in countries with extensive informality would be *to leverage such public financial support in order to encourage formality*: that is, to encourage participation by firms in wage subsidy programmes conditional on the employment being formal(ized). Doubtless this process sometimes already occurs;[2] sometimes, indeed, it is among the explicit aims of self-employment programmes, as with the programme Micro-empreendedor individual in Brazil mentioned in Chapter 7. However, there is no reason why wage subsidy programmes should not also be explicitly used in this way. Of course, this adds an additional consideration to programme design, as it needs to be sufficiently attractive for informal firms to formalize, or for formal firms employing informal workers to regularize their workforce, and attention needs to be paid to avoiding perverse incentives, encouraging "informalization" in order to obtain benefits. This is certainly an avenue worth further consideration. Recent evidence on the positive impact of payroll tax reductions in increasing both formal and permanent employment in Colombia (Kugler et al., 2017) provides further evidence in favour of adopting this type of approach.

8.3. Possible directions for future research work

8.3.1. Macroeconomic and sectoral policies

As regards fiscal policy, three future lines of research suggest themselves:

Owing to data constraints, the analysis presented here was restricted to higher-income European countries and, although there is no reason to suppose this not to be the case, it would be useful to confirm that discretionary fiscal policy can be equally – or possibly even more – effective in LMICs.

Further investigation of the mechanisms through which expansionary fiscal policy promotes youth employment would also usefully enhance our knowledge; in particular, understanding how the composition of fiscal policy is likely to affect its efficacy would make a significant contribution to understanding issues of better design as they relate to fiscal policy. In this regard it would be useful to look at the effectiveness, on the macroeconomic level, of expenditure on ALMPs in general and on wage subsidies in particular.

We also know relatively little about the distributional effects of fiscal policy, particularly as they affect young people. In the context of growing inequality,

---

[2] For example, in the former Yugoslav Republic of Macedonia, during the implementation of a large self-employment support programme coordinated by the UN Development Programme, it quickly became evident that many of the participants had already established informal businesses; accordingly, in later rounds of the programme two forms were developed, one explicitly aimed at formalization while the other was concerned with new start-ups.

it would be useful to examine the distributional impact of economic policies on youth labour markets.

As regards sectoral development, relatively little work has been undertaken on the effectiveness of these approaches with regard to youth employment. In particular, it would be useful to investigate the role that the promotion of green jobs can play for young people. Is there a trade-off between sustainability and job promotion in this respect, or, do green jobs promise a win–win solution for young people? Similarly, other sectors such as information and communications technology may well be worth investigating further. Having said that, it remains true that effective strategy will need to be based on a country-specific approach.

8.3.2. Labour market institutions

Our understanding of the interactions between labour market institutions and their impact on youth labour markets remains limited. We need to know much more about the complementarities between policies and programmes. Chapter 3 offered an example of the potential for knowledge-building efforts along these lines.

A second line of inquiry in this area concerns the impact of labour market institutions on inequality and disadvantage in youth labour markets. As with other policy areas, much knowledge development here has focused on average impacts, but it would be useful also to understand more about the distribution of impacts: do specific labour market institutions reduce or increase disadvantage in youth labour markets – and for whom?

8.3.3. Active labour market policies and programmes

We now know rather a lot about what works in respect of ALMPs for young people, and our knowledge is constantly expanding through the more widespread use of appropriate impact evaluations. As with labour market institutions, one area where very little is known is the distributional impact of different types of programme – which programmes help which groups in the youth labour market more? What, as a consequence, is the impact of specific programmes on youth labour market disadvantage? And what are the implications of this for the costs and benefits of different policies and programme designs in specific countries?

8.3.4. Self-employment and entrepreneurship

The evidence base on self-employment is improving steadily, but there remain some aspects of the major life course events (start up/failure) of the self employed and small businesses that remain largely unexplored. For instance, what are the consequences of business failure? The social, economic, health and well-being costs can be significant for the individual, and also for families and creditors who can be left with unpaid debts. There is little information on how often the end of a period of self-employment is followed by a seamless transition into another activity, or how often it can lead to extreme deprivation or even peonage. These issues need to be factored into the cost–benefit analysis of programmes if more start-ups mean more failures.

The SWTS has done much to clarify the nature of self-employment in developing countries, and to replace myths with facts. It is hoped that it will be repeated with an enhanced set of questions to determine more exactly the nature of the businesses of respondents who are not employees.

Perhaps one reason why our understanding of self-employment (and how to promote routes into self-employment in developing countries) is lacking lies in a prevalent mismatch between the phenomenon of self-employment and survey research methods. Employment is typically conceived of as a relationship between an individual and an employer, supplemented by relations with some other more peripheral actors (such as trade unions and factory inspectors). Yet self-employment is often a completely different type of labour-market status. Instead of "own-account workers" interacting autonomously with the market, the situation (in both developed and developing countries) is often better described as a complex network involving many codependent actors, and many of those links are with members of the same nuclear and extended families. We need to be far more aware of the ways in which the (actual and potential) self-employed are embedded in networks, and the abilities of those networks to provide skills, capital and other resources, before we start to intervene in that system through ALMPs for the self-employed. This will require both qualitative and quantitative research dedicated to gaining a thorough understanding of the nature of self-employment and the contexts in which it is being carried out, rather than simply adding a section on self-employment to surveys of employees.

8.3.5. Contractual arrangements and youth employment

Much remains to be understood regarding contractual arrangements for young people, and the need for such understanding is becoming more urgent. Non-standard forms of employment are ever more widespread – particularly among young people – and, with the additional impetus provided by technological change, the organization of work will continue to evolve, particularly for new entrants.

The focus in this book, specifically in Chapter 6, has been on contractual arrangements – and particularly on the interaction between temporary working arrangements and training. Future work needs to focus on specific emerging non-standard forms of employment which will increasingly affect young people's early – and perhaps also later – labour market experiences: not only the obvious example of internship, but also work-based forms of formal and informal learning more generally. Chapter 6 drew together existing evidence on internships and considered them from the juridical point of view. However, we still need to better understand which characteristics of internships determine positive subsequent labour market outcomes for young people. With the partial exception of work experience programmes as part of ALMPs, very little research has been undertaken with the aim of quantifying the impact of internships on the successful – or not – labour market integration of young people. In particular, we need to better understand what constitutes a quality internship.

8.3.6. Informality and the formalization of youth employment

Much progress has been made in understanding informal employment, albeit perhaps a little less so in respect of young people. However, there is a clear need for a better understanding of which types of policies work best in which circumstances. As repeatedly noted here, informal employment is a highly heterogeneous phenomenon, which means that solutions will also vary according to circumstances. As experience with specific strategies increases, it is important to evaluate these strategies and to use such evaluations to inform future policy initiatives.

As with the other areas of intervention outlined above, particular attention to the distributional impacts of formalization methods would also be extremely useful.

Appendix

This book makes extensive use of data from the ILO School-to-Work Transition Survey (SWTS). The SWTS was conducted in 34 countries under the "Work4Youth" (W4Y) project, on young people between 15 and 29 years old.

The W4Y project involved a partnership between the ILO Youth Employment Programme and the MasterCard Foundation. It had a budget of US$14.6 million and ran for five years to mid-2016. The main objective of the project was to strengthen the production of labour market information specific to youth and to work with policy-makers on the interpretation of the data, including transitions to the labour market, for the design or monitoring of youth employment policies and programmes.[1]

The SWTS was conducted in two rounds, the first round covering 28 countries between 2012 and 2013, and the second covering 25 countries between 2014 and 2015; in 19 of the 34 countries the survey was carried out in both rounds. More details about the countries considered in each sample, the regions covered and the survey itself are reported in table A1.

As stated above, the SWTS included 34 countries, but given some differences found between countries and/or between rounds of the survey for the same country, throughout the book there are some differences in the choice of countries for different analyses and statistics. For example, in Chapter 5 some of the statistics are based exclusively on the first round of the surveys due to the absence of the relevant information in the second-round database, and in Chapter 7 Samoa was excluded from some of the informality statistics – specifically, where a distinction is drawn between informal workers in the formal and informal economies – since this information was not collected in that survey. In each case, notes to tables indicate the specific data used.

In order to arrive at regional and "global" statistics, a uniform aggregation procedure was adopted. Base statistics were calculated for each survey. In countries where two rounds of the survey were conducted, "national" statistics were based on the unweighted average of the two samples. For countries where only one round was conducted, the country averages were taken directly from that survey. Once statistics by country were obtained, the regional information was calculated taking the unweighted average of the countries in each region; in other words, all countries were given the same weight. The same was done for the global statistics, with equal weight attributed to each of the five regions.

Major statistical indicators are reported by country in the following tables A2–A6.

---

[1]   For more information on the project and to gain access to the microdata, see: http://www.ilo.org/employment/areas/youth-employment/work-for-youth/lang--en/index.htm.

Table A1. The ILO School-to-Work Transition Survey: Meta-information

Region	Country	Survey date and sample size				Income status
		2012	2013	2014	2015	
SSA	Benin	6917		4305		Low-income
	Congo				3276	Lower-middle-income
	Liberia	1876		2416		Low-income
	Madagascar		3295		5044	Low-income
	Malawi	3102		3097		Low-income
	Sierra Leone				2708	Low-income
	United Rep. Tanzania		1988			Low-income
	Togo	2033		2238		Low-income
	Uganda		3811		3049	Low-income
	Zambia	3206		3225		Lower-middle-income
MENA	Egypt	5198		5758		Lower-middle-income
	Jordan	5405			3749	Upper-middle-income
	Lebanon			2616		Upper-middle-income
	Occupied Palestinian Territory		4320		4141	Lower-middle-income
	Tunisia		3000			Lower-middle-income
LAC	Brazil	3288				Upper-middle-income
	Colombia		6416			Upper-middle-income
	Dominican Republic				3554	Upper-middle-income
	El Salvador	3451		3604		Lower-middle-income
	Jamaica		2584		3666	Upper-middle-income
	Peru		2464			Upper-middle-income
EECA	Armenia	3216		2710		Lower-middle-income
	Kyrgyzstan		3930			Lower-middle-income
	Former Yugoslav Rep. Macedonia	2544		2474		Upper-middle-income
	Republic of Moldova		1158		1189	Lower-middle-income
	Montenegro				2998	Upper-middle-income
	Russian Federation	3890			3415	Upper-middle-income
	Serbia				0600	Upper-middle-income
	Ukraine		3526		3202	Lower-middle-income
AP	Bangladesh		9197			Lower-middle-income
	Cambodia	3552		3396		Lower-middle-income
	Nepal		3584			Low-income
	Samoa	2914				Lower-middle-income
	Viet Nam		2722		2229	Lower-middle-income

Note: Income status corresponds to the World Bank list of economies, Sep. 2016.

Table A2. Unemployment rate by sex and age group, SWTS countries (%)

Region	Country	Female			Male		
		15–19	20–24	25–29	15–19	20–24	25–29
SSA	Benin	3.6	8.3	8.8	5.9	19.0	16.4
	Congo	35.1	39.9	23.4	43.9	33.7	20.7
	Liberia	19.0	19.5	19.0	9.7	16.1	11.5
	Madagascar	1.2	4.1	1.5	1.3	3.4	1.7
	Malawi	7.0	9.7	8.3	4.0	8.0	3.2
	Sierra Leone	8.7	8.9	5.4	6.3	23.0	10.9
	United Rep. Tanzania	21.2	20.7	42.2	24.2	15.1	8.7
	Togo	2.5	7.2	6.7	6.4	8.9	8.8
	Uganda	6.3	7.3	6.1	5.2	5.7	3.6
	Zambia	15.5	19.5	19.0	14.5	18.6	11.2
MENA	Egypt	28.5	47.9	41.4	6.9	11.9	7.8
	Jordan	56.7	49.0	37.1	33.5	19.0	10.8
	Lebanon	41.6	24.2	10.5	18.3	12.9	6.2
	Occupied Palestinian Territory	53.9	64.6	48.2	37.6	31.3	22.8
	Tunisia	35.3	33.9	43.9	30.6	36.9	20.8
LAC	Brazil	36.5	24.2	14.2	24.5	13.1	7.8
	Colombia	17.6	20.0	10.6	16.3	11.8	5.1
	Dominican Republic	41.1	31.3	24.1	14.4	9.7	8.1
	El Salvador	26.7	31.7	20.9	15.5	18.8	9.3
	Jamaica	62.3	45.2	29.6	42.5	30.6	18.7
	Peru	12.0	17.6	8.0	13.9	10.1	3.9
EECA	Armenia	62.2	40.7	24.3	45.8	29.4	16.0
	Kyrgyzstan	4.3	6.2	2.1	3.4	6.5	1.8
	Former Yugoslav Rep. Macedonia	44.1	13.3	8.7	31.5	22.6	14.7
	Republic of Moldova	38.4	46.8	34.7	36.7	49.9	39.3
	Montenegro	57.7	38.8	32.3	66.2	43.2	41.9
	Russian Federation	34.8	12.0	7.8	33.3	13.7	7.0
	Serbia	59.2	41.7	30.8	28.1	36.0	22.0
	Ukraine	31.1	17.3	9.1	30.2	19.3	9.6
AP	Bangladesh	27.6	25.3	16.8	10.6	7.4	2.7
	Cambodia	2.3	3.2	1.3	2.0	3.5	1.1
	Nepal	26.8	24.5	16.3	23.6	21.6	10.0
	Samoa	33.5	22.5	12.9	16.3	16.2	11.7
	Viet Nam	4.1	4.0	2.1	2.4	4.5	2.1

Table A3. NEET rates by sex and age group, SWTS countries (%)

Region	Country	Female			Male		
		15–19	20–24	25–29	15–19	20–24	25–29
SSA	Benin	20.9	44.5	53.2	16.3	28.0	38.9
	Congo	16.1	39.3	40.9	16.2	21.0	30.8
	Liberia	17.5	30.2	30.0	9.8	19.6	14.8
	Madagascar	6.3	11.0	8.0	3.1	3.8	2.8
	Malawi	16.3	27.4	26.5	4.8	12.3	8.0
	Sierra Leone	13.9	16.0	19.0	5.5	15.1	15.5
	United Rep. Tanzania	39.8	42.6	47.4	26.2	20.6	13.8
	Togo	13.2	23.0	25.1	9.2	11.7	16.3
	Uganda	12.5	22.8	20.3	5.3	9.0	7.8
	Zambia	22.0	40.0	40.3	16.4	27.9	22.0
MENA	Egypt	25.4	62.3	75.2	4.6	21.8	10.2
	Jordan	19.9	51.4	73.0	15.5	15.2	12.9
	Lebanon	7.4	26.7	40.6	4.3	7.3	6.8
	Occupied Palestinian Territory	12.9	54.0	79.7	17.3	26.7	25.1
	Tunisia	20.5	37.9	64.2	12.8	28.6	24.9
LAC	Brazil	18.1	40.3	42.3	10.4	16.6	11.6
	Colombia	12.1	22.6	20.1	10.6	9.6	7.9
	Dominican Republic	13.5	28.6	35.4	7.5	9.7	9.8
	El Salvador	30.2	59.7	59.9	12.2	20.5	13.0
	Jamaica	26.5	47.0	42.2	22.0	35.5	26.4
	Peru	23.5	24.9	31.0	12.5	8.2	5.8
EECA	Armenia	10.5	47.2	56.5	11.7	21.8	23.4
	Kyrgyzstan	8.3	29.1	35.2	5.1	10.7	7.3
	Former Yugoslav Rep. Macedonia	13.9	33.9	46.1	11.8	33.1	36.9
	Republic of Moldova	10.3	29.0	54.3	8.9	28.7	30.4
	Montenegro	12.4	29.2	41.5	15.3	31.2	43.7
	Russian Federation	18.2	16.6	15.9	18.9	14.4	8.9
	Serbia	11.3	26.8	37.5	9.9	26.8	27.2
	Ukraine	5.7	20.8	23.7	4.4	23.4	26.0
AP	Bangladesh	47.2	73.6	75.7	15.0	13.7	9.3
	Cambodia	5.1	15.6	16.4	3.4	5.6	3.6
	Nepal	7.5	19.7	32.9	4.5	8.7	10.6
	Samoa	19.2	63.6	67.2	27.5	55.3	55.4
	Viet Nam	7.1	14.0	12.2	8.2	9.2	6.2

Table A4. Employment by sex and sector, SWTS countries (%)

Region	Country	Female			Male		
		Agriculture	Industry	Services	Agriculture	Industry	Services
SSA	Benin	16.2	12.6	71.2	30.1	21.5	48.4
	Congo	23.8	4.5	71.7	17.4	26.8	55.9
	Liberia	29.7	4.1	66.2	32.5	15.7	51.8
	Madagascar	71.3	10.9	17.9	75.8	9.4	14.8
	Malawi	54.3	11.6	34.2	51.5	17.6	30.9
	Sierra Leone	31.0	15.1	53.9	36.7	15.3	48.0
	United Rep. Tanzania	16.2	5.5	78.3	27.7	24.1	48.3
	Togo	41.3	17.5	41.3	52.9	14.8	32.4
	Uganda	62.2	5.3	32.6	55.0	14.3	30.7
	Zambia	28.1	6.1	65.9	31.4	17.0	51.6
MENA	Egypt	27.1	13.8	59.2	21.1	28.3	50.6
	Jordan	2.7	11.6	85.7	1.8	16.9	81.3
	Lebanon	2.0	6.8	91.2	2.5	16.5	81.1
	Occupied Palestinian Territory	7.3	11.8	80.9	7.5	36.6	55.9
	Tunisia	20.0	38.9	41.2	22.6	38.8	38.6
LAC	Brazil	2.6	10.5	86.9	10.3	33.8	55.9
	Colombia	0.1	38.3	61.6	0.9	55.4	43.7
	Dominican Republic	2.2	13.7	84.1	15.3	24.4	60.3
	El Salvador	11.2	15.3	73.5	45.8	17.7	36.4
	Jamaica	3.3	4.9	91.8	13.8	15.9	70.3
	Peru	5.5	15.6	78.9	5.1	30.8	64.1
EECA	Armenia	13.1	6.6	80.3	18.7	28.5	52.8
	Kyrgyzstan	55.2	10.0	34.8	39.5	27.3	33.3
	Former Yugoslav Rep. Macedonia	16.0	19.4	64.6	18.2	30.3	51.5
	Republic of Moldova	12.0	13.3	74.7	19.6	16.7	63.7
	Montenegro	0.5	4.5	95.1	1.6	16.8	81.6
	Russian Federation	8.4	13.9	77.7	10.2	41.0	48.8
	Serbia	8.1	14.8	77.1	18.6	29.3	52.1
	Ukraine	6.5	21.9	71.7	6.3	22.9	70.8
AP	Bangladesh	26.0	42.5	31.6	36.8	29.1	34.1
	Cambodia	46.1	18.8	35.1	51.4	19.5	29.1
	Nepal	53.0	9.2	37.8	40.1	17.4	42.5
	Samoa	2.8	9.6	87.6	7.0	22.2	70.8
	Viet Nam	31.6	32.2	36.2	34.47	32.4	33.1

Table A5. Employment by formality, sex and sector, SWTS countries (%)

Region	Country	Formality	Female			Male		
			Agriculture	Industry	Services	Agriculture	Industry	Services
SSA	Benin	Formal employment	4.9	19.3	6.7	6.5	14.8	13.4
		Informal employment in formal sector	5.8	1.6	5.7	6.7	15.3	18.5
		Informal sector	89.3	79.0	87.7	86.9	69.9	68.1
	Congo	Formal employment	2.6	9.0	5.8	8.1	12.8	13.0
		Informal employment in formal sector	2.1	18.3	13.6	1.2	29.3	33.0
		Informal sector	95.4	72.8	80.7	90.7	57.9	54.0
	Liberia	Formal employment	14.1	13.5	7.2	16.4	21.9	14.6
		Informal employment in formal sector	11.9	8.5	13.9	8.8	17.1	25.7
		Informal sector	74.0	78.0	78.9	74.8	61.0	59.7
	Madagascar	Formal employment	2.0	5.2	7.5	3.6	7.8	8.4
		Informal employment in formal sector	11.3	8.5	20.5	12.3	30.0	25.2
		Informal sector	86.7	86.2	72.0	84.2	62.2	66.4
	Malawi	Formal employment	3.6	7.8	4.3	5.4	7.4	5.7
		Informal employment in formal sector	3.4	9.0	5.2	6.7	10.8	17.1
		Informal sector	93.0	83.3	90.5	87.9	81.8	77.2
	Sierra Leone	Formal employment	2.3	3.7	5.6	6.5	10.4	9.2
		Informal employment in formal sector	20.4	19.7	14.6	22.0	33.3	27.1
		Informal sector	77.3	76.5	79.8	71.6	56.3	63.7
	United Rep. Tanzania	Formal employment	3.1	3.6	13.1	18.2	26.3	37.6
		Informal employment in formal sector	14.1	14.7	13.4	17.5	24.3	33.2
		Informal sector	82.8	81.8	73.5	64.2	49.4	29.2

Table A5. Employment by formality, sex and sector, SWTS countries (%) *(cont'd)*

Region	Country	Formality	Female			Male		
			Agriculture	Industry	Services	Agriculture	Industry	Services
	Togo	Formal employment	3.2	25.9	6.7	3.2	15.4	15.0
		Informal employment in formal sector	7.8	6.4	8.7	13.4	18.5	20.5
		Informal sector	89.1	67.8	84.6	83.4	66.1	64.5
	Uganda	Formal employment	6.1	8.3	9.0	5.3	9.2	14.2
		Informal employment in formal sector	8.5	13.5	19.1	12.8	46.2	22.7
		Informal sector	85.4	78.2	71.9	81.9	44.6	63.0
	Zambia	Formal employment	3.1	8.6	5.3	5.0	7.0	6.4
		Informal employment in formal sector	12.2	35.4	14.9	15.5	30.4	19.3
		Informal sector	84.7	56.0	79.8	79.5	62.6	74.3
MENA	Egypt	Formal employment	1.6	3.6	27.2	3.1	11.4	11.9
		Informal employment in formal sector	42.7	86.6	50.4	43.9	62.1	47.0
		Informal sector	55.7	9.8	22.5	53.0	26.4	41.1
	Jordan	Formal employment	0.0	52.5	54.3	6.2	24.9	59.5
		Informal employment in formal sector	47.6	42.4	40.8	46.0	48.5	32.6
		Informal sector	52.4	5.1	4.9	47.9	26.6	7.9
	Lebanon	Formal employment	0.0	28.2	37.1	11.8	24.2	46.9
		Informal employment in formal sector	13.1	60.7	37.4	27.1	34.8	27.5
		Informal sector	86.9	11.1	25.5	61.1	41.0	25.6

Table A5. Employment by formality, sex and sector, SWTS countries (%) (cont'd)

Region	Country	Formality	Female			Male		
			Agriculture	Industry	Services	Agriculture	Industry	Services
	Occupied Palestinian Territory	Formal employment	0.0	11.7	5.8	2.7	1.5	8.3
		Informal employment in formal sector	78.7	60.8	70.5	47.2	62.4	53.9
		Informal sector	21.3	27.6	23.7	50.1	36.2	37.8
	Tunisia	Formal employment	0.0	11.7	13.6	1.0	10.6	28.1
		Informal employment in formal sector	17.9	80.0	66.8	26.7	44.3	43.8
		Informal sector	82.1	8.3	19.7	72.3	45.2	28.1
LAC	Brazil	Formal employment	28.5	64.7	33.0	21.9	36.4	45.0
		Informal employment in formal sector	22.6	25.9	31.4	31.7	32.8	34.1
		Informal sector	48.9	9.4	35.6	46.4	30.8	20.9
	Colombia	Formal employment	64.7	53.5	53.2	50.5	56.2	60.8
		Informal employment in formal sector	35.3	24.9	28.0	27.7	27.2	22.2
		Informal sector	0.0	21.7	18.9	21.8	16.6	17.0
	Dominican Republic	Formal employment	18.3	36.2	21.1	3.0	25.2	17.1
		Informal employment in formal sector	24.2	53.7	38.6	37.8	43.8	41.7
		Informal sector	57.5	10.1	40.3	59.2	31.0	41.2
	El Salvador	Formal employment	4.4	14.7	9.4	1.3	10.7	13.8
		Informal employment in formal sector	50.5	32.4	29.0	20.6	44.7	51.5
		Informal sector	45.0	52.8	61.6	78.1	44.6	34.7

Table A5. Employment by formality, sex and sector, SWTS countries (%) *(cont'd)*

Region	Country	Formality	Female			Male		
			Agriculture	Industry	Services	Agriculture	Industry	Services
	Jamaica	Formal employment	2.1	37.5	28.9	5.2	20.8	25.3
		Informal employment in formal sector	16.0	51.1	34.7	6.2	46.9	45.3
		Informal sector	82.0	11.4	36.4	88.6	32.4	29.4
	Peru	Formal employment	14.9	19.7	15.2	0.0	16.8	18.5
		Informal employment in formal sector	45.8	56.5	53.4	45.8	54.7	50.3
		Informal sector	39.3	23.9	31.4	54.2	28.5	31.1
EECA	Armenia	Formal employment	0.7	52.5	48.3	1.5	24.3	42.1
		Informal employment in formal sector	6.9	36.4	42.6	7.3	56.0	46.4
		Informal sector	92.4	11.1	9.2	91.2	19.7	11.4
	Kyrgyzstan	Formal employment	6.2	23.1	39.5	12.6	16.7	36.0
		Informal employment in formal sector	5.8	60.9	25.2	9.8	50.1	26.3
		Informal sector	88.0	16.0	35.3	77.7	33.2	37.7
	Former Yugoslav Rep. Macedonia	Formal employment	1.3	66.8	65.3	4.2	51.5	62.8
		Informal employment in formal sector	34.6	32.3	29.9	29.5	37.7	32.7
		Informal sector	64.0	0.9	4.8	66.3	10.8	4.5
	Republic of Moldova	Formal employment	11.8	87.2	88.6	31.0	87.8	79.2
		Informal employment in formal sector	15.6	4.8	10.1	20.8	5.7	9.3
		Informal sector	72.6	8.0	1.3	48.2	6.5	11.5

Table A5. Employment by formality, sex and sector, SWTS countries (%) *(cont'd)*

Region	Country	Formality	Female			Male		
			Agriculture	Industry	Services	Agriculture	Industry	Services
	Montenegro	Formal employment	0.0	59.6	42.6	15.3	47.0	37.0
		Informal employment in formal sector	0.0	40.4	51.4	0.0	42.1	54.0
		Informal sector	100.0	0.0	6.0	84.7	10.9	9.0
	Russian Federation	Formal employment	15.2	61.9	52.0	14.9	53.1	50.9
		Informal employment in formal sector	4.5	24.9	26.8	13.4	26.8	22.6
		Informal sector	80.3	13.2	21.2	71.7	20.1	26.5
	Serbia	Formal employment	9.6	54.8	58.1	19.1	62.6	56.9
		Informal employment in formal sector	67.5	41.1	35.9	61.3	30.7	34.8
		Informal sector	22.9	4.1	6.0	19.6	6.7	8.3
	Ukraine	Formal employment	30.2	47.9	42.4	22.7	49.5	41.8
		Informal employment in formal sector	20.6	46.6	48.9	25.7	45.6	48.6
		Informal sector	49.2	5.4	8.6	51.5	4.9	9.5
AP	Bangladesh	Formal employment	1.9	2.0	14.0	1.7	3.0	9.5
		Informal employment in formal sector	13.4	78.6	29.0	38.4	82.0	41.0
		Informal sector	84.7	19.5	57.0	60.0	15.1	49.5
	Cambodia	Formal employment	0.7	6.5	4.1	1.1	4.8	5.2
		Informal employment in formal sector	17.5	58.3	23.9	15.7	64.4	37.8
		Informal sector	81.9	35.3	72.0	83.2	30.8	57.0

Table A5. Employment by formality, sex and sector, SWTS countries (%) *(concl.)*

Region	Country	Formality	Female			Male		
			Agriculture	Industry	Services	Agriculture	Industry	Services
	Nepal	Formal employment	0.9	6.2	12.1	2.9	8.0	15.6
		Informal employment in formal sector	9.5	22.6	51.0	14.9	47.3	49.8
		Informal sector	89.7	71.3	36.9	82.2	44.7	34.6
	Viet Nam	Formal employment	1.3	36.6	39.9	1.4	20.6	32.5
		Informal employment in formal sector	11.8	51.6	33.6	14.2	64.3	43.5
		Informal sector	86.9	11.8	26.6	84.4	15.2	24.0

Table A6. Education level by formality and sex, SWTS (%)

Region	Country	Education level	Female			Male		
			Formal employment	Informal employment	Informal sector	Formal employment	Informal employment	Informal sector
SSA	Benin	Up to primary	51.8	21.4	70.2	37.0	30.0	59.7
		Secondary	40.9	52.4	29.4	51.9	46.5	36.4
		Tertiary	7.3	26.2	0.4	11.1	23.5	3.9
	Congo	Up to primary	49.0	33.8	83.6	49.8	64.3	75.4
		Secondary	25.1	53.6	12.9	30.2	27.0	19.8
		Tertiary	25.9	12.6	3.5	20.0	8.6	4.9
	Liberia	Up to primary	66.4	36.7	53.4	43.4	14.3	43.3
		Secondary	33.7	58.1	42.5	51.9	79.1	54.1
		Tertiary	0.0	5.2	4.1	4.7	6.6	2.5
	Madagascar	Up to primary	41.0	51.8	66.0	39.7	50.7	69.0
		Secondary	42.3	42.9	33.7	55.3	47.0	30.3
		Tertiary	16.7	5.4	0.3	5.0	2.3	0.7
	Malawi	Up to primary	75.3	59.4	87.0	63.3	51.2	84.2
		Secondary	20.8	31.7	12.7	30.5	41.1	15.5
		Tertiary	3.9	8.9	0.3	6.2	7.7	0.3
	Sierra Leone	Up to primary	74.5	84.0	72.5	55.5	59.4	62.3
		Secondary	10.0	13.1	22.3	33.8	38.5	32.7
		Tertiary	15.5	2.9	5.2	10.7	2.0	5.0

Table A6. Education level by formality and sex, SWTS (%) *(cont'd)*

Region	Country	Education level	Female			Male		
			Formal employment	Informal employment	Informal sector	Formal employment	Informal employment	Informal sector
	Togo	Up to primary	60.8	50.4	67.3	38.8	42.6	58.1
		Secondary	32.1	42.6	31.5	45.6	49.5	39.0
		Tertiary	7.1	7.1	1.2	15.6	7.9	2.9
	Uganda	Up to primary	82.2	50.0	91.7	64.7	64.4	91.5
		Secondary	11.4	26.4	6.4	26.5	22.5	6.9
		Tertiary	6.4	23.6	2.0	8.7	13.1	1.6
	Zambia	Up to primary	7.4	9.9	34.8	15.3	11.6	24.9
		Secondary	78.9	85.2	64.5	69.3	85.0	74.3
		Tertiary	13.7	4.9	0.8	15.5	3.4	0.8
MENA	Egypt	Up to primary	4.4	24.1	41.3	16.9	34.8	43.7
		Secondary	34.9	34.3	47.3	47.7	48.7	49.6
		Tertiary	60.7	41.6	11.5	35.4	16.4	6.7
	Jordan	Up to primary	12.7	17.9	52.1	46.0	61.6	78.8
		Secondary	20.0	21.3	17.4	23.3	21.6	16.9
		Tertiary	67.3	60.8	30.5	30.7	16.8	4.3
	Lebanon	Up to primary	0.0	13.8	29.0	20.8	44.4	61.8
		Secondary	27.4	23.8	53.6	48.0	29.2	29.0
		Tertiary	72.6	62.4	17.4	31.3	26.5	9.2

Table A6. Education level by formality and sex, SWTS (%) (cont'd)

Region	Country	Education level	Female			Male		
			Formal employment	Informal employment	Informal sector	Formal employment	Informal employment	Informal sector
	Tunisia	Up to primary	14.5	36.0	51.0	20.2	43.2	61.9
		Secondary	31.9	41.8	44.8	47.8	38.6	32.7
		Tertiary	53.6	22.2	4.2	32.0	18.2	5.4
LAC	Brazil	Up to primary	19.5	28.7	51.8	26.5	41.5	60.4
		Secondary	69.2	61.7	46.7	64.7	54.6	38.8
		Tertiary	11.3	9.6	1.6	8.8	3.9	0.8
	Colombia	Up to primary	2.8	4.0	11.7	4.1	9.1	18.0
		Secondary	74.8	70.8	83.3	83.3	78.9	79.6
		Tertiary	22.4	25.2	5.0	12.6	12.0	2.4
	Dominican Republic	Up to primary	7.4	13.0	26.8	22.8	38.3	52.2
		Secondary	58.1	66.2	62.1	59.7	49.1	44.0
		Tertiary	34.4	20.8	11.1	17.5	12.6	3.8
	El Salvador	Up to primary	21.1	40.7	65.2	22.6	51.4	73.8
		Secondary	60.3	48.2	32.7	67.5	44.6	25.6
		Tertiary	18.6	11.1	2.1	10.0	4.0	0.6
	Jamaica	Up to primary	1.9	7.6	17.9	7.5	12.3	24.6
		Secondary	55.9	73.3	76.9	67.2	80.4	73.5
		Tertiary	42.2	19.1	5.2	25.3	7.4	2.0

Table A6. Education level by formality and sex, SWTS (%) (cont'd)

Region	Country	Education level	Female			Male		
			Formal employment	Informal employment	Informal sector	Formal employment	Informal employment	Informal sector
EECA	Armenia	Up to primary						
		Secondary	26.0	45.0	88.0	49.4	70.9	92.0
		Tertiary	74.0	55.1	12.0	50.6	29.1	7.2
	Kyrgyzstan	Up to primary	3.8	15.6	21.0	5.1	20.6	14.0
		Secondary	41.2	54.6	75.6	57.3	63.5	75.2
		Tertiary	55.0	29.7	3.4	37.6	15.9	10.8
	Former Yugoslav Rep. Macedonia	Up to primary	3.7	9.6	37.7	7.5	10.0	36.8
		Secondary	38.0	56.6	53.9	65.4	76.4	61.8
		Tertiary	58.3	33.8	8.3	27.1	13.6	1.4
	Republic of Moldova	Up to primary						
		Secondary	48.4	78.4	88.1	54.3	88.2	91.8
		Tertiary	51.6	21.6	11.9	45.7	2.2	5.5
	Montenegro	Up to primary	0.0	2.4	10.3	2.9	6.5	16.4
		Secondary	50.1	52.6	79.1	70.4	69.7	75.0
		Tertiary	49.9	45.1	10.6	26.7	23.8	8.6
	Russian Federation	Up to primary	1.1	0.4	6.2	2.1	3.9	7.9
		Secondary	44.4	56.4	72.2	65.4	74.2	79.4
		Tertiary	54.5	43.2	21.6	32.6	21.9	12.7

Table A6. Education level by formality and sex, SWTS (%) (concl.)

Region	Country	Education level	Female			Male		
			Formal employment	Informal employment	Informal sector	Formal employment	Informal employment	Informal sector
	Serbia	Up to primary	2.2	14.0	26.9	7.2	13.2	24.6
		Secondary	49.4	59.9	61.1	73.3	72.3	63.6
		Tertiary	48.4	26.1	12.0	19.5	14.6	11.8
	Ukraine	Up to primary	0.5	0.9	0.8	0.4	0.7	0.0
		Secondary	34.0	44.9	68.4	34.5	45.0	58.6
		Tertiary	65.5	54.2	30.7	65.1	54.3	41.4
AP	Bangladesh	Up to primary	14.2	49.1	49.6	23.1	63.2	55.3
		Secondary	42.2	46.5	50.4	67.9	34.7	43.4
		Tertiary	43.6	4.4	0.0	9.0	2.1	1.3
	Cambodia	Up to primary	27.6	49.7	59.0	33.1	45.1	54.5
		Secondary	49.5	44.0	39.8	48.6	45.7	43.6
		Tertiary	22.8	6.3	1.1	18.3	9.2	1.9
	Nepal	Up to primary	22.9	15.9	47.5	23.7	36.5	52.2
		Secondary	50.1	51.5	50.5	37.8	42.3	41.6
		Tertiary	27.0	32.6	2.0	38.5	21.2	6.2
	Viet Nam	Up to primary	9.8	23.2	32.5	7.8	30.6	35.6
		Secondary	62.5	69.6	65.3	65.1	64.0	63.4
		Tertiary	27.7	7.2	2.2	27.1	5.5	1.0

References

Aaviksoo, J.; Holm, J. 2013. *Praktika korraldamise ning läbiviimise tingimused ja kord* [Practice of organizing and carrying out the conditions and procedures], Statute of the Minister of Education and Science (Estonia) No. 32, 13 Sep. 2013.

Acemoglu, D.; Pischke, J.S. 1999. "The structure of wages and investment in general training", in *Journal of Political Economy*, Vol. 107, No. 3, pp. 539–972.

—; —. 2003. "Minimum wages and on-the-job training", in *Research in Labor Economics*, Vol. 22, pp. 159–202.

Aeberhardt, R.; Crusson, L.; Pommier, P. 2011. "Les politiques d'accès à l'emploi en faveur des jeunes: Qualifier et accompagner", in *INSEE, Portrait social* (Paris).

Afonso, A.; Agnello, L.; Furceri, D. 2010. "Fiscal policy responsiveness, persistence and discretion", in *Public Choice*, Vol. 145, Nos 3–4, pp. 503–530.

Agnello, L.; Furceri, D.; Sousa, R.M. 2013. "How best to measure discretionary fiscal policy? Assessing its impact on private spending", in *Economic Modelling,* Vol. 34, pp. 15–24.

Aleksynska, M.; Berg, J. 2016. *Firms' demand for temporary labour in developing countries: Necessity or strategy?*, Conditions of Work and Employment Series, No. 77 (Geneva, ILO).

Alesina, A.; Ardagna, S. 1998. "Tales of fiscal adjustments", in *Economic Policy*, Vol. 13, No. 27, pp. 489–545.

—; —; Perotti, R.; Schiantarelli, F. 2002. "Fiscal policy profits and investment", in *American Economic Review*, Vol. 92, No. 3, pp. 571–589.

—; Perotti, R. 1995. "Fiscal expansions and adjustments in OECD economies", in *Economic Policy*, Vol. 10, No. 21, pp. 207–247.

Allegretto, S.A.; Dube, A.; Reich, M. 2011. "Do minimum wages really reduce teen employment? Accounting for heterogeneity and selectivity in state panel data", in *Industrial Relations*, Vol. 50, No. 2, April, pp. 205–240.

Almeida, R.; Orr, L.; Robalino, D. 2014. "Wage subsidies in developing countries as a tool to build human capital: Design and implementation issues", in *IZA Journal of Labor Policy*, Vol. 3, No. 1, p. 12.

Andersen, O.D.; Kruse, K. 2016. *Key competences in vocational education and training: Denmark*, ReferNet Thematic Perspectives series (Thessaloniki, CEDEFOP). Available at: http://libserver.cedefop.europa.eu/vetelib/2016/ReferNet_DK_KC.pdf [2 Jan. 2017].

Angel-Urdinola, D.F.; Kuddo, K.; Semlali, A. 2013. *Building effective employment programs for unemployed youth in the Middle East and North Africa* (Washington, DC, World Bank). Available at: http://documents.worldbank.org/curated/en/2013/01/17966063/building-effective-employment-programs-unemployed-youth-middle-east-north-africa [1 Jan. 2017].

Arias-Vazquez, F.J.; Lee, J.N.; Newhouse, D. 2012. *The role of sectoral growth patterns in labour market development*, Policy Research Working Paper No. 6250 (Washington, DC, World Bank).

Astebro, T.; Bernhardt, I. 2005. "The winner's curse of human capital", in *Small Business Economics*, Vol. 24, No. 1, pp. 63–78.

Athayde, R. 2009. "Measuring enterprise potential in young people", in *Entrepreneurship Theory and Practice*, Vol. 33, No. 2, pp. 481–500.

Attanasio, O.; Kugler, A.; Meghir, C. 2011. "Subsidizing vocational training for disadvantaged youth in Colombia: Evidence from a randomized trial", in *American Economic Journal: Applied Economics*, Vol. 3, No. 3, pp. 188–220.

Autor, D.H.; Manning, A.; Smith, C.L. 2016. "The contribution of the minimum wage to US wage inequality over three decades: A reassessment", in *American Economic Journal: Applied Economics*, Vol. 8, No. 1, pp. 58–99.

Ayhan, S.H. 2013. "Do non-wage cost rigidities slow down employment? Evidence from Turkey", in *IZA Journal of Labor Policy*, Vol. 2, No. 1, p. 20.

Bacon, N. 2011. "Unpaid internships: The history, policy and future implications of fact sheet #71", in *Ohio State Entrepreneurial Business Law Journal*, Vol. 6, No. 1, pp. 67–96.

Baker & McKenzie. 2014. *Overview of labor and employment law in Latin America* (Ithaca, NY, Cornell University ILR School).

Baker, D.; Rosnick, D. 2014. *Stimulus and fiscal consolidation: The evidence and implications*, IMK Working Paper No. 135 (Dusseldorf, Hans-Böckler-Stiftung).

Ball, L.; DeLong, B.; Summers, L. 2014. *Fiscal policy and full employment* (Washington, DC, Center on Budget and Policy Priorities).

Banerjee, A.V.; Duflo, E.; Goldberg, N.; Karlan, D.; Osei, R.; Parienté, W.; Shapiro, J.; Thuysbaert, B.; Udry, C. 2015. "A multifaceted programme causes lasting progress for the very poor: Evidence from six countries", in *Science*, Vol. 348, No. 6236.

Barber, W. 1985. *From new era to new deal: Herbert Hoover, the economists and American economic policy 1921–1933* (Cambridge, Cambridge University Press).

Barza, R. 2011. *Essays in labor economics*, PhD diss. (Cambridge, MA, Harvard University).

Bassanini, A.; Duval, R. 2006. "The determinants of unemployment across OECD countries: Reassessing the role of policies and institutions", in *OECD Economic Studies*, Vol. 42, No. 1, pp. 7–86.

—; —. 2009. "Unemployment, institutions and reform complementarities: Re-assessing the aggregate evidence for OECD countries", in *Oxford Review of Economic Policy*, Vol. 25, No. 1, pp. 40–59.

Belman, D.; Wolfson, P.J. 2014. *What does the minimum wage do?* (Kalamazoo, MI, W.E. Upjohn Institute for Employment Research).

Bennet, A.M. 2011. "Unpaid internships and the Department of Labor: The impact of underenforcement of the Fair Labor Standards Act on equal opportunity", in *University of Maryland Law Journal of Race, Religion, Gender and Class*, Vol. 11, No. 2, pp. 293–313.

Berg, J. (ed.). 2015. *Labour markets, institutions and inequality: Building just societies in the 21st century* (Cheltenham, Edward Elgar).

—; Kucera, D. 2008. "Labour institutions in the developing world: Historical and theoretical perspectives", in J. Berg and D. Kucera (eds): *In defence of labour market institutions: Cultivating justice in the developing world* (Basingstoke, Palgrave Macmillan), pp. 9–31.

Bertola, G.; Blau, F.D.; Kahn, L.M. 2007. "Labor market institutions and demographic employment patterns", in *Journal of Population Economics*, Vol. 20, No. 4, pp. 833–867.

Betcherman, G.; Dar, A.; Olivas, K. 2004. *Impacts of active labor market programs: New evidence from evaluations with particular attention to developing and transition countries* (Washington, DC, World Bank, Social Protection and Labor).

—; Godfrey, M.; Puerto, S.; Rother, F.; Stavreska, A. 2007. *A review of interventions to support young workers: Findings of the Youth Employment Inventory*, Social Protection Discussion Paper No. 715 (Washington, DC, World Bank, Social Protection and Labor).

Biavaschi, C.; Eichhorst, W.; Giulietti, C.; Kendzia, M.J.; Muravyev, A.; Pieters, J.; Rodríguez-Planas, N.; Schmidl, R.; Zimmermann, K.F. 2012. *Youth unemployment and vocational training*, Discussion Paper No. 6890 (Bonn, IZA). Available at: http://ftp.iza.org/dp6890.pdf [2 Jan. 2017].

Blackburn, R. 1997. *Enterprise support for young people: A study of young business owners*, paper presented at 20th ISBA Conference, Belfast.

Blanchard, O.; Dell'Ariccia, G.; Mauro, P. 2010. *Rethinking macroeconomic policy*, IMF Staff Position Note 10/03 (Washington, DC, IMF).

Blattman, C.; Fiala, N.; Martinez, S. 2011. *Can employment programs reduce poverty and social stability? Experimental evidence from Uganda aid program*, mimeo (Washington, DC, World Bank).

—; —; —. 2014. "Generating skilled self-employment in developing countries: Experimental evidence from Uganda", in *Quarterly Journal of Economics*, Vol. 129, No. 2, pp. 697–752.

Blundell, R.; Costa Dias, M.; Meghir, C.; van Reenen, J. 2004. "Evaluating the employment impact of a mandatory job search program", in *Journal of the European Economic Association*, Vol. 2, No. 4, pp. 569–606.

Boeri, T. 2010. "Institutional reforms and dualism in European labor markets", in O. Ashenfelter and D. Card (eds): *Handbook of Labor Economics* (Amsterdam, Elsevier), pp. 1173–1236.

—; Conde-Ruiz, J.I.; Galasso, V. 2012. "The political economy of flexicurity", in *Journal of the European Economic Association*, Vol. 10, No. 4, pp. 684–715.

Boockmann, B. 2010. "The combined employment effects of minimum wages and labor market regulation: A meta-analysis", in *Applied Economic Quarterly*, Vol. 56, pp. 167–188.

Bördős, K.; Csillag, M.; Scharle, Á. 2015. *What works in wage subsidies for young people: A review of issues, theory, policies and evidence*, Employment Working Paper No. 199 (Geneva, ILO).

Braun, S. 2011. "The Obama crackdown: Another failed attempt to regulate the exploitation of unpaid internships", in *Southwestern Law Review*, Vol. 41, No. 2, pp. 281–307.

Bravo, D.; Rau, T. 2013. *Effects of large-scale youth employment subsidies: Evidence from a regression discontinuity design*, unpublished paper. Available at: http://faculty.arts. ubc.ca/nfortin/econ560/Rau_Bravo.pdf [2 Jan. 2017].

Brodaty, T. 2007. "La politique active de l'emploi en faveur des jeunes: Les dispositifs ont-ils touché leur cible?", in *Annales d'Économie et de Statistique*, Vol. 85, pp. 3–40.

Broecke, S. 2013. "Tackling graduate unemployment in North Africa through employment subsidies: A look at the SIVP programme in Tunisia", in *IZA Journal of Labor Policy*, Vol. 2, No. 1, pp. 1–19.

—; Forti, A.; Vandeweyer, M. 2017. "The effect of minimum wages on employment in emerging economies: A meta-analysis", in *Oxford Development Studies*, doi: 10.1080/13600818.2017.1279134.

Brown, A.J.G. 2015. "Can hiring subsidies benefit the unemployed?" in *IZA World of Labor*, 163, doi: 10.15185/izawol.163.

Brown, E.; DeCant, K. 2014. "Exploiting Chinese interns as unprotected industrial labor", in *Asian-Pacific Law and Policy Journal,* Vol. 15, No. 2, pp. 149–195.

Burchell, B.; Coutts, A.; Hall, E.; Pye, N. 2015. *Self-employment programmes for young people: A review of the context, policies and evidence*, Employment Policy Department, Youth Employment Programme, Working Paper No. 198 (Geneva, ILO).

Caliendo, M.; Künn, S.; Schmidl, R. 2011. *Fighting youth unemployment: The effects of active labor market policies*, Discussion Paper No. 6222 (Bonn, IZA).

Card, D.; Ibarrarán, P.; Regalia, F.; Rosas-Shady, D.; Soares, Y. 2011. "The labor market impacts of youth training in the Dominican Republic", in *Journal of Labor Economics*, Vol. 29, No. 2, pp. 267–300.

—; Kluve, J.; Weber, A. 2010. "Active labour market policy evaluations: A meta analysis", *Economic Journal*, Vol. 120, No. 548, pp. F452–F477.

—; —; —. 2015. *What works? A meta analysis of recent active labor market program evaluations*, Discussion Paper No. 9236 (Bonn, IZA). Available at: http://ftp.iza.org/ dp9236.pdf [2 Jan. 2017].

—; Kruger, A.B. 1995a. "Time series minimum wage-studies: A meta-analysis", in *American Economic Review*, Vol. 85, No. 2, pp. 238–243.

—; —. 1995b. *Myth and measurement: The new economics of the minimum wage* (Princeton, Princeton University Press).

Cavero, D.; Ruiz, C. 2016. *Do working conditions in young people's first jobs affect their employment trajectories? The case of Peru*, Work4Youth Publication Series No. 33 (Geneva, ILO).

China Briefing. 2014. *Learning from experience: The hows and whens of hiring interns in China*, 26 Nov. Available at: http://www.china-briefing.com/news/2014/11/26/hiring-interns-china.html.

Chletsos, M.; Giotis, G.P. 2015. *The employment effect of minimum wage using 77 international studies since 1992: A meta-analysis*, MPRA Paper No. 61321 (Munich Personal RePEc Archive, University Library of Munich).

Cho, Y.; Honorati, M. 2013. *Entrepreneurship programs in developing countries: A meta regression analysis*, Social Protection Discussion Paper No. 1302 (Washington, DC, World Bank, Social Protection and Labor).

—;—. 2014. "Entrepreneurship programs in developing countries: A meta regression analysis", in *Labour Economics*, Vol. 28, No. 1, pp. 110–130.

—; Margolis, D.; Newhouse, D.; Robalino, D. 2012. *Labor markets in low- and middle-income countries: Trends and implications for social protection and labor policies*, background paper for the World Bank 2012–2022 Social Protection and Labor Strategy, Social Protection and Labor Discussion Paper No. 1207 (Washington, DC, World Bank). Available at: http://siteresources.worldbank.org/SOCIALPROTECTION/Resources/SP-Discussion-papers/Labor-Market-DP/1207.pdf [2 Jan. 2017].

Choudhry, M.; Marelli, E.; Signorelli, M. 2012. "Youth unemployment and the impact of financial crises", in *International Journal of Manpower,* Vol. 33, No. 1, pp. 76–95.

Clauwaert, S.; Schömann, I. 2013. "The crisis and national labour law reforms: A mapping exercise", in *European Review of Labour and Research*, Vol. 19, No. 1, pp. 121–124.

Corseuil, C.H.; Foguel, M.; Gonzaga, G. 2013. *The effects of an apprenticeship program on wages and employability of youths in Brazil*, paper prepared for the CEDLAS-IRDC Regional Research Project on "Labour demand and job creation: Empirical evidence from firms in Latin America" (Rio de Janeiro). Available at: https://issuu.com/sae.pr/docs/efeitos_de_um_programa_-_en [2 Jan. 2017].

Costa Dias, M.; Ichimura, H.; van den Berg, G.H. 2013. "Treatment evaluation with selective participation and ineligibles", in *Journal of the American Statistical Association*, Vol. 108, No. 502, pp. 441–455.

Costanzi, R.N.; Barbosa, E.D.; da Silva Bichara, J. 2013. "Extending social security coverage to self-employed workers in Brazil", in *International Labour Review*, Vol. 152, Nos 3–4, pp. 549–557.

Council of the European Union. 1999. *Directive 1999/70/EC of 28 June 1999 concerning the framework agreement on fixed-term work* concluded by ETUC, UNICE and CEEP, *Official Journal of the European Communities*, L175, 10 July, pp. 43–48.

—. 2013. *On establishing a youth guarantee*, Council Recommendation No. 2013/C120/01 of 22 April (Brussels). Available at: http://ec.europa.eu/social/main.jsp?catId=1079.

Coutts, A. 2009. *Active labour market programmes and health: An evidence-base*. Review prepared for the Strategic Review of Health Inequalities in England Post 2010 (Marmot Review). Available at: http://www.instituteofhealthequity.org/Content/FileManager/pdf/economic-active-labour-market-full-report.pdf [2 Jan. 2017].

D'Arcy, C.; Gardiner, L. 2014. *Just the job – or a working compromise? The changing nature of self-employment in the UK* (London, Resolution Foundation). Available at: http://www.resolutionfoundation.org/wp-content/uploads/2014/05/Just-the-job-or-a-working-compromise-FINAL.pdf [2 Jan. 2017].

Davidsson, P. 2004. *Researching entrepreneurship*, International Studies in Entrepreneurship, Vol. 5 (Berlin and Heidelberg, Springer Science and Business Media).

Dawson, C.; Henley, A.; Latreille, P. 2009. *Why do individuals choose self-employment?* Discussion Paper No. 3974 (Bonn, IZA). Available at: http://ftp.iza.org/dp3974.pdf [2 Jan. 2017].

Daza Báez, N.; Gamboa, L. 2013. *Informal–formal wage gaps in Colombia*, Working Paper No. 301 (Verona, ECINEQ, Society for the Study of Economic Inequality).

Delajara, M.; Freije, S.; Soloaga, I. 2006. *An evaluation of training for the unemployed in Mexico*, Working Paper No. 35098 (Washington, DC, Inter-American Development Bank Publications).

Dema, G.; Diaz, J.J.; Chacaltana, J. 2015. *What do we know about first job programmes and policies in Latin America* (Lima, ILO Regional Office for Latin America and the Caribbean).

de Serres, A.; Murtin, F.; de la Maisonneuve, C. 2012. "Policies to facilitate the return to work", in *Comparative Economic Studies*, Vol. 54, No. 1, pp. 5–42.

De Stefano, V. 2014. "A tale of oversimplification and deregulation: The mainstream approach to labour market segmentation and recent responses to the crisis in European Countries", in *Industrial Law Journal*, Vol. 43, No. 2, pp. 253–285.

—. 2015. *Non-standard workers and freedom of association: A critical analysis of restrictions to collective rights from a human rights perspective*. CSDLE "Massimo D'Antona" Working paper No. 123/2015 (Catania, Centre for the Study of European Labour Law).

—. 2016. *The rise of the "just-in-time workforce": On-demand work, crowdwork and labour protection in the "gig-economy"*, Conditions of Work and Employment Series No. 71 (Geneva, ILO).

DiNardo, J.; Fortin, N.M.; Lemieux, T. 1996. "Labor market institutions and the distribution of wages, 1973–1992: A semiparametric approach", in *Econometrica*, Vol. 64, No. 5, pp. 1001–1044.

Divald, S. 2015. *Comparative analysis of policies for youth employment in Asia and the Pacific* (Geneva, ILO).

Doeringer, P.; Piore, M. 1971. *Internal labour markets and manpower analysis* (Lexington, KY, Heath Lexington Books).

Dorsett, R. 2006. "The New Deal for young people: Effect on the labour market status of young men", in *Labour Economics*, Vol. 13, No. 3, pp. 405–422.

Doucouliagos, H.; Stanley, T.D. 2009. "Publication selection bias in minimum-wage research? A meta-regression analysis", in *British Journal of Industrial Relations*, Vol. 47, No. 2, pp. 406–428.

Dube, A.; Lester, T.W.; Reich, M. 2010. "Minimum wage effects across state borders: Estimates using contiguous counties", in *Review of Economics and Statistics*, Vol. 92, No. 4, Nov., pp. 945–964.

Ebell, M.; O'Higgins, N. 2015. *Fiscal policy and the youth labour market*, Employment Working Paper No. 200 (Geneva, ILO).

Egebark, J.; Kaunitz, N. 2014. *Do payroll tax cuts raise youth employment?* IFN Working Paper No. 1001 (Stockholm, Research Institute of Industrial Economics).

Eichhorst, W.; Marx, P.; Tobsch, V. 2009. *Institutional arrangements, employment performance and the quality of work*, Discussion Paper No. 459 (Bonn, IZA).

—; Rinne, U. 2015. *An assessment of the youth employment inventory and implications for Germany's development policy*, IZA Research Report No. 67 (Bonn, IZA). Available at: http://www.iza.org/en/webcontent/publications/reports/report_pdfs/iza_report_67.pdf [2 Jan. 2017].

—; Rodríguez-Planas, N.; Schmidl, R.; Zimmermann, K. 2014. *A roadmap to vocational education and training around the world* (Bonn, IZA). Available at: http://www.iza.org/conference_files/worldb2014/1551.pdf [2 Jan. 2017].

Elbadawi, I.; Loayza, N.V. 2008. *Informality, employment and economic development in the Arab world*, paper presented at international conference on "The unemployment crisis in the Arab countries", Cairo, 17–18 March.

Elder, S.; Koné, K.S. 2014. *Labour market transitions of young women and men in sub-Saharan Africa*, Work4Youth Publication Series No. 9 (Geneva, ILO).

Elias, F. 2014. *Labor demand elasticities over the life cycle: Evidence from Spain's payroll tax reforms* (New York, NY, Columbia University). Available at: http://www.columbia.edu/~fe2139/JMP_FerranElias.pdf [2 Jan. 2017].

Eppel, R.; Mahringer, H. 2013. *Do wage subsidies work in boosting economic inclusion? Evidence on effect heterogeneity in Austria*, WIFO Working Paper No. 456 (Vienna, Austrian Institute of Economic Research).

Esping-Andersen, G. 1990. *The three worlds of welfare capitalism* (Cambridge, Polity).

European Centre for the Development of Vocational Training (CEDEFOP). 2012. *Italy: A new agreement on apprenticeship contracts*. Available at: http://www.cedefop.europa.eu/en/news-and-press/news/italy-new-agreement-apprenticeship-contracts [2 Jan. 2017].

European Commission (EC). 2010a. *Employment in Europe 2010*. Available at: http://ec.europa.eu/employment_social/eie/index_en.html [2 Jan. 2017].

—. 2010b. *An agenda for new skills and jobs: A European contribution towards full employment*. Communication from the Commission to the European Parliament, the Council, the European Economic and Social Committee and the Committee of the Regions. Available at: http://eur-lex.europa.eu/legal-content/EN/TXT/?uri=CELEX:52010DC0682 [2 Jan. 2017].

—. 2012a. *Apprenticeship supply in the Member States of the European Union,* Final Report (Brussels). Available at: ec.europa.eu/social/BlobServlet?docId=7717&langId=en [2 Jan. 2017].

—. 2012b. *Towards a Quality Framework on Traineeships*. Analytical document accompanying the Communication from the Commission to the European Parliament, the Council, the European Economic and Social Committee and the Committee of the Regions, *Towards a Quality Framework on Traineeships*, 5 Dec. Available at: www.adapt.it/englishbulletin/docs/comm_analytical_paper.pdf [2 Jan. 2017].

—. 2012c. *Towards a Quality Framework on Traineeships*. Communication from the Commission to the European Parliament, the Council, the European Economic and Social Committee and the Committee of the Regions. Second-stage consultation of the social partners at European level under Article 154 TFEU. Available at: http://eur-lex.europa.eu/legal-content/EN/TXT/?qid=1446711507815&uri=-CELEX:52012DC0728 [2 Jan. 2017].

—. 2012d. *Study on a comprehensive overview on traineeship arrangements in Member States,* Final Synthesis Report (Luxembourg, Publications Office of the European Union). Available at: ec.europa.eu/social/BlobServlet?docId=7754&langId=en [2 Jan. 2017].

—. 2013a. *Apprenticeship and traineeship schemes in EU27: Key success factors – A guidebook for policy planners and practitioners* (Brussels). Available at: http://www.bibb. de/dokumente/pdf/Guidebook_Apprenticeship_Schemes_EU27.pdf [2 Jan. 2017].

—. 2013b. *Proposal for a Council Recommendation on a Quality Framework for Traineeships*, COM/2013/0857 (Brussels). Available at: http://eur-lex.europa.eu/legal-content/EN/TXT/?qid=1408100798339&uri=CELEX:52013PC0857 [2 Jan. 2017].

European Employment Observatory Review. 2010. *Self-employment in Europe 2010* (Luxembourg, Publications Office of the European Union).

European Foundation for the Improvement of Living and Working Conditions (Eurofound). 2010. *Self-employed workers: Industrial relations and working conditions* (Dublin). Available at: http://www.eurofound.europa.eu/sites/default/files/ef_files/docs/comparative/tn0801018s/tn0801018s.pdf [2 Jan. 2017].

—. 2013. *Young people and temporary employment in Europe* (Dublin). Available at: http://www.eurofound.europa.eu/sites/default/files/ef_files/docs/erm/tn1304017s/tn1304017s.pdf [2 Jan. 2017].

—. 2015a. *Youth entrepreneurship in Europe: Values, attitudes, policies* (Dublin). Available at: http://www.eurofound.europa.eu/sites/default/files/ef_publication/field_ef_document/ef1507en.pdf [2 Jan. 2017].

—. 2015b. *New forms of employment* (Luxembourg, Publications Office of the European Union). Available at: http://www.eurofound.europa.eu/publications/report/2015/working-conditions-labour-market/new-forms-of-employment [2 Jan. 2017].

—. 2016. *Start-up support for young people in the EU: From implementation to evaluation* (Dublin).

European Parliament and Council of the European Union. 2001. "Recommendation of the European Parliament and of the Council on mobility within the community for students, persons undergoing training, volunteers, teachers and trainers", in *Official Journal of the European Communities*, L 215, 9 Aug. 2001, p. 30.

—; —. 2006. "Recommendation of the European Parliament and of the Council on transnational mobility within the community for education and training purposes: European Quality Charter for Mobility", in *Official Journal of the European Communities*, L394, 30 Dec., p. 5.

European Trade Union Confederation (ETUC). 2013. *Towards a European quality framework for traineeships and work-based learning* (Brussels). Available at: https://www.etuc.org/sites/www.etuc.org/files/publication/files/ces-brochure_unionlearn-uk-rouge.pdf [2 Jan. 2017].

Eyraud, F.; Saget, C. 2008. "The revival of minimum wage setting institutions", in J. Berg and D. Kucera (eds): *In defence of labour market institutions: Cultivating justice in the developing world* (Basingstoke, Palgrave Macmillan), pp. 100–118.

Ezrow, N.; Frantz, E. 2012. *Failed states and institutional decay: Understanding instability and poverty* (London, Bloomsbury).

Fatás, A.; Mihov, I. 2003. "The case for restricting fiscal policy discretion", in *Quarterly Journal of Economics*, Vol. 118, No. 4, pp. 1419–1447.

—; —. 2006. "The macroeconomic effects of fiscal rules in the US states", in *Journal of Public Economics*, Vol. 90, Nos 1–2, pp. 101–117.

Fay, R.G. 1996. *Enhancing the effectiveness of active labour market policies: Evidence from programme evaluations in OECD countries*, Labour Market and Social Policy Occasional Paper (Paris, OECD).

Feldstein, M. 1982. "Government deficits and aggregate demand", in *Journal of Monetary Economics,* Vol. 20, No. 1, pp. 1–20.

Fields, G. 2014. "Self-employment and poverty in developing countries: Helping the self-employed earn more for the work they do", in *IZA World of Labor*, May. Available at: http://wol.iza.org/articles/self-employment-and-poverty-in-developing-countries–1.pdf [2 Jan. 2017].

Freeman, R.B. 1996. "The minimum wage as a redistributive tool", in *Economic Journal*, Vol. 106, No. 436, pp. 639–649.

—. 2010. "Labor regulations, unions, and social protection in developing countries: Market distortions or efficient institutions?", in D. Rodrik and M. Rosenzweig (eds): *Handbook of Development Economics*, vol. 5 (Amsterdam, Elsevier), pp. 4657–4702.

Galasso, E.; Ravallion, M.; Salvia, A. 2004. "Assisting the transition from workfare to work: A randomized experiment", in *Industrial and Labor Relations Review*, Vol. 58, No. 1, pp. 128–142.

Gama, R.; Migliora, L.G. 2009. *Employment and benefits – Brazil: New internship law enacted* (London, International Law Office). Available at: http://www.international-lawoffice.com/newsletters/detail.aspx?g=27326165-5093-4648-b5a1-5b6e1c4aef5c [2 Jan. 2017].

Garganta, S.; Gasparini, L. 2015. "The impact of a social program on labor informality: The case of AUH in Argentina", in *Journal of Development Economics*, Vol. 115, Issue C, pp. 99–110.

Gatti, R.; Angel-Urdinola, D.F.; Silva, J.; Bodor, A. 2011. *Striving for better jobs – The challenge of informality in the Middle East and North Africa region* (Washington, DC, World Bank).

Gechert, S. 2015. "What fiscal policy is most effective? A meta-regression analysis", in *Oxford Economic Papers*, Vol. 67, No. 3, pp. 553–580.

Gersdorff, H. von; Benavides, P. 2012. "Complementing Chile's pensions with subsidized youth employment and contributions", in R. Hinz, R. Holzmann, D. Tuesta and N. Takayama (eds): *Matching contributions for pensions: A review of international experience* (Washington, DC, World Bank), pp. 179–192.

Giavazzi, F.; Pagano, M. 1990. "Can severe fiscal contractions be expansionary? Tales of two small European countries", in *NBER Macroeconomics Annual 1990*, Vol. 5, pp. 75–122.

—; —. 1996. "Non-Keynesian effects of fiscal policy changes", in *Swedish Economic Policy Review*, Vol. 3, No. 1, pp. 67–103.

Gilad, B.; Levine, P. 1986. "A behavioural model of entrepreneurial supply", in *Journal of Small Business Management*, Vol. 24, No. 4, pp. 45–54.

Gindling, T.H.; Newhouse, D. 2014. "Self-employment in the developing world", in *World Development*, Vol. 56, pp. 313–331.

Gineste, S. 2014. *Stimulating job demand: The design of effective hiring subsidies in Europe – France*, country background study for European Employment Policy Observatory Review.

Gopaul, S. 2013. *Feasibility study for a global business network on apprenticeship* (Geneva, ILO).

Green, F. 2013. *Youth entrepreneurship*, background paper for OECD Centre for Entrepreneurship, SMEs and Local Development (Paris, OECD). Available at: http://www.oecd.org/cfe/leed/youth_bp_finalt.pdf [2 Jan. 2017].

Grimm, M.; Paffhausen, A.L. 2015. "Do interventions targeted at micro-entrepreneurs and small and medium-sized firms create jobs? A systematic review of the evidence for low and middle income countries", in *Labour Economics*, Vol. 32, No. 1, pp. 67–85.

Groh, M.; Krishnan, N.; McKenzie, D.J.; Vishwanath, T. 2012. *Soft skills or hard cash? The impact of training and wage subsidy programs on female youth employment in Jordan*, Policy Research Working Paper No. 6141 (Washington, DC, World Bank). Available at: http://papers.ssrn.com/sol3/papers.cfm?abstract_id=2116139 [2 Jan. 2017].

Grubb, W.N.; Ryan, P. 1999. *The roles of evaluation for vocational education and training: Plain talk on the field of dreams* (Geneva, ILO).

Guajardo, J.; Leigh, D.; Pescatori, A. 2011. *Expansionary austerity: New international evidence*, Working Paper No. 11/158 (Washington, DC, IMF).

Hadjivassiliou, K.P.; Tassinari, A.; Eichhorst, W.; Wozny, F. 2016. *Assessing the performance of school-to-work transition regimes in the EU*, Discussion Paper No. 10301 (Bonn, IZA).

Hall, P.A.; Soskice, D. (eds). 2001. *Varieties of capitalism: The institutional foundations of comparative advantage* (Oxford, Oxford University Press).

Hassan, M.; Schneider, F. 2016. *Size and development of the shadow economies of 157 countries worldwide: Updated and new measures from 1999 to 2013*, Discussion Paper No. 10281 (Bonn, IZA).

Heckman, J.; Lochner, L.; Cossa, R. 2002. *Learning-by-doing vs. on-the-job training: Using variation induced by the EITC to distinguish between models of skill formation*, Working Paper No. 9083 (Cambridge, MA, NBER).

—; LaLonde, R.J.; Smith, J.A. 1999. "The economics and econometrics of active labor market programs", in *Handbook of Labor Economics*, Vol. 3 (Amsterdam, Elsevier), pp. 1865–2097.

Hodrick, R.J.; Prescott, E. 1980. *Post-war US business cycles: An empirical investigation*, Working Paper No. 45 (Pittsburgh, PA, Carnegie-Mellon University).

—; —. 1997. "Post-war US business cycles: an empirical investigation", in *Journal of Money, Credit, and Banking*, Vol. 29, No. 1, pp. 1–16.

Howell, D.R.; Baker, D.; Glyn, A.; Schmitt, J. 2007. "Are protective labor market institutions at the root of unemployment? A critical review of the evidence", in *Capitalism and Society,* Vol. 2, No. 1, pp. 1–73.

Ibarrarán, P.; Ripani, L.; Taboada, B.; Villa, J.M.; Garcia, B. 2014. "Life skills, employability and training for disadvantaged youth: Evidence from a randomized evaluation design", in *IZA Journal of Labor and Development*, Vol. 3, No. 1, p. 10.

—; Rosas-Shady, D.; Soares, Y. 2006. *Impact evaluation of a youth job training program in the Dominican Republic: Ex-post project evaluation report of the labor training and modernization project* (DR0134) (Washington, DC, Inter-American Development Bank). Available at: http://publications.iadb.org/handle/11319/4539 [1 Jan. 2017].

Ibourk, A. 2012. *Contribution of labour market policies and institutions to employment, equal opportunities and the formalization of the informal economy: Morocco*, Employment Working Paper No. 123 (Geneva, ILO). Available at: http://www.ilo.org/employment/Whatwedo/Publications/working-papers/WCMS_191244/lang--en/index.htm [2 Jan. 2017].

International Labour Office. 2002. *Decent work and the informal economy,* Report VI, International Labour Conference, 90th Session, Geneva, 2002 (Geneva). Available at: http://www.ilo.org/public/english/standards/relm/ilc/ilc90/pdf/rep-vi.pdf [4 May 2017].

—. 2005. *The employment relationship*, Report V(1), International Labour Conference, 95th Session, Geneva, 2006 (Geneva). Available at: http://www.ilo.org/public/english/standards/relm/ilc/ilc95/pdf/rep-v–1.pdf [2 Jan. 2017].

—. 2010. *Vulnerable employment and poverty on the rise*, Interview with ILO Chief of Employment Trends Unit, 26 Jan. Available at: http://www.ilo.org/global/about-the-ilo/newsroom/features/WCMS_120470/lang--de/index.htm [2 Jan. 2017].

—. 2011. *Upgrading informal apprenticeship systems*, Skills for Employment policy brief (Geneva). Available at: http://www.skillsforemployment.org/KSP/en/Details/ ?dn=FM11G_021426 [2 Feb. 2017].

—. 2012a. *The youth employment crisis: A call for action*, Resolution and Conclusions, International Labour Conference, 101st Session, Geneva, 2012 (Geneva). Available at: http://www.ilo.org/wcmsp5/groups/public/---ed_norm/---relconf/documents/ meetingdocument/wcms_185950.pdf [2 Feb. 2017].

—. 2012b. *The youth employment crisis: Time for action*, Report V, International Labour Conference, 101st Session, Geneva, 2012 (Geneva). Available at: http://www.ilo. org/wcmsp5/groups/public/---ed_norm/---relconf/documents/meetingdocument/ wcms_175421.pdf [2 Feb. 2017].

—. 2012c. *World of Work Report 2012: Better jobs for a better economy* (Geneva).

—. 2013a. *Global Employment Trends for Youth 2013: A generation at risk* (Geneva). Available at: http://www.ilo.org/wcmsp5/groups/public/---dgreports/---dcomm/ documents/publication/wcms_212423.pdf [2 Jan. 2017].

—. 2013b. *World of Work Report 2013: Repairing the economic and social fabric* (Geneva).

—. 2013c. *Women and men in the informal economy: A statistical picture* (second edition) (Geneva). Available at: http://www.ilo.org/wcmsp5/groups/public/---dgreports/--- stat/documents/publication/wcms_234413.pdf [2 Jan. 2017].

—. 2013d. *The informal economy and decent work: A policy resource guide, supporting transitions to formality*, Employment Policy Department (Geneva). Available at: http://www.ilo.org/wcmsp5/groups/public/---ed_emp/---emp_policy/documents/ publication/wcms_212689.pdf [2 Jan. 2017].

—. 2014a. *Fostering future entrepreneurs* (Geneva). Available at: http://www.ilo.ch/ wcmsp5/groups/public/---ed_emp/---emp_ent/---ifp_seed/documents/publication/ wcms_175469.pdf [2 Jan. 2017].

—. 2014b. *Global Employment Trends 2014: Risk of a jobless recovery?* (Geneva). Available at: http://www.ilo.org/moscow/information-resources/publications/WCMS_ 385999/lang--en/index.htm [2 Jan. 2017].

—. 2014c. *Jobs and skills for youth: Review of policies for youth employment of the Russian Federation*, Youth Employment Programme, mimeo (Geneva). Available at: http://ilo.org/wcmsp5/groups/public/---dgreports/---dcomm/---publ/documents/ publication/wcms_233953.pdf [2 Jan. 2017].

—. 2015a. *Global Employment Trends for Youth 2015*, Employment Policy Department (Geneva). Available at: http://www.ilo.org/wcmsp5/groups/public/---dgreports/--- dcomm/---publ/documents/publication/wcms_412015.pdf [2 Jan. 2017].

—. 2015b. *Employment protection legislation: Summary indicators in the area of terminating regular contracts (individual dismissals)*, Inclusive Labour Markets, Labour Relations and Working Conditions Branch (INWORK) (Geneva). Available at: http://www.ilo.org/wcmsp5/groups/public/@ed_protect/@protrav/@travail/ documents/publication/wcms_357390.pdf [2 Jan. 2017].

—. 2015c. *Jobs and skills for youth: Review of policies for youth employment of Nepal* (Geneva). Available at: http://www.ilo.org/wcmsp5/groups/public/---ed_emp/documents/publication/wcms_502340.pdf [2 Jan. 2017].

—. 2015d. *Jobs and skills for youth: Review of policies for youth employment of Kazakhstan* (Geneva). Available at: http://www.ilo.org/wcmsp5/groups/public/---europe/---ro-geneva/---sro-moscow/documents/publication/wcms_385997.pdf [2 Jan. 2017].

—. 2015e. *Boosting youth employment through public works*, background paper prepared for the "What works in youth employment" knowledge-sharing event, Addis Ababa, 29–30 June.

—. 2015f. *Non-standard forms of employment.* Report for discussion at the Meeting of Experts on Non-Standard Forms of Employment, Feb. (Geneva).

—. 2015g. *Revision of the International Classification of Status in Employment* (ICSE- 93), discussion paper, Working Group for the Revision of ICSE-93, Geneva, 6–8 May.

—. 2015h. *Youth and informality: Promoting formal employment among youth – Innovative experiences in Latin America and the Caribbean* (Lima, ILO Regional Office for Latin America and the Caribbean). Available at: http://www.ilo.org/wcmsp5/groups/public/---americas/---ro-lima/documents/publication/wcms_361990.pdf [2 Jan. 2017].

—. 2016a. *World Employment and Social Outlook: Trends for youth 2016* (Geneva).

—. 2016b. *Non-standard employment around the world: Understanding challenges, shaping prospects* (Geneva). Available at: http://www.ilo.org/wcmsp5/groups/public/---dgreports/---dcomm/---publ/documents/publication/wcms_492373.pdf [2 Jan. 2017].

—. 2016c. *What works? Active labour market policies in Latin America and the Caribbean*, ILO Studies on Growth with Equity (Geneva). Available at: http://www.ilo.org/wcmsp5/groups/public/---dgreports/---dcomm/---publ/documents/publication/wcms_534326.pdf [2 Jan. 2017].

—. Forthcoming. *Quality apprenticeships: A policy brief*, Skills and Employability Branch (Geneva).

—; World Bank/International Bank for Reconstruction and Development (IBRD). 2013. *Possible futures for the Indian apprenticeship system,* Options paper for India (New Delhi). Available at: http://www.ilo.org/wcmsp5/groups/public/---asia/---ro-bangkok/---sro-new_delhi/documents/publication/wcms_234727.pdf [2 Jan. 2017].

International Monetary Fund (IMF). 2012. *IMF Outlook for sub-Saharan Africa: Maintaining growth in an uncertain world* (Washington, DC).

—. 2014. *Fiscal monitor – Back to work: How fiscal policy can help* (Washington, DC).

—. 2015. *Fiscal monitor – Now is the time: Fiscal policies for sustainable growth* (Washington, DC).

Islam, R.; Islam, I. 2015. *Employment and inclusive growth* (London, Routledge).

Jacobi, L.; Kluve, J. 2006. *Before and after the Hartz Reforms: The performance of active labour market policy in Germany*, Discussion Paper No. 2100 (Bonn, IZA). Available at: http://ftp.iza.org/dp2100.pdf [2 Jan. 2017].

Jeannet-Milanovic, A.; Rosen, A. 2016. *Contractual arrangements for young people*, mimeo (Geneva, ILO).

Jeppesen, E.; Siboni, A. 2015. *The Danish apprenticeship system: Lessons for possible adaptations in other countries,* mimeo (Geneva, ILO).

Jimeno-Serrano, J.F.; Rodriguez-Palenzuela, D. 2002. *Youth unemployment in the OECD: Demographic shifts, labour market institutions, and macroeconomic shocks,* Working Paper No. 155 (Brussels, European Central Bank).

Junankar, P.N. 2013. *Is there a trade-off between employment and productivity?* Discussion Paper No. 7717 (Bonn, IZA).

—. 2016. *Sectoral employment patterns and youth employment: An analysis of issues, theory, policies and evidence,* background paper for ACI2 (ILO, Geneva).

Kaldor, N. 1967. *Strategic factors in economic development* (Ithaca, NY, Cornell University Press).

Kapsos, S. 2005. *The employment intensity of growth: Trends and macroeconomic determinants,* Employment Strategy Papers No. 12 (Geneva, ILO).

Keynes, J.M. 1936. *The general theory of employment, interest and money* (London, Macmillan).

Khandker, S.R.; Koolwal, G.B.; Samad, H.A. 2010. *Handbook on impact evaluation: Quantitative methods and practices* (Washington, DC, World Bank).

Kluve, J. 2010. "The effectiveness of European active labor market programs", in *Labour Economics*, Vol. 17, No. 6, pp. 904–918.

—. 2014. "Youth labor market interventions", in *IZA World of Labor*, Dec.

—; Puerto, S.; Robalino, D.; Romero, J.M.; Rother, F.; Stöterau, J.; Weidenkaff, F.; Witte, M. 2016a. *Interventions to improve the labour market outcomes of youth: A systematic review of training, entrepreneurship promotion, employment services, mentoring, and subsidized employment interventions* (Oslo, Campbell Collaboration). Available at: http://campbellcollaboration.org/lib/project/306/ [2 Jan. 2017].

—; —; —; —; —; —; —; —. 2016b. *Do youth employment programs improve labor market outcomes? A systematic review,* Discussion Paper No. 10263 (Bonn, IZA).

—; Schmidt, C.M. 2002. "Can training and employment subsidies combat European unemployment?", in *Economic Policy,* Vol. 17, No. 35, pp. 409–448.

Knight, G.M. 2002. *Evaluation of the Australian wage subsidy special youth employment and training program, SYETP* (Sydney, University of Sydney, School of Economics and Political Science). Available at: http://www.psi.org.uk/docs/2004/genevieve-PhDfull.pdf [2 Jan. 2017].

Kolev, A.; Saget, C. 2005. *Towards a better understanding of the nature, causes and consequences of youth labor market disadvantage: Evidence for south-east Europe,* Social Protection Discussion Paper No. 0502 (Washington, DC, World Bank, Social Protection and Labor).

Kring, S.; Breglia, M.G. 2015. *Jobs and skills for youth: Review of policies for youth employment of Indonesia* (Geneva, ILO).

Kucera, D.; Roncolato, L. 2008. "Informal employment: Two contested policy issues", in *International Labour Review*, Vol. 147, No. 4, pp. 321–348.

—; —. 2015. "Structure matters: Sectoral drivers of growth and the labour productivity-employment relationship", in I. Islam and D. Kucera (eds): *Beyond macroeconomic stability: Structural transformation and inclusive development* (Basingstoke, Palgrave Macmillan), pp. 133–197.

—; —. 2016. "The manufacturing–services dynamic in economic development", in *International Labour Review*, Vol. 155, No. 2, pp. 171–199.

Kugler, A.; Jimeno, J.F.; Hernanz, V. 2002. *Employment consequences of restrictive permanent contracts: Evidence from Spanish labor market reforms*, Discussion Paper No. 657 (Bonn, IZA).

—; Kugler, M.; Prada, L.O.H. 2017. *Do payroll tax breaks stimulate formality? Evidence from Colombia's reform*, Working paper No. 23308 (Cambridge, MA, NBER).

Lang, C.; Schömann, I.; Clauwaert, S. 2013. *Atypical forms of employment contracts in times of crisis*, Working Paper No. 2013.03 (Brussels, European Trade Union Institute).

La Porta, R.; Shleifer, A. 2008. "The unofficial economy and economic development", in *Brookings Papers on Economy Activity*, Fall, pp. 343–362.

—; —. 2014. "Informality and development", in *Journal of Economic Perspectives*, Vol. 28, No. 3, pp. 109–126.

Larsson, L. 2003. "Evaluation of Swedish youth labor market programs", in *Journal of Human Resources*, Vol. 38, No. 4, pp. 891–927.

Lechner, M.; Wunsch, C. 2009. "Are training programs more effective when unemployment is high?" in *Journal of Labor Economics*, Vol. 27, No. 4, pp. 653–692.

Le Deist, F.; Winterton, J. 2011. *Synthesis report on comparative analysis of the development of apprenticeship in Germany, France, the Netherlands and the UK: Comparative analysis of apparent good practice in apprenticeship system* (Toulouse, Leonardo da Vinci Transfer of Innovations Project Devapprent). Available at: http://www.adam-europe.eu/prj/7158/prd/8/1/deva_comp_EN_final.pdf [2 Jan. 2017].

Leonard, M.; Stanley, T.D.; Doucouliagos, H. 2014. "Does the UK minimum wage reduce employment? A meta-regression analysis", in *British Journal of Industrial Relations*, Vol. 52, No, 3, pp. 499–520.

Levinsohn, J.; Pugatch, T. 2014. "Prospective analysis of a wage subsidy for Cape Town youth", in *Journal of Development Economics*, Vol. 108, May, pp. 169–183.

—; Rankin, N.; Roberts, G.; Schöer, V. 2014. *Wage subsidies and youth employment in South Africa: Evidence from a randomised control trial*, Stellenbosch Economic Working Papers No. *WP02/2014*. Available at: http://www.ekon.sun.ac.za/wpapers/2014/wp022014 [2 Jan. 2017].

Loayza, N.V.; Raddatz, C. 2010. "The composition of growth matters for poverty alleviation", in *Journal of Development Economics*, Vol. 93, pp. 137–151.

—; Servén, L.; Sugawara, N. 2009. *Informality in Latin America and the Caribbean*, Policy Research Working Paper No. 4888 (Washington DC, World Bank).

Losch, B. 2016. *Structural transformation to boost youth labour demand in sub-Saharan Africa: The role of agriculture, rural areas and territorial development*, Employment Working Paper No. 204 (Geneva, ILO).

Marcén, M. 2014. "The role of culture on self-employment", in *Economic Modelling*, Vol. 44, Supp. 1, pp. S20–S32.

Martin, J.P.; Grubb, D. 2001. "What works and for whom: A review of OECD countries' experiences with active labour market policies", in *Swedish Economic Policy Review*, Vol. 8, No. 2, pp. 9–56.

Martin, R.; Nativel, C.; Sunley, P. 2003. "The local impact of the New Deal: Does geography make a difference?", in R. Martin and P.S. Morrison (eds): *Geographies of labour market inequality* (London, Routledge), pp. 175–207.

Matsumoto, M.; Hengge, M.; Islam, I. 2012. *Tackling the youth employment crisis: A macroeconomic perspective*, Employment Working Paper No. 124 (Geneva, ILO).

McCaig, B.; Pavcnik, N. 2015. "Informal employment in a growing and globalizing low-income country", in *American Economic Review*, Vol. 105, No. 5, pp. 545–550.

McCann, D. 2008. *Regulating flexible work* (Oxford, Oxford University Press).

McKenzie, D.; Woodruff, C. 2014. "What are we learning from business training and entrepreneurship evaluations around the developing world?", in *World Bank Research Observer*, Vol. 29, No. 1, pp. 48–82.

McKinsey Global Institute (MGI). 2012. *Africa at work: Job creation and inclusive growth* (Brussels, San Francisco and Shanghai, MGI).

McMillan, M.S.; Rodrik. D. 2011. *Globalization, structural change and productivity growth*, Working Paper No. w17143 (Cambridge, MA, NBER).

McVicar, D.; Podivinsky, J.M. 2010. *Are active labour market programs least effective where they are most needed? The case of the British New Deal for Young People*, Working Paper No. 16/10 (Melbourne Institute of Applied Economic and Social Research, University of Melbourne).

Meager, N.; Bates, P.; Cowling, M. 2003. "An evaluation of business start-up support for young people", in *National Institute Economic Review*, Vol. 186, No. 1, Oct., pp. 70–83.

Mirza-Davies, J. 2016. *Apprenticeships policy in England*, Briefing Paper No. 03052 (London, House of Commons Library).

Morosini, V. 2013. *Apprenticeships and new incentives for employers: Italy promotes the employment of young people and women* (Rome and Milan, Toffoletto De Luca Tamajo e Soci). Available at: http://www.lexology.com/library/detail.aspx?g=ae1b 40fe-2d02-4714-9fe4-074b334b6043 [2 Jan. 2017].

Moscariello, V.; O'Higgins, N. 2017. *Minimum wages and youth employment: A meta-analysis*, forthcoming Employment Working Paper (Geneva, ILO).

Nataraj, S.; Perez-Arce, F.; Kumar, K.B.; Srinivasan, S.V. 2014. "The impact of labor market regulation on employment in low-income countries: A meta-analysis", in *Journal of Economic Surveys*, Vol. 28, No. 3, pp. 551–572.

Neri, M.C. 2012, *As razões da educação professional: Olhar da demanda* [The rationale for vocational education: A look at demand] (Rio de Janeiro, FGC Social, Centro de Políticas Sociais).

Neumark, D.; Grijalva, D. 2013. *The employment effects of state hiring credits during and after the Great Recession*, Working Paper No. 18928 (Cambridge, MA, NBER).

—; Salas, J.M.I.; Wascher, W. 2013. *Revisiting the minimum wage–employment debate: Throwing out the baby with the bathwater?* Discussion Paper No. 7166 (Bonn, IZA).

—; Wascher, W. 2004. "Minimum wages, labor market institutions, and youth employment: A cross-national analysis", in *Industrial and Labor Relations Review*, Vol. 57, No. 2, pp. 223–246.

—; —. 2007. *Minimum wages and employment*, Discussion Paper No. 2570 (Bonn, IZA).

Ñopo, H. 2008. "Matching as a tool to decompose wage gaps", in *Review of Economics and Statistics*, Vol. 90, No. 2, pp. 290–299.

Nordman, C. J.; Rakotomanana, F.; Roubaud, F. 2016. *Informal versus formal: A panel data analysis of earnings gaps in Madagascar*, Discussion Paper No. 9970 (Bonn, IZA).

O'Higgins, N. 2001. *Youth unemployment and employment policy: A global perspective* (Geneva, ILO).

—. 2003. *Trends in the youth labour market in developing and transition countries.* Social Protection Discussion Paper No. 0321 (Washington, DC, World Bank, Social Protection and Labor).

—. 2010. *The impact of the economic and financial crisis on youth employment: Measures for labour market recovery in the European Union, Canada and the United States*, Employment Working Paper No. 70 (Geneva, ILO).

—. 2012. "This time it's different? Youth labour markets during 'The Great Recession'", in *Comparative Economic Studies*, Vol. 54, No. 2, pp. 395–412.

—. 2014. "Institutions and youth labour markets in Europe during the crisis", in L. Mamica and P. Tridico (eds): *Economic policy and the financial crisis* (London, Routledge), pp. 90–113.

—. 2015. "Ethnicity and gender in the labour market in central and south east Europe", in *Cambridge Journal of Economics*, Vol. 39, No. 2, pp. 631–654.

—. 2017. "Youth unemployment", in A. Furlong (ed.): *Handbook of youth and young adulthood*, 2nd edn (Abingdon, Routledge), pp. 141–155.

—; Pica, G. 2017. *Complementarities between labour market institutions and their causal impact on youth labour market outcomes*, Employment Working Paper (Geneva, ILO).

O'Leary, C.J. 1998. *Evaluating the effectiveness of active labor programs in Hungary*, Technical Report No. 98-013 (Kalamazoo, MI, W.E. Upjohn Institute for Employment Research).

—. 2014. *Going it alone* (London, Demos).

—; Eberts, R.W.; Hollenbeck, K. 2011. *What works for whom in public employment policy?* Technical Report No. 12-2011 (Kalamazoo, MI, W.E. Upjohn Institute for Employment Research). Available at: http://works.bepress.com/randall_eberts/116 [2 Jan. 2017].

Organisation for Economic Co-operation and Development (OECD). 2007. *Going for growth* (Paris).

—. 2009. *Is informal normal? Towards more and better jobs in developing countries* (Paris).

—. 2012. *Policy brief on youth entrepreneurship: Entrepreneurial activities in Europe* (Paris). Available at: http://www.oecd.org/cfe/leed/Youth%20entrepreneurship%20 policy%20brief%20EN_FINAL.pdf [2 Jan. 2017].

—. 2014a. *The missing entrepreneurs: Policies for inclusive entrepreneurship in Europe* (Paris). Available at: http://www.oecd-ilibrary.org/docserver/download/8412061e. pdf?expires=1439752169&id=id&accname=oid007055&checksum=8798155D30 52367EEF9844943F00C511 [2 Jan. 2017].

—. 2014b. *Investing in youth: Brazil* (Paris). Available at: http://www.oecd-ilibrary.org/ social-issues-migration-health/investing-in-youth-brazil_9789264208988-en [2 Jan. 2017].

—. 2014c. *G20–OECD–EC conference on quality apprenticeships for giving youth a better start in the labour market*, background paper (Paris). Available at: http://www. oecd.org/els/emp/G20-OECD-EC%20Apprenticeship%20Conference_Issues%20 Paper.pdf [2 Jan. 2017].

Oskamp, F.; Snower, D. 2006. *The effect of low-wage subsidies on skills and employment*, Working Paper (Kiel, Kiel Institute for the World Economy).

Palmi Reig, M.A. 2012. *Balance bibliográfico sobre la legislación para promover el empleo juvenil en América Latina*, mimeo, Youth Employment Programme (Geneva, ILO).

Parker, S. 2004. *The economics of self-employment and entrepreneurship* (Cambridge, Cambridge University Press).

Paulin, J.F.; Thivin, S. 2010. *L'étudiant en entreprise. Enjeux et cadre juridique de l'alternance* (Paris, Wolters Kluwer).

Pavlopoulos, D. 2009. *Starting your career with a temporary job: Stepping-stone or dead end?*, SOEP Papers on Multidisciplinary Panel Data Research No. 228 (Berlin, Deutsches Institut für Wirtschaftsforschung).

Peprah, J.; Afoakwah, C.; Koomson, I. 2015. "Savings, entrepreneurial trait and self-employment: Evidence from selected Ghanaian universities", in *Journal of Global Entrepreneurship Research*, Vol. 5, No. 1, pp. 2–17.

Perlin, R. 2012. *Intern nation: How to earn nothing and learn little in the brave new economy* (London and New York, Verso).

Perry, G.E.; Maloney, W.F.; Arias, O.S.; Fajnzylber, P.; Mason, A.D.; Saavedra-Chanduvi, J. 2007. *Informality: Exit and exclusion* (Washington, DC, World Bank).

Pessoa e Costa, S.; Robin, S. 2009. *An illustration of the returns to training programmes: The evaluation of the "qualifying contract" in France* (Louvain, Université Catholique de Louvain, Institut de Recherches Economiques et Sociales). Available at: http://sites.uclouvain.be/econ/DP/CIACO/CIACO-2009038.pdf [2 Jan. 2017].

Pohl, A.; Walther, A. 2007. "Activating the disadvantaged – Variations in addressing youth transitions across Europe", in *International Journal of Lifelong Education*, Vol. 26, No. 5, pp. 533–553.

Poschke, M. 2013. "Entrepreneurs out of necessity: A snapshot", in *Applied Economics Letters*, Vol. 20, No. 7, pp. 658–663.

Premand, P.; Brodmann, S.; Almeida, R.; Grun, R.; Barouni, M. 2011. *Entrepreneurship training and self-employment among university graduates: Evidence from a randomized trial in Tunisia*, Discussion Paper No. 7079 (Bonn, IZA). Available at: http://ftp.iza.org/dp7079.pdf [2 Jan. 2017].

Quintini, G.; Martin, S. 2006. *Starting well or losing their way? The position of youth in the labour market in OECD countries* (Paris, OECD).

—; —. 2014. *Same but different: School-to-work transitions in emerging and advanced economies*, Social, Employment and Migration Working Papers No. 154 (Paris, OECD). Available at: http://dx.doi.org/10.1787/5jzbb2t1rcwc-en [2 Jan. 2017].

Raffe, D. 2011. "Cross-national differences in education–work transitions", in M. London (ed.): *The Oxford handbook of lifelong learning* (New York, Oxford University Press), pp. 312–328.

Ranhhod, A.; Finn, A. 2014. *Estimating the short run effects of South Africa's employment tax incentive on youth employment probabilities using a difference in difference approach*, Working Paper No. 134 (Cape Town, Southern Africa Labour and Development Research Unit).

—; —. 2015. *Estimating the effects of South Africa's youth employment tax incentive: An update*, Working Paper No. 152 (Cape Town, Southern Africa Labour and Development Research Unit).

Rani, U.; Belser, P.; Oelz, M; Ranjbarr, S. 2013. "Minimum wage coverage and compliance in developing countries", in *International Labour Review*, Vol. 152, Nos 3–4, pp. 381–410.

Richard, D. 2012. *The Richard review of apprenticeships* (London, School for Startups). Available at: https://www.gov.uk/government/uploads/system/uploads/attachment_data/file/34708/richard-review-full.pdf [2 Jan. 2017].

Richardson, J. 1998. *Do wage subsidies enhance employability? Evidence from Australian youth,* Discussion Paper No. 387 (London, London School of Economics and Political Science, Centre for Economic Performance).

Riley, R.; Bondibene, C.R. 2017. "Raising the standard: Minimum wages and firm productivity", in *Labour Economics*, Vol. 44, pp. 27–50.

Røed, K.; Raum, O. 2006. "Does labour market training speed up the return to work?", in *Oxford Bulletin of Economics and Statistics*, Vol. 68, No. 5, pp. 541–568.

Roger, M.; Zamora, P. 2011. "Hiring young, unskilled workers on subsidized open-ended contracts: A good integration programme?" in *Oxford Review of Economic Policy*, Vol. 27, No. 2, pp. 380–396.

Rosin, A.; Muda, M. 2013. "Labour law status of a trainee: The Estonian situation with comparative insights from Finland, France and the US", in *European Labour Law Journal*, No. 4, pp. 292–312.

Royal Society of Arts (RSA). 2014. *Salvation in a start-up: The origins and nature of the self-employment boom*. Available at: https://www.thersa.org/discover/publications-and-articles/reports/salvation-in-a-start-up/ [2 Jan. 2017].

Rustico, L. 2013. *Youth employment and training in Italy and in Britain: Laws, policies and practices*, International PhD School, "Human capital formation and labour relations", University of Bergamo, 25th Session. Available at: https://aisberg.unibg.it/retrieve/handle/10446/28667/11605/rustico_tesi_10_1_13.pdf [2 Jan. 2017].

Ryan, P. 2001. "The school-to-work transition: A cross-national perspective", in *Journal of Economic Literature*, Vol. 39, No. 1, pp. 34–92.

—. 2011. *Apprenticeship: Between theory and practice, school and workplace*, Leading House Working Paper No. 64 (Zurich and Bern, University of Zurich and University of Bern).

Sawyer, M. 2012. "The tragedy of UK fiscal policy in the aftermath of the financial crisis", in *Cambridge Journal of Economics*, Vol. 36, No. 1, pp. 205–221.

Schneider, F. 2005. "Shadow economies around the world: What do we really know?", in *European Journal of Political Economy*, Vol. 21, No. 3, pp. 598–642.

Schöer, V.; Rankin, N. 2011. *Youth employment, recruitment and a youth-targeted wage subsidy: Findings from a South African firm level survey* (Johannesburg, World Bank, Human Development Unit, Africa Region). Available at: http://www-wds.worldbank.org/external/default/WDSContentServer/WDSP/IB/2012/09/18/000386194_20120918011506/Rendered/PDF/726010WP00PUBL05B0Youth0employment.pdf [2 Jan. 2017].

Shapiro, A.F. 2013. *The business cycle consequences of informal labor markets* (College Park, MD, Digital Repository of the University of Maryland).

Sheehan, M.; McNamara, A. 2015. *Business start-ups and youth self-employment: A policy literature review synthesis report*, STYLE Working Papers WP7.1 (Brighton, CROME, University of Brighton). Available at: http://www.style-research.eu/wordpress/wp-content/uploads/ftp/D_7_1_Business_Start-Ups_Youth_Self-Employment_Policy_Literature-Review_FINAL.pdf [2 Jan. 2017].

Shehu, D.; Nilsson, B. 2014. *Informal employment among youth: Evidence from 20 school-to-work transition surveys*, Work4Youth Publication Series No. 8 (Geneva, ILO).

Sianesi, B. 2008. "Differential effects of active labour market programs for the unemployed", in *Labour Economics*, Vol. 15, No. 3, pp. 370–399.

Smith, C. 2006. *International experience with worker-side and employer-side wage and employment subsidies, and job search assistance programmes: Implications for South Africa* (Pretoria, Employment Growth and Development Initiative, Human

Sciences Research Council). Available at: http://www.hsrc.ac.za/en/research-data/ ktree-doc/1318 [2 Jan. 2017].

Smith, E.; Kemmis, R.B. 2013. *Towards a model apprenticeship framework: A comparative analysis of national apprenticeship systems* (New Delhi, ILO and World Bank). Available at: http://www.ilo.org/wcmsp5/groups/public/---asia/---ro-bangkok/---sro-new_delhi/documents/publication/wcms_234728.pdf [2 Jan. 2017].

Souitaris, V.; Zerbinati, S.; Al-Laham, A. 2007. "Do entrepreneurship programmes raise entrepreneurial intention of science and engineering students? The effect of learning, inspiration and resource", in *Journal of Business Venturing*, Vol. 22, No. 4, pp. 566–591.

Steedman, H. 2012. *Overview of apprenticeship systems and issues: ILO contribution to the G20 task force on employment*, Skills and Employability Department (Geneva, ILO). Available at: http://www.ilo.org/wcmsp5/groups/public/---ed_emp/---ifp_skills/ documents/genericdocument/wcms_190188.pdf [2 Jan. 2017].

Stewart, A.; Owens, R. 2013. *Experience or exploitation? The nature and prevalence of unpaid work experience, internships and trial periods in Australia* (Adelaide, University of Adelaide).

Storey, D.J.; Greene, F.J. 2010. *Small business and entrepreneurship* (Harlow, Prentice-Hall).

Tatomir, S. 2015. *Self-employment: What can we learn from recent developments?* Quarterly Bulletin Q1 (London, Bank of England). Available at: http://www.bankofengland.co.uk/publications/Documents/quarterlybulletin/2015/q105.pdf [2 Jan. 2017].

Tičar, L. 2013. "Relationship between state law, collective agreement and individual contract: Case of Slovenia", in György Kiss (ed.): *Recent developments in labour law* (Budapest, Akadémia Publisher), pp. 44–62. Available at: http://mta-pte.ajk. pte.hu/downloads/MTA-PTE_Labour_Law_Research-Luka_ABSTRACT.pdf [2 Jan. 2017].

Trades Union Congress (TUC). 2014a. *More than two in five new jobs created since mid-2010 have been self-employed* (London). Available at: https://www.tuc.org.uk/ economic-issues/economic-analysis/labour-market/labour-market-and-economic-reports/more-two-five-new [2 Jan. 2017].

—. 2014b. *Government cuts in vital health and safety 'red tape' threaten lives at work* (London). Available at: https://www.tuc.org.uk/workplace-issues/health-and-safety/ workers-memorial-day/government-cuts-vital-health-and-safety-%E2%80%98red [2 Jan. 2017].

Treu, T. 2007. *Labour law and industrial relations in Italy*, 2nd edition (The Hague, Kluwer Law International).

Tros, F. 2012. *The effects of legislation on youth employment contracts in Europe* (Amsterdam, Amsterdam Institute for Advanced Labour Studies).

Van der Sluis, J.; van Praag, M.; Vijverberg, W. 2005. "Entrepreneurship selection and performance: A meta-analysis of the impact of education in developing economies", in *World Bank Economic Review*, Vol. 19, No. 2, pp. 225–261.

Viollaz, M.; Ham, A.; Cruces, G. 2012. *Scarring effects of youth unemployment and informality: Evidence from Argentina and Brazil,* working paper (La Plata, Argentina, Center for Distributive, Labor and Social Studies).

Visser, J. 2016. ICTWSS database on the institutional characteristics of trade unions, wage setting, state intervention and social pacts in 34 countries between 1960 and 2012 (Amsterdam, Amsterdam Institute for Advanced Labour Studies). Available at: http://www.uva-aias.net/en/ictwss.

Wang, C.Y. 2014. *Apprenticeships in China: Experiences, lessons and challenges,* presentation made at OECD. Available at: http://www.oecd.org/els/emp/C_WANG-Apprenticeships%20in%20China%20Update.pdf [2 Jan. 2017].

Wang, J.; Bao, C.; Cao, J.; Kring, S. 2016. *Jobs and skills for youth: Review of policies for youth employment of China* (Geneva, ILO).

Webb, M.; Sweetman, A.; Warman, C. 2012. *How targeted is targeted tax relief? Evidence from the unemployment insurance youth hires program,* Economics Department Working Paper No. 1298 (Ontario, Queen's University).

Williams, C.C.; Lansky, M.A. 2013. "Informal employment in developed and developing economies: Perspectives and policy responses", in *International Labour Review,* Vol. 152, Nos 3–4, pp. 355–380.

World Bank. 2006. *World Development Report* 2007: *Development and the next generation* (Washington, DC).

—. 2007. *World Development Report 2008: Agriculture for development* (Washington, DC).

—. 2010. *Active labour market programs for youth. A framework to guide youth employment interventions* (Washington, DC). Available at: https://openknowledge.worldbank.org/handle/10986/11690 [2 Jan. 2017].

—. 2012a. *Striving for better jobs: The challenge of informality in the Middle East and North Africa region* (Washington, DC). Available at: http://www-wds.worldbank.org/external/default/WDSContentServer/WDSP/IB/2012/03/21/000333037_2 0120321002602/Rendered/PDF/675900WP0P11320y0paper0text09021011.pdf [2 Jan. 2017].

—. 2012b. *In from the shadow: Integrating Europe's informal labor* (Washington, DC). Available at: https://openknowledge.worldbank.org/bitstream/handle/10986/9377/706020PUB0EPI0067902B09780821395493.pdf?sequence=1 [2 Jan. 2017].

Yarrow, C.; Pugh, A. 2013. "You're hired: An employer's guide to apprenticeships", Lexology Bircham Dyson Bell. Available at: http://www.lexology.com/library/detail.aspx?g=f07a5253-cd8c-4eef-9b59-e9011863423f [2 Jan. 2017].